THE RACE TO ZERO

THE RACE TO ZERO

How ESG Investing Will Crater the Global Financial System

PAUL H. TICE

NEW YORK · LONDON

First American edition published in 2023 by Encounter Books, an activity of Encounter for Culture and Education, Inc., a nonprofit, tax exempt corporation.
Encounter Books website address: *www.encounterbooks.com*

Manufactured in the United States and printed on acid-free paper. The paper used in this publication meets the minimum requirements of ANSI/NISO Z39.48–1992 (R 1997) (*Permanence of Paper*).

FIRST AMERICAN EDITION

LIBRARY OF CONGRESS CATALOGING-IN-PUBLICATION DATA IS AVAILABLE

Information for this title can be found at the Library of Congress website under the following ISBN 978-1-64177-347-8 and LCCN 2023053914.

For Pat, Matt, and Andrew,
My one thing in life

CONTENTS

INTRODUCTION

A BEST-LAID PLAN

The whole secret lies in confusing the enemy, so that he cannot fathom our real intent.
Sun Tzu, *The Art of War*

The game is afoot.
Arthur Conan Doyle, *The Return of Sherlock Holmes*

As a rule, most financial crimes tend to be limited affairs. If you are planning a bank holdup or an airport heist, secrecy and simplicity are both key, as is keeping the number of players involved to a bare minimum. Keep it simple, stick to the plan, and don't talk too much. Otherwise, before long, dead bodies are turning up in freezer trucks, garbage dumpsters, and pink Cadillacs, just like in the 1990 mob movie *Goodfellas.*

Speed of execution is also critical, as is having a good getaway strategy. Smash-and-grab jewel thieves know to keep the car engine running. Pickpockets hit their mark and then quickly fade into a crowd of tourists after multiple handoffs to accomplices. Hustlers and swindlers always need to keep moving on to the next town since confidence games cannot be sustained for long. Eventually, the people catch on, alarm bells go off, and the law shows up.

The same criminal rules of secrecy, simplicity, and speed apply to investment scams. Whether pump-and-dump stock market schemes or the classic Ponzi variety of investor fraud, most have relatively short shelf lives and are inherently unsustainable given that they wither in the full sunshine of public disclosure and market transparency. Getting in and out of the market and having an exit plan are paramount because it is only a matter of time before the window of opportunity closes.

ZZZZ Best Co., the carpet cleaning company founded by the teenager Barry Minkow and taken public back in the mid-1980s, rose to a nearly $300 million stock valuation on the back of falsified financial statements before collapsing into bankruptcy just months after its initial public offering (IPO). Enron Corp. and WorldCom Inc. were both able to keep their respective accounting frauds – hiding balance sheet debt in the former case and capitalizing operating expenses in the latter – going for slightly longer during the Internet-crazed dot-com market bubble of the late 1990s before meeting the same Chapter 11 fate over 2001–2002. Insiders at all three companies, though, were able to liquidate stock holdings at artificially inflated prices for years before the end came.

The fraud innovator Charles Ponzi was only able to keep his international postage stamp scheme going for roughly seven months back in 1920 before it came crashing down around his ears. A century later, 30-year-old Sam Bankman-Fried added a technology twist by setting up FTX Trading Ltd., a cryptocurrency exchange with more than one million users. Over the course of three years, the youthful, wild-haired savant diverted billions of dollars of customer funds into his other business ventures and his own personal pockets before FTX was forced to file for bankruptcy in November 2022.

In terms of size, scope, and staying power, however, Bernie Madoff is still the category leader when it comes to robbing Peter to pay Paul. Madoff stole an estimated $65 billion from mostly sophisticated institutions and individual investors and kept his private market fraud going for some 17 years, only being exposed when the entire global financial system came crashing down in 2008. Sometimes the process of market discovery can take a while, but in the end, the truth will out around most investment rackets.

With this in mind, the latest fraud being perpetrated on the financial markets, sustainable investing, is truly remarkable in that it breaks all of the rules when it comes to investment schemes. Its core premise is overly complex, its execution is elaborate, and its scale is global. Moreover, the entire swindle is playing out in the open, in full view of the investment community and the general public. To add insult to injury, the con is being perpetrated by people with little to no experience in finance and, even though there are grifters galore around sustainability, it is not primarily about making money – at least not for those market players being suckered into the trade.

Sustainable investing is based on the theory that subjective environmental, social, and governance (ESG) factors should drive corporate policy and investment decisions, as opposed to objective financial metrics and returns. The master ESG list is kept, not by financial market participants, but rather by an informal working group comprised of the United Nations (UN), the World Economic Forum (WEF), liberal politicians, academics, environmental activists, social justice warriors, and the media. It is an extensive and ever-changing list of corporate demands, with new ESG controversies being added on a regular basis. While climate change remains the highest-priority ESG issue, the target list hits most liberal hot buttons including diversity, union power, gender-pay equality, executive compensation, and corporate tax responsibility. Essentially, sustainable investing redefines all of the core tenets of progressive ideology over the past 100 years as corporate policy goals and investment criteria, wrapping the entire package with a thin veneer of morality and collective responsibility.

Wall Street research analysts, traders, and portfolio managers are now being asked to willingly suspend disbelief and forgo the traditional financial approach that they have used for decades to analyze, value, and trade company securities. Rather than comparing leverage metrics, cash flow margins, and earnings momentum, market participants are now sizing up carbon footprints, checking on water and electricity usage, and making sure companies are paying their "fair share" of corporate taxes. Analysts and portfolio managers must now know the gender, racial, ethnic, and demographic composition of every company's board of directors and its underlying workforce, as well as who gets paid what and whether employees truly enjoy working at a company. Instead of focusing on quarterly earnings trends and annual investment horizons, they must now consider very long-term forecasts – over 10, 20, and 30 years – for climate change and other ESG factors, given the futurism intrinsic to the sustainability argument. If English were to be replaced as the global business language with either Aramaic or Sanskrit, the effect on the global financial system would be no less jarring.

While catching fire and spreading rapidly across Wall Street in recent years, the ESG movement has been decades in the making. With deep progressive roots stretching all the way back to 19th-century Marxism, the doctrine of sustainability was crystallized in the 1980s when the liberal streams of environmentalism and anticapitalism were first crossed, mainly as a means of reining in corporations and bringing the financial markets to heel. The term "sustainability" was originally coined in the 1987 report "Our Common Future," issued by the UN's Brundtland Commission, which also decreed that the business sector is responsible for helping to solve all the world's human and social problems in a clear rejection of traditional shareholder capitalism in favor of the stakeholder capitalism pushed by Klaus Schwab through the WEF and the Davos Manifesto. Over the past 40 years, the UN and its member governments and supranational affiliates have taken the lead in pushing the sustainability agenda, using climate change as its core thesis and moral exoskeleton.

Sustainable investing stands Milton Friedman's simple but sage advice about corporate social responsibility – that profit maximization in the context of open and free competition should be a company's main priority – completely on its head by arguing that companies should be run for the benefit of society, rather than for the employees and managers doing the actual work or the shareholders and bondholders providing the investment capital. Effectively, it places the weight of all the world's sins and deficiencies on the backs of the corporate sector – as opposed to the government sphere, where it rightly belongs – and enlists the asset management industry as its Praetorian Guard to enforce its strictures and serve as society's bill collector. Any company that does not fully embrace all of the progressive elements embedded in the ESG orthodoxy is deemed unsustainable and not worthy of client service, customer patronage, or, most importantly, market financing.

Thus far, empirical studies have shown only a tenuous linkage between ESG factors and corporate performance, which is not surprising given the array of subjective, morally relative topics animating sustainability activists. At best, ESG factors represent a source of potential negative-event risk that affects a small subset of issuers, rather than a positive catalyst for improved operating and financial performance or a new, more enlightened way of analyzing companies. In the absence of hard data showing that a sustainable approach leads to better corporate results or greater investor returns, ESG advocates qualify their performance promises with "may" or "can" and give vague assurances about "doing well by doing good." Alternatively, they try to make their case by citing metadata studies, which are basically the analytical equivalent of Bigfoot sightings.

Most of the efforts to make the economic case for ESG are half-hearted at best. Much like the climate change agenda at its core, the sustainability movement has developed into a kind of religion for the financial markets, walking by faith more than logic at this point. In place of reasoned arguments, it relies on emotion and moral suasion – after all, ESG also goes by the name of responsible investing – and uses schoolyard tactics such as peer pressure and public shaming to force compliance and capitulation, often hiding behind youth activists and children to plead its case. ESG controversies – which are the stock-in-trade of the movement – can be manufactured out of whole cloth by a flash mob protesting at a company's headquarters or annual shareholder meeting. ESG opponents across Wall Street run the risk of being canceled for speaking out or questioning the sustainability orthodoxy – especially when it comes to climate action and the need to reduce carbon dioxide emissions. As with every other progressive cause to date, the sustainable investment movement will eventually stop debating and simply resort to government force to impose its proprietary system of morality on the global financial markets.

Sustainable investing is a scam because it is not about generating excess returns for investors or furthering ethical goals such as improving society or saving the planet; rather, it is about determining the allocation of capital and investment flows across the corporate sector. It is liberal progressive politics masquerading as finance whose objective is to create a compliant corporate sector that serves as both Greek chorus and funding source for the environmental and social causes championed by government and the elite class. It is socialism disguised as a new form of capitalism. The sustainable investment movement represents an integral component of the closely coordinated and synchronized 2030 agendas of both the UN and the WEF, with a reengineering of the global financial markets notably being a prerequisite of the Great Reset Initiative of the latter.

The ultimate goal of sustainable investing is to control the entire global financial system, which is the one remaining segment of society that progressives have yet to put under their collective thumb. Since the

1980s, the rolling liberal takeover has included the estates of education (both universities and K–12 public schools), government (with its permanent regulatory state), organized religion (watered-down orthodoxy), the arts (Hollywood and the music industry), and all forms of media (traditional as well as social), with major components of the economy (electric power, health care, and banking) also being indirectly controlled through regulation.

Even though the financial markets are also highly regulated – increasingly so over the past decade since the 2008 global financial crisis – such rules only ensure fair disclosure and dealing and a level playing field for all market participants. They control how companies are allowed to finance themselves through the markets; they do not determine the cost of capital or decide which companies are allowed to access the financial markets. This is where sustainable investing comes in. ESG criteria are meant to tilt the investment playing field and serve as the discriminant filter for market access and pricing going forward. To facilitate this new enlightened system, every financial market and market participant must get on board. For the scheme to work, it will need to ensnare every financial market – debt and equity, public and private – and eventually impact every investor – both passive and active, institutional and retail – including the approximately one-third of working-age Americans who currently have funded 401(k) retirement accounts.

In the years since the 2015 signing of the Paris Agreement and the corollary release of the UN's Sustainable Development Goals (SDGs), the market objective has been to spread the ESG gospel and integrate sustainability across the global financial system. Almost overnight, a cottage industry of ESG specialist firms and service providers has sprung up to facilitate this integration, aided and abetted in the process by a steady stream of confirmatory research out of the many sustainable business centers now resident in the halls of academia. So far, the buy side of Wall Street – investment management firms, insurance companies, and pension funds – has taken the lead doing the missionary work of engaging with companies on ESG disclosure and compliance. Harassing and haranguing corporate management teams to set and hit sustainability targets for their businesses is what passes for active ownership these days in the brave new world of ESG investing.

Superimposing sustainability onto the financial markets has led to a paralysis of analysis across Wall Street, wasting time, energy, and money while distracting from the real fundamental and technical drivers of the markets. Even though stakeholder capitalism based on ESG factors constrains both companies and investors alike, to date there has been little public resistance or analytical pushback across Wall Street. Since sustainability policy is mainly set by liberal CEOs and driven top-down from the corporate suite at most companies, banks, and asset management firms, this tends to cut down on dissent from business line managers and the rank and file. While most of the take-up has been concentrated in Europe, where the ESG force is strong among European companies, financial institutions, and investment firms, the pressure is now building across the US market.

As proof that ESG is gaining traction, business leaders now regularly and reflexively take a public stand on all the cultural and political issues of the day – including climate change, critical race theory, LGBTQ+ rights, gun control laws, COVID-19 vaccine mandates, and the Russia–Ukraine war, almost always staking out a position on the left side of the debate. Whether Apple Inc. on transgender bathroom policy in North Carolina or The Coca-Cola Company on voting requirements in Georgia or The Walt Disney Company on parental education rights in Florida, CEOs now feel compelled to weigh in on every social headline and donate corporate money to every liberal cause. In 2020, after the death of George Floyd, US corporations sent millions of dollars to Black Lives Matter, the NAACP, the Equal Justice Initiative, and other so-called antiracism organizations. In 2022, when Roe v. Wade was overturned by the Supreme Court and the issue of abortion was returned to state legislatures, scores of American companies including The Goldman Sachs Group Inc. immediately announced plans to cover abortion-related travel expenses for their employees.

While confirming that the Pavlovian ESG exercise is working, such public displays of woke capitalism are basically an outward symptom of the problem. These virtue-signaling acts mainly serve as a distraction from the real sustainability threat now occurring behind the scenes as ESG metastasizes across the financial markets. And for all the focus on company resolutions, proxy fights, and board control during the annual shareholder meeting season, the main ESG battle is taking place not in the public equity markets but in the less transparent credit markets, given that bank loans and institutional bonds are the main source of liquidity for most companies and the cheapest source of capital with which to fund ongoing operations and acquisition-related growth. The ESG goal is to choke off debt capital to certain industries and companies by either driving up their cost of capital to prohibitive levels or branding these issuers as basically unworthy of financing at any price. No amount of management compliance, increased ESG disclosure, or vocal public support for liberal causes will stop what is coming for those politically incorrect businesses targeted by the ESG activists.

Sustainable investing is all about picking corporate winners and losers, with the choice being made from without the financial markets. Given that climate change is the top priority of the ESG movement – in many ways, the concept of sustainability was created to co-opt the private sector into the public sector's climate crusade – the biggest corporate losers will be oil, gas, and coal companies, fossil-fuel-based power generators, organic chemical and steel manufacturers, and heavy industry in general. These companies, with their large carbon footprints, are the main targets for the sustainability mob, to be made an ESG example of for the educational benefit of other sectors. On the flip side, the most-favored ESG industries will include green energy and renewable power players benefiting from the politically driven energy transition, as well as most technology and consumer goods companies by virtue of their asset-light business models. Also, consistent with the bipolar UN approach to climate change, the ESG rules are typically applied more harshly to large-cap public industrial companies trading in the developed markets of North America and Europe, as opposed to smaller, private issuers in the riskier emerging market regions of Asia, Africa, and Latin America.

Now, like most religious belief systems, the morality-driven sustainability movement is moving from evangelism to a more puritanical phase, with the expansive ESG bureaucracy now starting to ossify and become more exclusionary, prescriptive, and compulsory on the back of regulatory mandates. Financial regulators are starting to mandate climate and other ESG disclosures, with Europe again taking the lead and the United States now following suit. Recent criminal and regulatory investigations of investment management firms looking for evidence of "greenwashing" would seem to indicate that government officials are aiming to lay the predicate for ESG fund mandates and reporting requirements as a means of "protecting investors." Fiduciary rules are being rewritten not just to allow but even require an ESG approach by fund managers. The current wave of sustainable finance regulations now hitting the global markets will usher in the next, more rigid stage of the ESG movement – one where voluntary participation and bespoke integration is replaced by standardization and coercion. Based on the current industry trajectory, by 2030 the iron curtain of sustainability will have fully descended across Wall Street.

In the long wake of the 2008 global financial crisis, a hyperregulated and compliance-cowed Wall Street sets up as a vulnerable target for the sustainable shakedown. After years of being criticized for taking government bailout money and wrecking Main Street, Wall Street firms – like the rest of corporate America – have tried to leverage the virtue-signaling aspects of ESG so as to burnish the industry's image. At the same time, investment banks and asset managers have focused on the short-term profit potential of sustainable investing – including underwriting green bonds and raising capital for dedicated ESG funds with higher fee structures – rather than the negative long-term implications for the financial markets, in the process losing the forest for the trees. By viewing sustainability chiefly as a financing problem to be solved and a revenue-generating opportunity to be exploited, both sell-side and buy-side financial firms are losing sight of the bigger picture and effectively getting played.

Wall Street has experienced investment fads before, but the current ESG craze is unique in that it is not a market or asset bubble that will eventually burst, allowing the industry to move on. Unlike Dutch tulips in the 1630s, South Sea Company shares in the 1720s, Japanese stocks in the 1980s, or the US housing market in the 2000s, sustainability is not meaningfully affecting asset prices. While it is a crowded trade, it is not being driven by irrational exuberance, so there is nothing to pop; there is no natural safety valve for the financial markets.

The running joke on Wall Street is that it is usually a good time to sell whenever market prognosticators are telling you to buy because there has been a paradigm shift in a particular market, industry, or product, and "this time is different." With the sustainable investment movement, however, this investment trope will finally prove accurate. A global financial system where every trade, investment, and portfolio decision is viewed through a subjective multivariate moral prism applied by third-party sustainability experts will represent a paradigm shift that fundamentally changes Wall Street. In industry jargon, there will be no mean reversion with ESG. Past a certain point – which is rapidly approaching – there will be no unwinding of the sustainability trade. With each passing year of capitulation and conformity, it becomes that much harder for the financial industry to walk back its previous praise and support of the ESG argument. ESG investing has kicked off a race to the bottom for Wall Street and a downward market spiral that will eventually crater the global financial system.

While an immediate concern for Wall Street players and those already invested in the financial markets, inevitably the sustainability movement – if left unchecked – will impact the broader US economy and touch every American as politically incorrect industries and companies get cut off from financing and either grow more slowly or simply go away. This, in turn, will lead to a narrowing of consumer choices and an increase in the cost of everything, which the world is already starting to see. Since oil and gas energy is used to make and transport most goods, the economic impact will be felt broadly if the ESG movement ultimately succeeds in its primary goal of canceling out fossil fuel companies.

The final market countdown to 2030 has already begun. Wall Street ignores the long-term threat posed by ESG and the sustainable investment movement at its own peril.

CHAPTER 1

SUSTAINABILITY: A THEORY ABOUT EVERYTHING

The best way to destroy the capitalist system is to debauch the currency.
Vladimir Lenin

The bigger the humbug, the better people will like it.
P. T. Barnum

By all outward appearances, the 1980s were a tough decade for liberal progressives. By then, the crowning government achievements of the Progressive Era at the turn of the 20th century, the New Deal age of the 1930s, and even the Great Society period of the 1960s had either faded into distant memory or fallen into disrepute. Despite a burgeoning government bureaucracy and a sharp increase in US federal spending on social welfare programs, the number of American families living in poverty – particularly single-parent households – had remained stubbornly high. This, in turn, led to a host of other social pathologies, including increased high school dropout rates, rising homelessness, a public housing crisis, rampant drug use, and skyrocketing crime in US cities. Ronald Reagan became the 40th US president and won two landslide elections based on his promise to put an end to "Trust me" government.

Eight years of supply-side economics and muscular American foreign policy under the Reagan administration and the steady decline and sudden fall of the Soviet Union – symbolized by the toppling of the Berlin Wall in 1989 – only served to reinforce the strength of capitalism and individual freedoms over communism, socialism, and other failed collectivist approaches. As chronicled by the British historian Paul Johnson in *Modern Times*, moral relativism during the 20th century led to the rise of totalitarian government regimes around the globe between the 1920s and the 1980s, all of which were intent on creating their own versions of heaven on earth. These "despotic utopias,"[1] which included Nazi Germany, the Soviet Union, and Communist China plus all their respective allies and satellites, offered clear examples of what happens when absolute government force is combined with a blank sheet upon which to redraw society and its economic underpinnings. It is estimated that more than 100 million people perished at the hands of progress-minded communist and socialist dictators during the last century, through a combination of political persecution, military aggression, and sheer economic incompetence.[2]

Undeterred by such bad press, the progressive movement simply slipped into the background to consolidate its position and take the fight for power and control to a different front. Even as the rest of the world was busy celebrating the imminent end of the Cold War and the forthcoming freedom of nearly 300 million people trapped in the Soviet system, progressives were commencing a rearguard action to lay siege to the main structural pillars of Western society: public schools and universities, churches, mass media, the arts, and big business. While the deconstruction and hollowing out of these institutions from the inside would take several years and multiple generations to complete, much of the planning and groundwork occurred during the 1980s, an era ostensibly characterized by conservative politics.

It was during this period that the doctrine of business sustainability was originally conceived, mainly as a means of reining in corporations and eventually bringing the financial markets to heel. The term "sustainability," which previously had been used mainly as an ecological and biological term to describe the natural world, was first applied to the corporate sector in the 1987 report "Our Common Future" issued by the World Commission on Environment and Development of the United Nations, the collective political body created out of the ashes of World War II. The 1987 UN commission is more commonly known as the Brundtland Commission since the body was chaired by Gro Harlem Brundtland, the prime minister of Norway, who began her political career as the Norwegian minister of the environment back in the 1970s. The

Brundtland Commission was the follow-on to the United Nations Conference on the Human Environment held in Stockholm back in 1972, which helped launch the world environmental movement and led to the formation of the United Nations Environment Programme (UNEP). It was at the 1972 conference that the antagonistic relationship between the natural environment and economic development was first established, and environmental issues were made an integral part of the international agenda.

The 23-member Brundtland Commission was originally tasked with coming up with proposals for balancing the competing goals of economic development and environmental protection in the developing world – specifically, actionable steps for driving economic growth across lower-income countries that would not place undue pressure on "the planet's lands, waters, forests, and other natural resources."[3] Of these two goals, the former was clearly the more pressing at the time. During the 1980s, the sovereign debt crisis triggered by Mexico's 1982 default on its external debt led to a lost decade of development across Latin America, Africa, and the rest of the emerging markets. Shut off from the international debt markets, foreign capital inflows dried up, economic growth stalled, and poverty levels increased across most of the third world. Leveraging the existing network of multilateral credit agencies, including the World Bank and all its regional development lending counterparts, seemed like an obvious solution to the problem of economic development.

Instead, the Brundtland Commission chose to focus on how environmental degradation had "become a survival issue for developing nations" due to "the downward spiral of linked ecological and economic decline in which many of the poorest nations are trapped."[4] Rather than analyzing how market-based reforms – as demonstrated by the Asian Tiger model – could lay the foundation for a virtuous economic cycle and improve living standards in a greater number of developing countries, the UN panel instead emphasized the vicious "links between poverty, inequality and environmental degradation."[5] The commission's work was doubtless influenced by the environmental headlines of the times – including the 1983–1985 Ethiopian drought, the 1984 San Juanico liquid petroleum gas tank farm explosion, the 1984 Bhopal pesticide chemical plant leak, and the 1986 Chernobyl nuclear power plant disaster – even though all these events were caused by either natural phenomena or human operating error, from which no meaningful development-policy conclusions could be drawn.

As with the Stockholm Conference 15 years earlier, environmental issues were also top of mind for the Brundtland Commission, even though many of the dire environmental predictions made by the likes of Rachel Carson (*Silent Spring*, 1962), Paul Ehrlich (*The Population Bomb*, 1968), Edward Goldsmith (*A Blueprint for Survival*, 1972), and the Club of Rome (*The Limits of Growth*, 1972) had not panned out over the interim two decades. Nonetheless, the final report of the Brundtland Commission was infused with the same antihuman environmentalism of the earlier UN conference, including its irrational fear of overpopulation and overwhelming pessimism about mankind's prospects. Even though its authors viewed the 1987 report as carrying "a message of hope," "Our Common Future" channeled the same Malthusian spirit of Stockholm by positing that a resource-constrained planet requires a new kind of sustainable growth that is less material- and energy-intensive and "more equitable in its impact."[6] Placing a self-imposed limit on economic development, mainly through the application of an environmental brake, stood in sharp contrast with the limitless view of human progress and economic expansion based on science and technology advancements that had endured for more than 200 years since the Enlightenment.

Moreover, rather than sticking to its original remit – economy versus ecology in the developing world – the final 374-page report issued by the Brundtland Commission employed a wider lens to frame the problem and used a very broad brush to draw its conclusions. In the Brundtland formulation, sustainable development is development that "meets the needs of the present without compromising the ability of future generations to meet their own needs."[7] At first glance, this working definition seemed like a simple paraphrasing of the theme of the 1972 Stockholm Conference: What should be done to maintain the Earth as a place suitable for human life not only now, but also for future generations?

However, on closer inspection, the Brundtland sustainability doctrine represented a clear escalation of the UN's previous environmental mandate. First, the commission redefined the term "environment" to include not just natural factors but also all human social and political dimensions. As the report stated, the environment is "where we all live" and "does not exist as a sphere separate from human actions, ambitions, and needs."[8]

Second, using a unitarian approach, the report forever linked this expanded definition of "environment" with "development," forging the two as inseparable concepts that must be looked at from a global perspective across both developing and industrialized countries. As the commission noted, "The integration of environment and development is required in all nations, rich and poor" which, in turn, will require "changes in the domestic and international policies of every nation."[9] Over time, the burden of sustainable development has fallen harder on the backs of industrialized nations than of developing countries, which is counterintuitive but consistent with the rich-man, poor-man economic policies and Lilliputian politics that have dominated the UN since the days of Dag Hammarskjöld. Ever since the reverse takeover of the UN by the Bandung Generation of third-world member nations during the 1950s and 1960s,[10] income redistribution has been an important component of most UN policies and programs. To justify the need for a wealth-transfer solution, the Brundtland Report reinforced the global tension between developing countries mainly in the Southern Hemisphere (the so-called Global South) and developed nations concentrated in the Northern Hemisphere (mainly Europe and North America), placing much of the blame for the world's environmental problems on the unsustainable patterns of energy and raw material consumption in the North.

Third, the Brundtland Commission recalibrated the argument around pollution of the natural environment and protection of the planet, bringing the abstract concept of global warming and man-made climate change to the forefront of sustainable development. Such a reset did not come as a surprise given that, up until then, the sustainable descriptor had been mainly used by environmentalists as a slur against the resource-depleting hydrocarbon sector – particularly, integrated and independent oil companies. The Brundtland Report notably referred to the fossil fuels industry as a "continuing dilemma,"[11] both because of its finite recoverable reserve base and the increase in atmospheric carbon dioxide and other greenhouse gases that resulted from the burning of oil, gas, coal, and other hydrocarbons, the latter of which purportedly raised average global temperatures and altered the world's climate system. While it was still the early days of the UN-led climate crusade – the UN's Intergovernmental Panel on Climate Change (IPCC) would not hold its first meeting until the following year – this anchoring of the sustainability movement to the environmental cause of climate change was a deliberate move that would have broad and long-lasting implications, particularly for the corporate sector. Notably, the Brundtland Commission gave rise to two new environmental verticals within the UN bureaucracy: one for sustainable development through the United Nations Commission on Sustainable Development and its successor, the High-Level Political Forum on Sustainable Development (HLPFSD); the other for climate change through the IPCC and the United Nations Framework Convention on Climate Change (UNFCCC). After her star turn with "Our Common Future," Gro Harlem Brundtland would go on to serve as the UN special envoy on climate change.

Lastly and most importantly, the Brundtland doctrine of sustainable development designated the business sector as a responsible party for all the world's environmental and other problems. Even as the commission renewed calls for increased multilateral cooperation and a hardening of "political will" to promote sustainable development and "enforce the common interest," the report also co-opted corporations into the "common cause" and the progressive fight against climate change and sundry other social issues.[12] The framing of this argument was subtle but deliberate, the corporate equivalent of a "Kick Me" sign being placed on the back of an unsuspecting middle schooler. Besides government officials and policymakers, the Brundtland Report was also specifically addressed to "private enterprise, from the one-person business to the great multinational company with a total economic turnover greater than that of many nations," with the clear messaging that industry "should accept a broad sense of social responsibility and ensure an awareness of environmental considerations at all levels."[13] The new "triple bottom line" for companies included ledgers for social and environmental performance as well as economic profit and loss. And all this corporate altruism came with an invoice attached, given that "sustainable development must be powered by a continuing flow of wealth from industry."[14]

The corporate social responsibility inherent to the Brundtland definition of sustainable development explicitly rejected the shareholder capitalism theory of business ethics espoused by Milton Friedman, winner of the 1976 Nobel Memorial Prize in Economic Sciences and the leading proponent of the neoclassical economic thought prevalent at the time. As summarized in his 1970 essay in the *New York Times*, Friedman believed that "there is one and only one social responsibility of business – to use its resources and engage in activities designed to increase its profits so long as it stays within the rules of the game, which is to say, engages in open and free competition, without deception or fraud."[15] This was the complete and unabridged version of the Friedman Doctrine, although critics have deceptively truncated this statement to read that a corporation's only goal is to maximize its profit.

In Friedman's view, the "acceptance by corporate officials of a social responsibility other than to make as much money for their stockholders as possible" is a "fundamentally subversive doctrine" that will "thoroughly undermine the very foundations of our free society." When corporate executives exercise a distinct "social responsibility," they are no longer acting as the agents of the company's stockholders or its customers or employees; rather, they are behaving more like civil servants imposing a tax and spending someone else's money for a social cause favored by government and other activists. While often used by shortsighted managers as "moral cloaks" to generate goodwill and ward off public criticism, the doctrine of social responsibility is basically "hypocritical window dressing" that only serves to reinforce the "already too prevalent view that the pursuit of profits is wicked and immoral and must be curbed and controlled by external forces." Lastly, Friedman recognized the corporate social responsibility movement for what it was: a system built on conformity and, basically, socialism in disguise.[16]

Friedman believed that there was no need for the business sector to seek moral redemption through extracurricular social activities because free-market capitalism has always been the most moral economic system known to man, as well as a precondition for political freedom. This view was grounded in the moral, economic, and political philosophy of the great Enlightenment thinkers Adam Smith, David Hume, and John Locke, all of whom extolled the virtues of liberty, property rights, and economic freedom and the dynamic self-regulating nature of the market mechanism in their writings. In *An Inquiry into the Nature and Causes of the Wealth of Nations*, Smith argued that the pursuit of individual self-interest in economic life – the metaphorical invisible hand – leads to a public good and a betterment of the community and society.[17] In his *Essays, Moral, Political, and Literary*, Hume opined that "industry, knowledge, and humanity, are linked together by an indissoluble chain" and that modern commerce and trade promoted peace, civility, and moral refinement.[18] In his *Second Treatise of Government*, Locke wrote that the accumulation of wealth and private property through labor or industriousness were moral activities that increased "the common stock of mankind."[19] All three philosophers believed that morality was the natural state inherent to humans, informing all their economic and commercial dealings.

Friedman's views about morality and capitalism also drew from the work of contemporaries such as Friedrich Hayek, the Austrian economist and recipient of the 1974 Nobel Memorial Prize in Economic Sciences, who wrote in *The Road to Serfdom* that free markets built on self-interest, competition, and individual rights and responsibilities were the best economic approach and obviated the need for "conscious social control," while adding that collectivist systems were "destructive of all morals" and the central direction of all economic activity according to a single plan inevitably leads to dictatorship.[20] Friedman's free-market economics were also echoed – and amplified – by the Russian philosopher Ayn Rand, who gave a more robust and full-throated moral defense of capitalism in her various political essays and published books. In her 1961 essay "America's Persecuted Minority: Big Business," she wrote, "All the evils, abuses, and iniquities, popularly ascribed to businessmen and to capitalism, were not caused by an unregulated economy or by a free market, but by government intervention into the economy."[21] Or as she put it more bluntly in her epic 1957 novel *Atlas Shrugged*, "Run for your life from any man who tells you that money is evil. That sentence is the leper's bell of an approaching looter."[22]

Even though Milton Friedman's economic theories represented orthodox thought at the time and his teachings predominated in the curriculum of most US business schools during the second half of the 20th century, the Brundtland Commission rejected his views about shareholder capitalism – interestingly, the words "shareholder" and "capitalism" appear nowhere in the final UN report – and instead chose to embrace the relatively new but complementary theory of stakeholder capitalism to help make its altruistic argument around sustainability. Stakeholder capitalism theory, which had been making the rounds in management circles since the 1960s, argues that modern enterprises must serve not only shareholders but all company stakeholders – including employees, suppliers, and customers as well as the state, the economy, and society at large.

One of the leading champions of stakeholder capitalism is Klaus Schwab, author of the 1971 book *Modern Company Management in Mechanical Engineering*, which laid out his initial views on the topic. That same year Schwab founded the European Management Forum, which holds its annual meeting in the ski resort of Davos, Switzerland, and which was subsequently renamed the WEF in 1987. An industrial engineer and economist by training, the German-born Schwab believes that capitalism needs to be improved upon by adopting the corporatist model prevalent in Germany and other Western European nations during the postwar period. Under corporatism, businesses, labor, and the state all cooperate and work together to safeguard social order, with government appointees and union representatives often sitting on company boards. Since companies are both social organisms and trustees of society, business owners have an obligation to use their private property in a moral fashion. Such a business approach creates strong linkages between companies and their communities and local institutions such as government, schools, and health organizations. As Schwab writes, "The wider economy, the state and society expect that the company will contribute to the improvement of public well-being."[23] As Schwab has noted, it was "quite natural" during the 1950s and 1960s for a company and its executives to consider not just shareholders but everyone who had a stake in the success of the firm, because "one person or entity could only do well if the whole community and economy functioned."[24] Since 1973, the membership of the WEF, which purportedly includes thousands of multinational corporations and global financial institutions, has pledged its allegiance to the concept of stakeholder capitalism by being signatories to the Davos Manifesto, which notably states that companies must "serve society."[25]

While doubtless influenced by an engineering flow-chart mindset and a Prussian need to order society, the corporatism underlying the Schwab stakeholder approach is basically a collectivist political ideology with a dark lineage. Fundamentally, it is fascism once-removed, bearing a strong resemblance to the German Corporation Law of 1937 passed by Adolf Hitler's National Socialist government, which was designed to force all forms of economic activity – especially large-scale businesses – to adhere to the Nazi rule of "public welfare before individual gain." Under the 1937 law, the German state supplanted liberal market convention and laissez-faire policies to become the guiding power over the national economy and ensure that all business activities remained in socially correct channels, consistent with the other Nazi slogan: "Politics leads economics and not vice versa." Notably, the law freed German corporate managers and directors of their specific fiduciary duty to shareholders by substituting a general duty to all stakeholders.[26]

In an interesting genealogical twist, Schwab's father, Eugen, who was also an industrial engineer, actively supported the German war effort during World War II. The elder Schwab worked for the Swiss industrial manufacturer Escher Wyss & Cie., and moved his family back to Germany after the Nazi Party rose to power during the 1930s to serve as the commercial manager of the Swiss company's factory in Ravensburg. The plant run by Schwab's father supplied military armaments and aircraft parts to the Wehrmacht and used approximately 200 forced laborers from nearby Nazi camps in its production process. Under the senior Schwab's management, the Ravensburg branch of Escher Wyss was awarded the title of "National Socialist Model Company" by Adolf Hitler. Apart from the Schwab-run munitions factory, the Escher Wyss industrial conglomerate was also deeply involved in the Nazi atomic weapons program since the hydroelectric power turbines that it manufactured helped produce the heavy water needed to turn common uranium into plutonium. After the war ended, Eugen Schwab was exonerated under the denazification program run by the Allies after filling out two questionnaires in 1946.[27]

Similarly, the fascist Italian government of Benito Mussolini pushed a state-directed economy as a "third way" between liberal capitalism and communism or socialism. In 1933, Italy formed the Institute for Industrial Reconstruction, a government holding company that assumed control of roughly three-quarters of the Italian industrial and agricultural economy by working through the state-owned banking system, much as the 1937 German law did.[28] Echoing Mussolini, Schwab has described stakeholder capitalism as a third economic model and a better alternative to either shareholder or state-owned capitalism. Despite this public spin, the Schwab brand of stakeholder capitalism equates to a gradual Fabian approach to achieving socialism; its concept of public–private partnership is basically the public sector directing the private sector, similar to a general partner–limited partner structure. It is ironic that Western Europe won the military battle against Nazi Germany and Fascist Italy during World War II but then lost the economic peace by adopting in its aftermath democratic socialism as its dominant political system, with all the state economic control that this political choice entailed.

Since the early 1970s, the popularity of stakeholder capitalism has steadily grown, typically adding more followers during periods of economic stress or market excess. This was the case during the 1980s when stakeholder capitalism and sustainable development first became intertwined with the release of the 1987 Brundtland Report. At the time, the world was dealing with a banking-related sovereign debt crisis across the developing world, even as Wall Street was posting outsized industry profits on the back of a wave of merger and acquisition (M&A) activity, most of which was hostile in nature and driven by charges of poor corporate governance. The 1980s were also the decade of leveraged buyouts and junk bonds. Such a financial backdrop, along with the mounting environmental emergency of man-made global warming, provided the pretext and helped bolster the argument for a new business approach.

As symbiotic ideologies holding similar anticapitalist views and using the same progressive lexicon when it came to the business sector, sustainable development and stakeholder capitalism were a natural fit. Even though the UN and the WEF already traveled in the same multilateral circles and attended the same international conferences (including Davos), the activist agendas of both groups have become more closely aligned and synchronized since the release of "Our Common Future." The UN now regularly talks about stakeholders when it frames sustainable development, while the WEF highlights sustainability in its discussions of stakeholder capitalism. Both organizations go on ad nauseam about global warming and the climate emergency, often completing each other's sentences.

Since this marriage of convenience, the Schwab brand of stakeholder capitalism has been revised to reflect the main sustainability goals of the UN, as described in Schwab's updated book on the subject *Stakeholder Capitalism: A Global Economy that Works for Progress, People and Planet,* which was published in 2021. In line with the increasing globalization of trade and business seen during the second half of the 20th century, the original focus of stakeholder capitalism on strategic management and local issues has been replaced with a global corporate agenda organized around two primary stakeholders: people and the planet. As Schwab writes, it is incumbent on good global corporate citizens to place the "well-being of people and planet" at the center of their business operations given the interconnectedness of the world's societies and the fact that "the planet ... is the central stakeholder in the global economic system."[29] This global stakeholder reorganization, in turn, significantly expanded the number of constituencies in need of business attention and required a reordering of the focus list of pressing social issues, mainly to move climate issues to the forefront and prioritize the environmental agenda of the UN.

While the Brundtland Report provided a broad sustainability framework, stakeholder capitalism theory has served as the atomizer to push the macro-level concept of sustainable development down to the company level – the lowest common denominator of economic activity. As opposed to a top-down system directly imposed by national governments, sustainability has now become an international bottom-up movement driven by socially conscious corporations, some signing up willingly and others joining under duress. To achieve a sustainable planet and global economy, each individual company must do its part not just by engaging with civil society, but also by internalizing a global stakeholder mindset and becoming a "sustainable business" in its own right. Even though most business leaders don't have the requisite skill set for understanding and solving the world's problems, this argument has particularly resonated with semiautonomous professional management teams running large publicly traded corporations with diluted shareholder ownership structures, most of which are based in the industrialized world and trade in the developed markets of North America and Europe. With corporate sustainability now the main frame of reference, business behavior can be more easily controlled through the imposition of a sustainability test – or, said another way, a progressive loyalty test – to ensure that companies are focusing on "social values."[30] Now almost every corporate action is looked at through a prism of sustainability that includes a cost–benefit analysis of its externalities on the natural, human, social, and political environment.

What exactly does it mean to be a sustainable business? While somewhat of a moving target, broadly speaking, it means subscribing to the liberal global agenda set by the UN and the WEF. Over the past three decades, the definition of sustainable business has proven malleable and changed with the tastes of the times as progressives have gradually filled in all the missing colors to reveal the entire picture. With the Brundtland Report serving as an organic foundational document and a living constitution for the movement – the concepts of fairness, equity, and inclusiveness permeate its pages – sustainability has become the equivalent of an open-ended springing lien for companies, perpetually adding new obligations to the social balance sheet of business. While climate change has remained the focal point and the animating force behind the sustainability movement since the 1980s, over time all the core tenets of progressive ideology have been added to the list – including union power, human rights, gender-pay equality, tax fairness, social justice, and diversity, equity, and inclusion – and redefined as corporate policy goals.

Like every other progressive ideal, sustainability has proven a very long game for the UN, with the timetable largely dictated by developments and progress on the parallel climate change front. More than 25 years after the release of "Our Common Future," the UN finally followed up with a master list of sustainable business goals. Seeking to capitalize on the momentum resulting from the 2015 signing of the Paris Agreement, the HLPFSD released its SDGs for 2030 that same year. These included 17 interlinked global goals designed to "transform the world" and serve as a "blueprint to achieve a better and more sustainable future for all." The 17 SDGs, which UN leaders have dubbed a "master plan for humanity," read like a progressive bucket list and include the following goals: #1 No Poverty, #2 Zero Hunger, #3 Good Health and Well-being, #4 Quality Education, #5 Gender Equality, #6 Clean Water and Sanitation, #7 Affordable and Clean Energy, #8 Decent Work and Economic Growth, #9 Industry, Innovation and Infrastructure, #10 Reduced Inequalities, #11 Sustainable Cities and Communities, #12 Responsible Consumption and Production, #13 Climate Action, #14 Life Below Water, #15 Life on Land, #16 Peace, Justice and Strong Institutions, and #17 Partnerships for the Goals.[31]

Climate action (SDG #13) provides the intersectional glue for the entire progressive agenda embedded in the UN's sustainability program, with each individual cause drawing strength and further validation from the moral imperative of saving the planet from fossil fuels because, in the UN's telling, climate change also affects global health, poverty, hunger, and national security, and "its adverse impacts undermine the ability of all countries to achieve sustainable development."[32] In the words of UN Secretary-General António Guterres, "Climate action is the 21st century's greatest opportunity to drive forward all the Sustainable Development Goals."[33] Notably, 12 of the 17 SDGs directly involve taking action on climate change – in addition to climate change having its own goal. As with the 2030 SDGs, the climate change calendar also has an arbitrary self-imposed 2030 deadline, so both UN programs are now sprinting toward the same finish line like partners in a three-legged race. In addition to this starting framework of 17 climate-centric SDGs, 169 specific individual targets were also released to foster further alignment with the UN at the industry and company level, along with 232 metrics against which to measure progress.

Over the past eight years, the WEF has also taken a number of steps to keep pace with the UN, while at the same time upping the ante on sustainability. In 2017, the WEF published a white paper on resetting the "global operating system" to achieve the UN's SDGs. In 2019, the WEF formed a strategic partnership with the UN to advance the UN's 2030 Agenda for Sustainable Development, which included the WEF promise to help finance the UN's climate change agenda and help the UN "meet the needs of the Fourth Industrial Revolution," which is the term coined by the WEF's Klaus Schwab to describe the current historical period that we are living in – one "characterized by a range of new technologies that are fusing the physical, digital and biological worlds, impacting all disciplines, economies and industries, and even challenging ideas about what it means to be human." In the 2016 book that he wrote on the subject, Schwab discusses how recent advancements in artificial intelligence (AI), robotics, blockchain, the Internet of Things (IoT), three-dimensional (3D) printing, genetic engineering, quantum computing, and other technologies are driving the Fourth Industrial Revolution and rapidly changing society, while providing the means to the end of "digital governance," a cryptic phrase evoking the technology-enabled surveillance state of China, whose economy Schwab has openly praised as a "role model" for other nations to follow. The Schwab book includes ominous-sounding chapters on "Implantable Technologies," "Designer Beings," "Smart Cities," "The Connected Home," "3D Printing and Human Health," and "Neurotechnologies."[34]

In 2020, the WEF followed up with the official launch of its Great Reset Initiative at the group's 50th annual meeting, which took place virtually in June of that year at the height of the COVID-19 pandemic. While described as an economic recovery plan drawn up by the WEF in response to COVID-19 – barely three months after the pandemic officially started – the Great Reset involves an extreme makeover of the global economy and human society using the pandemic as justification. As Schwab has noted, "The pandemic represents a rare but narrow window of opportunity to reflect, reimagine, and reset our world." In his view, "gradual measures and ad hoc solutions are not enough," so "new foundations must be laid to support the economic and social system" and "make the world more sustainable and resistant to sudden changes in external conditions," including those increasingly from climate change. The WEF has laid out three core objectives for the Great Reset program, all of which echo the 2030 agenda of the UN. First, shareholder capitalism must be replaced by stakeholder capitalism so that all companies work for the "common good" rather than short-term profits and immediate benefits alone. Second, a "more resilient, equitable and sustainable" economic and financial system must be constructed based on ESG criteria and metrics. Last, many of the technological innovations inherent to the Fourth Industrial Revolution must be harnessed for "the public good," to nourish "greener, smarter and fairer growth."[35] While benignly described as a simple reboot, the Great Reset represents a major reworking of the world economy and global financial system using many of the government measures rolled out during the COVID-19 pandemic – including lockdowns, forced vaccines, and digital passports – as a policy template for the coming climate emergency and other sustainability challenges. In the 50 years since he founded the WEF in 1971, Klaus Schwab has now completed the jump from industrial engineering to bio- and social engineering.

As the concept of sustainability has changed over time from a macroeconomic development theory to a matter of corporate policy and, more recently, an investment approach, its evolution has been strongly influenced along the way by historical and cultural events, especially during the formative years of the movement during the 1980s. Consider the central premise of sustainability – not compromising the ability of future generations to meet their own needs – as it applies to individual businesses, which is predicated on the ability to see into the distant future and divine in the here and now what corporate operating and strategic actions will prove sustainable over the long term. In this regard, the movement is borrowing from some of the blockbuster time-traveling movies of the 1980s such as the *Back to the Future* trilogy with Michael J. Fox and Christopher Lloyd and the *Terminator* movie series starring Arnold Schwarzenegger. While the darker, dystopian mood of the latter is clearly more consistent with the messaging of the movement, the premise of sustainability is basically a rip-off of the plot of *Back to the Future Part II.* Viewers will recall that, in the 1989 sequel, Biff Tannen uses a sports almanac listing the results of major sporting events from 1950 to 2000 to go back in time, alter the historical line, and make himself rich and powerful. In a nutshell, sustainability activists are arguing that they have the equivalent of Biff's sports almanac for 2050–2100 showing what will happen to the world if companies don't act now on climate change and other pressing issues. Of course, DeLorean time machines don't exist, which is unfortunate for environmentalists given that, in the future, they apparently use recycled household waste to generate the requisite 1.21 gigawatts of power needed to run the flux capacitor.[36]

This hasn't stopped sustainability activists, though, from using computer models and financial Excel spreadsheets to predict the future, Nostradamus-style. Long-dated forecasts put down on paper now take on a life and reality of their own, whether projections of average global temperatures and carbon emissions in 2100 or renewable power generation and electric vehicle (EV) demand estimates for 2050. Much like climate change theory, sustainability is predicated on unknowable and unverifiable outcomes decades down the road; however, speculating about the 21st-century future is probably preferable for progressive liberals to defending the historical track record of collectivist economic approaches during the 20th century. With the future, you can forever adjust your forecasts, timing, and confidence ranges and never be proven wrong, which is the most brilliant conceit of the sustainability movement: it is nonempirical and immune to deductive logic. Challenging the sustainability argument invariably degenerates into the equivalent of an unwinnable medieval debate about the number of angels that can dance on the head of a pin.

If the situation comedy *Seinfeld*, which debuted in 1989, was basically a "show about nothing," as highlighted in the self-aware 43rd episode of the series,[37] then sustainability can rightly be viewed as a theory about everything and an organizing principle for all things progressive. Using the broad enabling language of the Brundtland Report, every progressive ideal – from labor rights to climate action and social justice – has now been given eternal life by being rebranded as a sustainable goal for the world. Rather than defending each idea on its own merits, the entire sustainability agenda is offered up en bloc, with no line-item veto allowed. Since sustainability is an a priori ideology, no proof of concept or performance track record is necessary, with all the collectivist failures of the 20th century being chalked up to problems of execution rather than fatal flaws of logic. By touching every aspect of economic life and subsuming every business around the world, sustainability creates the mother of all corporate bureaucracies by swallowing up every other existing program, including the expansive diversity complex built out over the past 50 years on the back of equal opportunity laws and affirmative action programs. In the new progressive hierarchy, everything now reports to the Chief Sustainability Officer.

Sustainability is just the latest in a long series of fixes to be proposed for the capitalist model. Even though free-market capitalism has led to a dramatic rise in living standards and an amazing increase in human prosperity and freedom over the past two centuries, the system has been subject to regular attack almost since the beginning of the First Industrial Revolution. Most of these criticisms have been opportunistically timed around periods of economic shock, social transition, and financial market volatility to help make the political case for a new paradigm by exploiting a temporary crisis or extreme cycle turn. Karl Marx called for a revolution by the proletariat class of workers and an overthrow of the capitalist system in response to the difficult employment and living conditions for most factory workers in Europe during the 19th century. At the turn of the 20th century, American Progressives called in government support – mainly in the form of trust-busting statutes and new problem-solving regulatory bodies manned by technical experts – to reform capitalism from within by addressing such moral deficiencies as its extreme concentration of economic wealth and the poor workplace health and safety standards resulting from industrialization. During the first half of the 20th century, global military conflicts such as World War I and worldwide economic shocks such as the Great Depression were used to double down on both of these approaches, either by scrapping capitalism altogether and replacing it with the central planning of communism and socialism – a concept mainly test-run in Europe, with catastrophic results – or significantly increasing government regulation and intervention in the economy, as was seen in the US with the federal bureaucratic surge that occurred during the Franklin Delano Roosevelt administration.

The history of anticapitalism is now repeating itself with sustainability, which borrows elements from both the totalitarian and reformist approaches of the past. Sustainability seeks to work within the capitalist system to harness its productive capacity and create a virtual state-directed global economy, one where social pressure is used to align government and business interests and control private property. Under the moral cover of a looming environmental crisis and the existential threat of climate change, it seeks to impose a comprehensive set of liberal policy values on all companies. It is basically an attempt to build a totalitarian system of conformity across the business sector based on moral suasion, thereby avoiding the administrative cost and public sector responsibility associated with outright state ownership or direct government intervention. It embraces both state and progressive priorities but is mainly the fabrication of a permanent supranational bureaucracy of technocrats residing at multilateral agencies led by the UN and international NGOs such as the WEF, which effectively insulates it from accountability at the ballot box. In Friedman's words, it is "an attempt to attain collectivist ends without collectivist means."[38]

The theory of sustainability has been years in the making, slowly evolving and picking its spots since the release of "Our Common Future" in 1987. Rounding out the 1980s flashback theme, now like the last five minutes of an episode of *The A-Team*, the sustainability plan is coming together quickly as the timeline has been accelerating since 2015. With the all-important 2030 deadline fast approaching, we are already well into what the UN has described as the "Decade of Action," with less than "ten years to transform our world."[39] With its global scope, decentralized method of attack, and insidious appeal to business ethics, sustainability represents the most formidable threat to free-market capitalism ever seen. What better way to destroy capitalism than by paralyzing the invisible hand described by Adam Smith through the imposition of a moral test with global purview for every business decision? Depending on how things play out over the next few years, sustainability with a stakeholder focus may become capitalism's end stage as the last remaining structural pillar of society falls to the progressive agenda.

CHAPTER 2

IT'S ALL ABOUT CLIMATE CHANGE

Unthinking respect for authority is the greatest enemy of truth.
Albert Einstein

Back off, man. I'm a scientist.
Bill Murray, *Ghostbusters*

In 1970, the Clean Air Act (CAA) was passed with nearly unanimous bipartisan support in the US Congress and signed into law by, of all people, President Richard Nixon, who then went on to establish the Environmental Protection Agency (EPA) by executive order. This was followed by the passage of the Clean Water Act (CWA) in 1972, the Endangered Species Act in 1973, and the Toxic Substances Control Act in 1976. Even as the Democrat and Republican parties publicly battled over the Vietnam War and Watergate, there was broad political consensus about the need to clean up the environment in this country.

And then, a terrible thing happened: the environmental movement actually succeeded and got what it wanted. America's air got demonstrably cleaner, with the combined emissions of criteria air pollutants – particulates (PM2.5 and PM10), sulfur dioxide (SO_2), nitrogen oxide (NOx), volatile organic compounds (VOCs), carbon monoxide (CO), and lead (Pb) – dropping by 33% between 1970 and 1990, on the way to a 78% decline by 2021.[1] Companies stopped dumping chemicals in rivers and streams, with the percentage of dissolved oxygen deficits and the share of unfishable waters both decreasing almost every year between 1962 and 1990, with each halving over the period.[2] Endangered species like the American bald eagle, the timber wolf, and the gray whale all made dramatic population comebacks by the early 1990s.

Not willing to let a good government bureaucracy go to waste, environmental activists and politicians went back to the drawing board to come up with a problem that would require almost infinite government resources but could never be solved: global warming and man-made climate change. Somewhere back in the early 1980s, environmentalism was hijacked by the global warming crowd, which had been growing and gaining converts throughout the 1960s and 1970s. For the past 40 years, this insular group has been driving the psychedelic policy bus and setting the environmental agenda, lecturing the world at every turn about the existential threat posed to the planet and the human race by greenhouse gas emissions (mainly carbon dioxide) from fossil fuels, with the volume cranked up to 11 in recent years.

The theory of the greenhouse effect, which hypothesizes that the accumulation of certain gases – chiefly carbon dioxide, but also methane and water vapor – in the Earth's atmosphere leads to a warming of the planet, was first proposed at the turn of the 20th century by the American geologist Thomas Chamberlin and the Swedish chemist Svante Arrhenius. But without the instrumentation to measure and prove the hypothesis, it was largely overlooked by the scientific community until being revisited during the mid-20th century. In the 1960s, the modern environmental movement was just taking off and global warming theory – with its implications of impending planetary doom – fit in perfectly with the negativity of the times.

In 1965, the issue of global warming rose to prominence when it was publicly raised with the Johnson administration in the White House report "Restoring the Quality of Our Environment," which was prepared by the President's Science Advisory Committee. The report included a 23-page appendix on atmospheric carbon dioxide that was prepared by a subpanel of scientists including Roger Revelle of Harvard University and Charles D. Keeling of the Scripps Institution of Oceanography, both of whom had been doing research on carbon dioxide since the late 1950s. Among other things, the section highlighted the "possibility of climatic change resulting from changes in the quantity of atmospheric carbon dioxide," with the burning of fossil fuels cited as the main source of the incremental carbon dioxide that was being added to the ocean–atmosphere–biosphere system. While sometimes resorting to hyperbolic language – "Man is unwittingly conducting a vast geophysical experiment" – the report also noted the uncertainties associated with the theory of anthropogenic global warming, with most of its findings couched in conditional terms. Apart from warning about the possible effects of increased atmospheric carbon dioxide – including the melting of the Antarctic ice cap, rising sea levels, warming ocean waters, and the increasing acidity of freshwater sources – the report also flagged other potential sources of carbon dioxide than fossil fuels as well as potential mitigation strategies including geoengineering.[3]

By the end of the 1960s, though, global warming was still an idea in search of data and proof and an organized following. Even though the 1965 White House report referred to carbon dioxide as an "invisible pollutant," the 1970 CAA did not include carbon dioxide on its original list of 189 hazardous air pollutants to be regulated by the EPA. In fact, throughout the 1970s, environmentalists were far more concerned about the prospects of global cooling and another potential ice age rather than a warming planet. Between 1945 and 1975, there had been a discernible cooling trend in average global temperatures. Moreover, the reflective properties of aerosol and particulate pollution – both of which were more pressing environmental issues at the time – were thought to more than offset the radiation-absorbing characteristics of atmospheric carbon dioxide. In 1973, *Saturday Review* ran an article titled "The Ice Age Cometh," which was followed by a 1974 *Time* magazine piece posing the same question, "Another Ice Age?" and a 1975 *Newsweek* article on "The Cooling World." This set the tone for most of the climate coverage during the decade.

When the next ice age didn't arrive by the 1980s, the script was permanently flipped from global cooling to global warming, although the messaging has been tweaked over time to rebrand the crisis as man-made climate change. Ever since, the party line has been that the greenhouse gas effect caused by the burning of fossil fuels is warming up the planet and altering the world's climate systems, with the UN controlling both the climate change research program and the public relations campaign. In 1988, a year after the Brundtland Commission issued its seminal report on sustainability, the UN's IPCC, a joint effort between the UNEP and the UN's World Meteorological Organization (WMO), held its first meeting. This was followed quickly by the release of the IPCC's First Assessment Report (AR1) on the global climate in 1990, with a new assessment report being issued every six years to keep the issue of climate change front and center with the public. The Fourth Assessment Report (AR4) issued in 2007 won the IPCC the Nobel Peace Prize that year for the group's "efforts to build up and disseminate greater knowledge about man-made climate change, and to lay the foundations for the measures that are needed to counteract such change."[4] The latest Sixth Assessment Report (AR6) has been released in serial fashion like a Stephen King horror novel since 2021, with the latest synthesis or greatest-hits version coming out in March 2023.

The IPCC's climate research efforts are supported by similarly expansive climate bureaucracies at many of its member governments. The US established its US Global Change Research Program (USGCRP) in 1990, currently spanning 14 regulatory agencies, with the National Oceanic and Atmospheric Administration (NOAA), the National Aeronautics and Space Administration (NASA), and the EPA being the most important. Every four years, the USGCRP issues its own National Climate Assessments, with the fifth US report now due out sometime in late 2023. Both the UN and its member countries have also worked closely with colleges and universities around the world to ensure a steady stream of corroborative climate research – all funded by government and multilateral grants. This insular global network of climate research universities includes Caltech, Harvard, MIT, Penn State, and Yale in the US and the universities of Cambridge, East Anglia, Exeter, and Oxford in the UK.

To complement its climate research and reporting program, for the past 30 years the UN has been signing up its member countries for international environmental treaties to reduce global greenhouse gas emissions working through its UNFCCC framework, which was kicked off in 1992 at the UN's Earth Summit in Rio de Janeiro, Brazil. This was followed by the signing of the Kyoto Protocol in 1997 and the ratification of the landmark Paris Agreement in 2015. Every year since 1995, the UNFCCC parties have held annual Conference of the Parties (COP) meetings to provide updates on signatory progress toward the latest treaty goals. It is noteworthy that one of the first moves by the UN when it assumed control of the climate change movement back in the 1980s was to start working on limiting greenhouse gas emissions – and, by extension, hydrocarbon production and consumption – immediately through its UNFCCC treaty-making construct, rather than trying to get a better handle on the climate data and the science – both of which were still lagging at the time, with little consensus on the nature of the threat or the urgency of the problem. Even as the UN was starting to beat the drum for global emissions reduction targets, the US was largely ignoring the issue. Despite two legislative shots over 20 years at amending the 1970 CAA – the first in 1977 and the second in 1990 – the US federal government both times failed to add carbon dioxide to the list of EPA-regulated air pollutants.

To prove the causal relationship between fossil fuels, greenhouse gas emissions, and anthropogenic global warming, climate change proponents mainly focus on seven key indicators: atmospheric carbon dioxide levels, average global surface temperatures, average ocean water temperatures, average sea levels, polar ice cap levels, species and biodiversity loss, and the incidence of extreme weather events. Due to the limits of technology, clean, consistent, and directly measured data only go back about 60 years or less for many of these metrics. For all of them, the long-term trend is distorted by changes in instrumentation and data sources over time. For some indicators, measurement problems persist to the current day.

Digging into the data from the perspective of a Wall Street financial analyst – which seems appropriate given that climate change is the main bill of goods being sold by sustainable investing – highlights just how weak the analytical framework is for the climate change argument. Anyone who has taken high school biology, chemistry, and physics can understand the scientific concepts and immediately see the loopholes in the underlying data, even though the expert keepers of the climate research do not make it easy on members of the public trying to form their own independent view of the subject. Finding the raw data is often a *Where's Waldo* exercise. Most of the climate data is densified, distorted, and misrepresented to exaggerate the problem, including the use of provocative and highly misleading hockey stick charts that would never be allowed in a Wall Street research report. Every IPCC and USGCRP publication contains thousands of pages of climate minutiae. If climate change were an investment pitch, it would be over after the first meeting, with the deal team sent back to the drawing board with instructions to clean up its supporting data, tighten up its thesis, and work on its presentation.

As the first step in the chain of causality, atmospheric carbon dioxide levels are at the core of the argument that greenhouse gases are warming up the planet. Since 1958, NOAA's Mauna Loa Observatory in Hawaii has been continually monitoring atmospheric carbon dioxide levels using infrared sensors. Since carbon dioxide is not evenly distributed across the globe, NOAA also measures carbon dioxide, methane, and other greenhouse gas concentrations at about 100 sites worldwide through its Global Greenhouse Gas Reference Network, although the Mauna Loa data series is the longest one available and the benchmark for the climate industry. Based on Mauna Loa measurements, the amount of atmospheric carbon dioxide has increased from 316 parts per million (ppm) in March 1958 to 419 ppm in December 2022,[5] with the graph scale always compressed to sharply increase the slope of the curve to exaggerate the recent trend. How significant is a 33% increase in carbon dioxide levels over the past 60 years? For that matter, how dangerous is carbon dioxide when, even after this recent rise, it has only moved from the equivalent of 0.03% to 0.04% of the volume of the atmosphere, which is still approximately zero?

Here more of a historical context would help to answer such questions. Unfortunately, prior to the 1950s, there are no consistent direct measurements to use, so historical carbon dioxide levels must be interpolated from natural records such as Arctic and Antarctic ice cores and primordial tree rings using paleoclimatology proxies. Such indirect historical data is not directly comparable to the modern track record compiled by the Mauna Loa facility, although much is made of the sharp hockey stick pattern that results from grafting the two disparate data series together in Frankenstein fashion, which is a common presentation feature of many climate metrics. Probably the most notable takeaway from the longer-dated, pre-1950 historical record gleaned from ice cores and tree rings is the regular oscillating pattern for carbon dioxide levels over the past 800,000 years.[6] This would seem to imply a natural planetary cycle for atmospheric carbon dioxide levels that predates the Industrial Revolution and the use of fossil fuels beginning in the late 19th century. This would be consistent with the short-term natural cycling seen in the recent Mauna Loa data, which shows clear seasonal and diurnal patterns of variability in modern atmospheric carbon dioxide levels. However, since natural cyclicality in carbon dioxide would be fatal to the global warming argument, these oscillations are largely ignored by the climate community, with little attention paid to the scientific fact that the Earth's natural carbon cycle releases and absorbs roughly 10 times as much carbon dioxide as that from fossil fuels and other human sources in any given year.[7]

The next most important indicator is average global surface temperatures given the need to establish the critical link between rising carbon dioxide levels and rising world temperatures. But when it comes to taking the world's temperature, there are problems with both the current and historical readings, as well as with how the data is shown to the public. Given the wide range of temperatures posted across the planet – including a roughly 100°F differential between the equator and the polar ice caps – the concept of an average global temperature is fairly meaningless. Nonetheless, global surface temperatures are calculated by averaging both land and sea surface temperatures, with the mean weighted based on the 70–30 split of the planet between oceans and terra firma. Land surface temperatures are captured by weather stations located around the world, which typically take readings two meters above the ground every few hours each day for real-time collection by geostationary satellites. The current network of land weather stations includes approximately 40,000 sites globally and is maintained by NOAA and other national weather services as part of the International Surface Temperature Initiative (ISTI).[8]

There are several problems associated with the surface temperature readings taken by these land stations. First, locating these stations near developed urban areas tends to distort their temperature readings due to the workings of urban heat islands, where pavements, buildings, and other hard surfaces trap heat and machinery and equipment produce heat. Some of these land stations were originally located at airports and other industrial sites, while others were placed in rural settings only to see urban sprawl slowly encroach on them over time. A 2022 report by the Heartland Institute found that the temperature data from an estimated 96% of land weather stations in the US were corrupted by some form of heat bias.[9] Moreover, a 2020 study by the University of Exeter in the UK found that, over the 1983–2017 period, land surface temperatures had increased by 0.25°C more at night versus the day over more than half of the planet,[10] which would seem to be consistent with increased urbanization and heat-trapping hardscapes slowly cooling after sunset. Second, there is the problem of spatial coverage and the random distribution of the current monitoring system. Not surprisingly, coverage is best for the developed areas of the globe such as North America, Europe, and North Asia, but more sparse and uneven for other parts of the world, especially as you go back in time. Only about 3,000 current land stations have data going back as far as 1900, with few instrumental measurements for land surface temperature existing prior to 1850.

Since there is no way to measure temperature just above the ocean's surface as is done with land readings, scientists are forced to use a different approach with sea surface temperatures, which highlights how apples and oranges are being mixed to calculate average global surface temperatures, both in the present and the past. Since the 1980s, sea surface temperatures have been measured by satellites using infrared and microwave radiometers that capture readings for the top one-millimeter slice of the ocean surface, with NOAA tracking comprehensive data for the entire globe. Prior to the 1980s, sea surface temperatures were estimated using thermometers attached to either buoys or the intake ports of large ships, which results in an even more random pattern of readings in terms of water depth and geographical location. As with land station measurements, historical sea surface temperature readings are also skewed toward the developed Northern Hemisphere and, while stretching back to the mid-1700s, are particularly sketchy during the World War II period and prior to 1920. Importantly, the effect of such suspect historical measurement data for sea surface temperatures is amplified due to the 70% ocean weighting used in the calculation of average global surface temperatures.

To go further back in time, scientists are forced to use temperature proxy data from the same ice cores and tree rings used to interpolate historical carbon dioxide levels. Interestingly, the same oscillating pattern found in the interpolated data for atmospheric carbon dioxide is also seen in the inferred temperature record, which would seem to imply similar natural cyclicality in the Earth's temperature independent of human activity. Over the past 800,000 years, carbon dioxide levels have tended to track ice age and interglacial periods – lower when colder and higher when hotter – although the relationship between the two – whether coincident or causal and, if causal, which way – cannot be discerned from the synchrony of the available data.[11] Some scientists believe that atmospheric carbon dioxide follows rather than leads temperature and biosphere changes. Moreover, it seems clear that the Earth has been much hotter in the prehuman, preindustrial past than it has been in the modern postindustrial period since 1880. Based on the latest NOAA data, the average world surface temperature approximated 58.6°F in 2022,[12] which is only about 1.6°F higher than the estimated average for the 20th century and still relatively cool from a historical perspective in the context of the current interglacial period. In golfing terms, a temperature reading of 58.6°F would still be chilly if you were playing 18 holes.

However, such a sanguine view is not how the temperature data is portrayed by the experts. Rather than simply showing a straight average absolute temperature for the entire world – again, as meaningless as that one number would be – NOAA and the other tracking agencies instead calculate the temperature anomaly at each land and sea data collection point, which represents the difference between the current measurement and a subjectively defined and constantly changing long-term average period for that site. Often, the temperature margin of error at each site is larger than the anomaly calculated, which means actual cooling could be reported as warming and vice versa. All of these thousands of anomalies are then averaged to come up with a global mean temperature anomaly which, not surprisingly, results in a hockey stick chart when graphed using a compressed y-axis scale over the period since 1880. Typically, a line showing carbon dioxide levels is overlaid with a similarly compressed vertical scale on the standard temperature anomaly chart to visually reinforce the correlation between the two climate variables. Getting your hands on the raw temperature data behind the anomalies is no mean feat. For those looking to do their own calculations, NASA's website includes a patronizing primer on "The Elusive Absolute Surface Air Temperature," which assures readers, in Jedi Knight fashion, that what they are really looking for are temperature anomalies rather than absolute temperature data.[13]

Besides surface temperatures, average ocean temperatures are also tracked as a key climate change indicator because, as the argument goes, the oceans absorb an estimated 90% of the excess heat trapped in the atmosphere by greenhouse gases. In turn, increased ocean heat content leads to rising sea levels, the melting of ocean-terminating glaciers and ice sheets at both poles, and adverse effects on aquatic flora and fauna such as coral reefs. Calculating an average ocean temperature is arguably an even more pointless exercise than for surface temperatures given that oceans cover 70% of the planet's roughly 200 million square miles, reach a maximum depth of 36,000 feet in the western part of the Pacific Ocean, and have an estimated volume of some 321 million cubic miles (per NOAA). Moreover, from a temperature perspective, the ocean is stratified like a three-layer cake. In the top mixed layer of the ocean that runs from the surface down to about 200 meters, water temperatures are not evenly distributed (as anyone who has gone to the beach at Coney Island could tell you) and mainly influenced by sunlight radiation, circulation currents (such as the Gulf Stream in the Atlantic Ocean and El Niño and La Niña in the Pacific Ocean) and churning storms. Between 200 and 1,000 meters below the surface sits the thermocline layer, where sunlight rarely penetrates and temperatures range from 55°F to 39°F, dropping in line with water depth. Approximately 90% of the ocean's volume is located in the zone below the thermocline layer, which starts at a depth of some 1,000 meters below the surface, is not well mixed, and maintains a fairly uniform average water temperature ranging from 32°F to 39°F.[14] Obviously, reducing all this natural temperature variation into one global number provides little informational content.

Since 1999, a system of Argo diving robotic floats developed by the Scripps Institution of Oceanography has been deployed across the world's oceans to capture temperature, salinity, and other ocean data down to depths of 1.2 miles below the surface. Some newer-model floats go down as far as 3.7 nautical miles or more than one league under the sea. Approximately 4,000 Argo floats are currently in the field feeding real-time data up to satellites, with more than half of these floaters being supplied by NOAA. The current Argo floater network provides fairly good spatial coverage of the world's oceans, although with 140 million square miles of ocean surface, each float has to cover an average 35,000-square-mile range, with floater distribution somewhat thinner in the Arctic and the Antarctic Oceans. Before the Argo floater system was up and running, deeper ocean temperatures were primarily measured by bottles, cylinders, and probes deployed by ships along major shipping routes. As with sea surface temperatures, the number and quality of the deep ocean temperature readings decline sharply as you go back in time, with a step change in the mid-20th century and no meaningful data points prior to 1900.[15]

Rather than presenting an average temperature for the world's oceans, though, NOAA and other national meteorological agencies convert their temperature readings into aggregate heat content statistics to show an incrementally large – and largely abstract – number expressed in watts per square meter or zettajoules, extrapolating out from the top 2,000 meters to the full depth of the ocean. For good measure, an extra layer of opacity is added by presenting this gigantic heat content figure in terms of an anomaly versus some long-term average period, as is done with land and sea surface temperatures, rather than an absolute number. For example, based on the latest available NOAA disclosure, over 1993–2021, the full ocean heat-gain rate was estimated to have been in the range of 0.64–0.80 watts per square meter, using an arbitrary 1955–2006 reference period for anomaly purposes.[16] Since 1955, the heat content of the first 2,000 meters of ocean depth has increased by 345 zettajoules.[17] Presenting the data in this way results in a hockey stick chart, with the hosel of the stick located at the point where the modern and historical data series attach, as with all the other climate metrics.

Since warming oceans lead to melting ice caps and rising sea levels, these are the next two metrics tracked by the IPCC and the rest of the climate industry. Satellites have been used to monitor the size and thickness of sea ice in both the Arctic and Antarctic regions since 1979. Data from weather stations, ship logs, ice cores, and ocean sediment samples has been cobbled together to reconstruct estimates – albeit just for the Arctic – going back to about 1900, which is as far back as any historical record goes. Based on recent satellite imaging, over the past four decades, Arctic sea ice has receded while Antarctic sea ice levels have remained remarkably constant. Between 1979 and 2021, the minimum extent of Arctic summer ice declined by roughly 30%, while winter ice extent only decreased by about 10%. Moreover, the Arctic ice lows were reached a few years ago and have been expanding of late. Since 2012, Arctic summer ice minimum extent has increased by roughly 35–40%.[18] This same unexplained short-term variability in Arctic sea ice levels can also be seen in the reconstructed historical data for the region. Meanwhile, at the South Pole, one recent study published in May 2023 by *The Cryosphere* scientific journal found that overall, the Antarctic ice shelf had grown slightly by 5,305 square kilometers or roughly 0.4% between 2009 and 2019.[19] However, all this uncertainty – Antarctic sea ice staying power and recent Arctic sea ice recovery – gets lost in the public climate reporting about melting ice caps. And yes, conjoining the modern satellite data with the reconstructed history results in another hockey stick chart with the blade of the chart turning downward in 1979 where the two separate data series meet.

Since the early 1990s, satellites have also been used to measure mean global sea levels, which are ostensibly rising due to the combination of thermal expansion and melting sea ice. Prior to the 1990s, tidal gauges located in harbors and along coastlines were used to measure sea levels going as far back as 1700, although data quality (sediment distortion) and geographical coverage (mostly Northern Hemisphere) were both limited prior to 1850. Combining these two disparate series of measurements, though, creates the necessary hockey stick pattern. Global sea levels rose by an average of 1.7 millimeters per year over the 1880–2000 period, with the annual pace accelerating from 1.2 millimeters in the latter 19th century to 1.9 millimeters during the second half of the 20th century. Based on satellite data, since 1993 the seas have been rising at an average annual rate of 3.3 millimeters, roughly double the 1880–2000 pace.[20] Even with this recent reported acceleration, an average annual increase in mean sea level of 3.3 millimeters is still imperceptible to the naked eye and equates to only about one foot of rise over nearly 100 years, which hardly seems catastrophic. Globalizing a particularly local climate issue such as sea level results in another theoretical math exercise that calculates an average number for 140 million square miles of ocean. Nonetheless, climate scientists still recommend that people defer to these measurements rather than relying on their lying eyes by using historical photographs of coastal areas to gauge whether the seas are rising or not.

Species and biodiversity loss is another factor tracked by climate scientists as a coincident indicator of man-made climate change. For years, the UN and other climate alarmists have been describing global warming as an impending "mass extinction event." In a 2019 report, the UNEP put some numbers on the problem, finding that some one million animal and plant species are now "threatened with extinction, many within decades," with climate change being the main culprit. Based on UNEP estimates, more than 40% of amphibian species, roughly 33% of reef-forming corals, and more than one-third of all marine mammals are currently threatened. Moreover, the report found that the rate of species extinctions is accelerating, with the average abundance of native species in most major land-based habitats having fallen by at least 20% since 1900.[21] The problem with all these dire UNEP warnings about climate-driven species loss, though, is the lack of particulars to demonstrate the general trend.

Originally, polar bears were the public animal face of the climate movement as their numbers and habitat were both purportedly shrinking due to the melting northern polar ice cap. Sad pictures of solitary polar bears floating on ice rafts in the Arctic Ocean were ubiquitous, tugging at the public's heartstrings. Environmental groups such as the World Wildlife Fund (WWF) raised millions of dollars using the polar bear as their poster child. As the WWF warned in a 2006 article, polar bears were set to become "one of the most notable and dramatic casualties of global warming," and fossil fuel addiction was what was driving polar bears to extinction.[22] New WWF members can still receive a stuffed polar bear toy as a gift for joining, and symbolically adopt a polar bear in the wild in return for donating. The only problem is polar bears are in no danger of extinction. Fifty years ago they were, due to overhunting. But after a worldwide hunting ban went into effect in 1976, the polar bear population quickly recovered, and their numbers have steadily increased over the past 40 years despite rising global temperatures. Based on data tracked by the Polar Bear Specialist Group (PBSG), a part of the International Union for the Conservation of Nature and Natural Resources, the total number of polar bears across 19 discrete Arctic subpopulation groups has increased from an estimated range of 20,000–25,000 in the 1980s to 25,000–30,000 as of 2021.[23] So, climate activists stopped talking about polar bears and shifted the focus to the Great Barrier Reef, the world's largest coral system located off the eastern coast of Australia, where rising sea temperatures and increased ocean acidification are reportedly causing severe coral loss and a bleach-out of the colorful underwater animal refuge. However, the data doesn't back up this environmental claim either, as coral cover has been recovering over the past four decades. In its latest annual report on coral reef conditions, the Australian Institute of Marine Science (AIMS) found that in 2022 the Great Barrier Reef registered its highest levels of coral cover yet recorded in its northern and central regions over the past 36 years of monitoring.[24]

Lastly, extreme weather events – mainly hurricanes, floods, blizzards, tornadoes, heat waves, droughts, and wildfires – are regularly presented as real-time proof that climate change is already occurring, even though weather and climate are not the same thing. Such weather phenomena – even wildfires – are naturally occurring events that tend to move in longer-dated cycles over a period of decades. In the US, there has been no discernible increase in the frequency or intensity of severe weather events over the past few decades, which anyone over the age of 30 should already realize. Since 1900, the number of major (Category 3 or higher) landfalling hurricanes in the US has averaged less than one per year. Despite the press hype, so-called Superstorm Sandy was only a Category 1 storm when it hit the greater New York City area right at high tide during a full moon in 2012. Since 1900, only four Category 5 hurricanes have made landfall in this country. Similarly, the number of severe (EF3 or higher) tornadoes in the US has declined since the particularly active period from the 1950s through the 1970s, with overall tornadic activity remaining roughly constant over the past 60 years. Over the past century, the country has experienced periodic heat waves and regional droughts during the 1930s, the 1950s, the 2000s, and the 2010s – interspersed with unusually cool and wet conditions during the 1980s and 1990s – although nothing since compares to the Dust Bowl devastation during the Great Depression. The number of acres burned by US wildfires, mainly in the western portion of the country, has declined significantly since the early 1900s, including over the past 30 years. All this data is available on the NOAA website.[25]

Most importantly, the number of annual US deaths from natural disasters has declined by roughly 50% since the early 1900s to a run rate of less than 400 currently. Globally, the annual number of disaster-related deaths has dropped by a factor of 10 over the past 100 years, from an average of more than 500,000 during the 1920s to less than 50,000 per annum during the 2010s, which notably equates to only about 0.1% of total worldwide deaths in any given year.[26] And while storm-damage costs are often cited as evidence that weather is getting more extreme due to climate change, almost all of the inflation-adjusted increase in storm insurance and liability costs is attributable to population growth and increased development, particularly around coastal areas.

Apart from the data limitations associated with all the key climate indicators, there is also a significant degree of uncertainty about how the Earth's complex climate systems work, what the feedback loops are, and what other factors – both natural and man-made – may be coming into play besides the knee-jerk assumption of fossil fuel combustion. One study published in the February 2022 volume of *Health Physics* found that only 23% of the total carbon dioxide accumulated in the world's atmosphere between 1750 and 2018 was due to the burning of fossil fuels.[27] Apart from the natural cyclicality seen in the interpolated historical carbon dioxide and temperature record, how much of the modern-day increase in atmospheric carbon dioxide levels has been caused by global deforestation? Since 1880, the world has lost nearly 1.1 billion hectares of forested land for agriculture and firewood, an area larger than the size of the US, which has released sequestered carbon while eliminating ongoing photosynthetic carbon removal.[28] How much of the jump in average surface temperatures since 1880 is owing to changes in the Earth's solar orbit and increased solar irradiance since 1850, when the Little Ice Age in the Northern Atlantic that began back in the 14th century finally ended?

Water vapor is also a powerful greenhouse gas, so how has the hydrologic cycle affected recent global temperature readings? For all the focus on melting polar sea ice due to the loss of its heat-reflecting properties, clouds – which are formed out of water vapor – also reflect heat and typically cover approximately 70% of the Earth's surface. Not enough research has been conducted to date on the trend in cloud cover, how water vapor and cosmic rays affect cloud formation, and how clouds behave at different altitudes, all of which appear to be critical climate factors. Like the line from the 1966 Joni Mitchell classic "Both Sides Now," climate scientists "really don't know clouds at all." As far back as 1995, a study by the Department of Energy found that minor changes in the microphysical properties of the Earth's cloud cover – particularly droplet size, concentration, and absorption – would have the same planetwide warming effect as a doubling of atmospheric carbon dioxide levels.[29] More recently, a 2021 study found that reforestation leads to an increase in highly reflective low-level cloud cover,[30] which begs the question as to whether deforestation has led to a decrease in cloud cover over the past century, further contributing to global warming.

For that matter, what impact has the increased global volcanic activity since the 1980s had given that such eruptions mainly release water vapor and particulate emissions, as evidenced by the 1991 eruption of Mount Pinatubo in the Philippines, which NASA has noted resulted in a measurable cooling of the Earth's surface for a period of almost two years? On the particulate front, since particulates such as soot and aerosols also reflect heat – recall the premise of the global cooling hysteria of the 1970s – how much of the recent increase in average global surface temperatures is because real air pollution (i.e., particulate matter) has been reduced sharply in recent decades, particularly in the US and other developed countries?

These uncertainties have not stopped climate scientists from plugging the current body of suspect data into computer models to generate long-range climate forecasts for the planet through the year 2100 and beyond. Since there is, at best, only about 30 to 60 years' worth of clean data for most input metrics, these climate models are extrapolating out from an infinitesimally small time period in the context of 200,000 years of human history on a 4.6-billion-year-old planet. Moreover, these are two-way models that project both forward and backward given the need to fill in and smooth out historical data gaps. It is the equivalent of a Wall Street equity analyst building out a 100-year company revenue and earnings model based on a few days' worth of actual and unaudited financial results, and then hitting the Excel F9 recalculate button every quarter when his forecast missed. No trader or investor would commit capital based on such a 100-year financial spreadsheet, so it is fair to ask why major global economic decisions are now being made based on the very long-range projections generated by climate models.

Not surprisingly, these climate models have had a weak forecasting track record to date. On Wall Street, research analysts who consistently miss with their company and market calls are quickly tuned out by clients and eventually flushed out of the industry. The same rules, though, do not apply to climate scientists perennially missing the mark. Like Goldilocks, the IPCC's first five assessment reports were all over the map in terms of predicting the actual global warming trend seen over the

1970–2016 period, with AR1 in 1990 coming in 17% too hot, AR2 in 1995 28% too cold, AR3 in 2001 14% too cold, AR4 in 2007 8% too hot, and AR5 in 2013 16% too hot.[31] Notably, these IPCC misses were for a relatively short and contemporaneous forecast period. The margin of error would be far greater shooting at a long-range target in the distant future like the year 2100.

Most climate models missed the global warming hiatus that occurred between 1998 and 2013, as initially reported in the IPCC's AR5. When AR5 was released in 2013, it was the equivalent of dropping a Bengal tiger into the baboon exhibit at the Bronx Zoo, with climate scientists running around screaming for months trying to explain away the 15-year pause in global warming. This lull in temperature rise was eventually "corrected" after the fact by simply switching out the historical sea surface temperature data to replace warmer readings taken from ship intakes with colder readings taken from ocean buoys, which highlights another problem with climate models and climate science in general. Whenever the climate models do not spit out the desired projections or miss the actual mark, either the historical data is manipulated or other subjective manual adjustments are made to the model to force-fit the result, raising questions of objectivity and confirmation bias. As George Orwell wrote in *Nineteen Eighty-Four*, "Who controls the past controls the future: who controls the present controls the past."

With such a fail-safe, though, the confidence of climate scientists and policymakers in the predictive power of their simulation models has only grown over time. In the policymaker summary for the physical science section of its AR6 released in 2021, the IPCC tightened up its previous conditional language and stated that it is "unequivocal that human influence has warmed the atmosphere, ocean and land," and that "human-induced climate change" is already occurring in every region across the globe. Moreover, the report stated categorically that natural drivers have "little effect on long-term global warming." All of the five main emissions-driven climate scenarios laid out in AR6 were deemed very likely with a greater than 90% probability, although this was only after widening out the confidence ranges for each to make sure that each projection landed somewhere in the future fairway. And by doing so, many of the confidence ranges have a high degree of overlap.[32]

The latest IPCC report noted with metaphysical certitude that "global warming of 1.5°C and 2°C will be exceeded during the 21st century unless deep reductions in carbon dioxide and other greenhouse gas emissions occur in the coming decades." And if such warming targets are exceeded, the effects on the Earth's climate systems would be catastrophic and "irreversible for centuries to millennia," with severe coastal flooding, widespread food shortages, forced migration waves, and biodiversity and species losses becoming the norm by 2100. These are the same 1.5°C and 2°C global temperature goals that every UN member signed up for under the UNFCCC's Paris Agreement in 2015, measured in terms of mean temperature anomaly against an 1850–1900 baseline and based on melded and highly flawed land and sea surface temperature data. Moreover, these targets are completely arbitrary numbers set mainly for political reasons. They are designed to be tripped – most likely during the first half of the 21st century – which, in turn, will only heighten the sense of urgency and increase the pressure on national governments to cut greenhouse gas emissions and throw more money at the problem. Cumulative global warming since the late 19th century was 1.0°C as of the signing of the Paris Agreement and 1.1°C as of the 2021 release of the initial installment of the IPCC's AR6.

Reducing the goals of the climate change movement to just two numbers is also meant to simplify a very complex issue for the public to gin up popular support for the cause. The UN-led climate change program has always been more about marketing the message than perfecting the science. For the past four decades, the UN has not deviated from its original conclusion – greenhouse gas emissions from fossil fuels production must be curtailed to save the planet from climate disaster – despite gaping holes in the argument and growing uncertainties about the accuracy of climate models and the quality of the underlying data. Rather than engaging in a debate about the merits and methodology, the public relations strategy has focused on conflating climate with weather, citing every extreme (and not-so-extreme) weather event as a sign of man-made climate change to play on people's emotions, and shouting down any opposing or contradictory view.

As with sustainable development, climate change sets up as another UN money game where the dichotomy between developed and developing nations rationalizes a flow of funds from the former to the latter. Because climate change disproportionately affects poorer countries in the

Southern Hemisphere – many of which are said to be at risk of washing away from severe storms or sinking into the ocean due to rising sea levels – climate action becomes a matter of justice and equity, echoing the language of the Brundtland Report. To drive this point home, another climate marketing gimmick used by the UN is the concept of a carbon budget for the planet. If Earth exceeds its allocated budget for carbon emissions, then the impact on climate will be catastrophic. Because this carbon budget is cumulative, industrialized nations have already used up most of the allowable balance. As a simple matter of fairness, these richer nations are the ones that should be shouldering the lion's share of global emissions reductions required to stay within budget, while also sending money in the form of reparation payments to poorer countries to help fund their transition to a low-carbon economy. The IPCC has been reporting an estimated carbon budget for the planet since 2013. In AR6, the UN estimated that the cumulative carbon balance since 1850 stood at roughly 2,390 gigatons of CO_2 equivalent (GtCO_2e) as of 2019, leaving only 500 GtCO_2e of remaining budget as of 2020 for the world to have a 50–50 chance to hit the UN's 1.5°C Paris temperature target. By the start of 2023, this headroom had shrunk to an estimated 380 GtCO_2e based on a roll-forward of the IPCC's numbers by the Global Carbon Project, a climate NGO focused on environmental research.[33] While useful for a household living paycheck to paycheck with little savings in the bank, the idea of a fixed carbon budget for a carbon-based planet is nonsensical, although it does further highlight how climate change is an anti-industrial policy with a scientific wrapper and basically a device to beggar rich developed nations.

Regular IPCC predictions of climate Armageddon by 2100 if global warming and greenhouse gas emissions continue unchecked feed this public narrative and keep the issue of climate change front and center. In this process, the UN serves as both the main Cassandra and the chief calendar-keeper, with the year 2030 now set as the latest climate tipping point for the planet, with the rhetoric ratcheting up accordingly. In its AR6 release over 2021–2022, which UN Secretary-General António Guterres described as a "code red for humanity,"[34] the IPCC stated that global greenhouse gas emissions must peak before 2025 at the latest and must be reduced by 45% by 2030 versus a 2010 baseline to avoid an "unlivable world."[35] In November 2022 at the kick-off for COP27 in

Sharm el-Sheikh, Egypt, Guterres again warned the world, "We are on a highway to climate hell with our foot on the accelerator."[36] Other than pushing back the planetary deadline, not much has changed about the UN's climate scaremongering since 1989 when Noel Brown, the director of the New York office of the UNEP, publicly warned that "entire nations could be wiped off the face of the Earth by rising sea levels" if the global warming trend was not reversed by the year 2000.[37]

Helping on the messaging front has been the positive feedback loop around climate change that has formed in recent decades among the UN and other supranational agencies, national governments, colleges and universities, K–12 public schools, and the news media to help indoctrinate the masses and keep the public in a constant state of alarm. By the time college students graduate, most have filed away man-made climate change alongside gravity as a scientific fact. Broadcast media channels colorize weather maps in Ted Turner fashion with scary shades of red and orange to reinforce the global warming message, while reports of hurricanes occurring in hurricane zones during hurricane season are now treated as unexpected news. Almost every day, month, and year is now reported as the hottest on record by meteorologists.

Despite this built-in support network, the climate change movement has been trying to shut down public dissent for the past two decades. In 2007, when he shared the Nobel Peace Prize with the IPCC, Al Gore famously declared in his global warming documentary *An Inconvenient Truth* that the science around climate change had been settled. Ever since, the climate industry has endeavored to present a unified front and project an overwhelming scientific consensus to reinforce its appeal to authority. Since 2013 – the same year that the IPCC famously blew the temperature call with AR5 – it has been widely reported that 97% of climate scientists agree that human activities are causing anthropogenic global warming. This headline number was based on a research study published that year by the Skeptical Science website, which, despite its misleading name, is actually an antiskeptic outfit aimed at countering climate "misinformation." The Skeptical Science study looked at 11,944 climate research papers published in the *Environmental Research Letters* journal between 1991 and 2011 and first categorized each publication as either endorsing global warming or rejecting or expressing no opinion on the theory before subjectively characterizing the climate change view of each author. Only 33% of the papers included in the 21-year sample endorsed global warming theory and, of these, 97% agreed with the consensus view that human activity is the cause. This is the "97% scientific consensus" number that has been consistently reported in the press without mentioning the fact that two-thirds of the climate papers included in the study were agnostic on the subject of man-made climate change.[38]

Recently, this flawed consensus study was updated by Cornell University's Alliance for Science research institute, a climate advocacy group funded by the Bill and Melinda Gates Foundation. The lead author for the 2021 study was Mark Lynas, a self-described environmental activist. The Cornell study analyzed 88,125 climate-related scientific studies published in the *Environmental Research Letters* journal between 2012 and 2020. Of these, a random 3,000-paper sample was selected and whittled down to 2,718 publications, which the authors then categorized as either endorsing global warming theory (31%) or rejecting or expressing no opinion on the topic (69%) before subjectively characterizing the view of each paper, as in the previous study. This manual filtering process yielded four papers that either implicitly or explicitly rejected the theory of anthropogenic global warming, so four out of 2,718 works out to a 99.85% consensus, even though 1,869 of the total papers in the sample expressed no view on the subject. Using a second automated methodology, the entire batch of 88,125 papers was screened using skeptical keywords such as "natural cycles" and "cosmic rays," with the top 1,000 most skeptical papers manually reviewed. Of these, only 28 were found to reject man-made climate change out of hand. Adding three skeptical papers found in the random sample, 31 divided by 88,125 works out to an upper limit of 99.97% for the scientific consensus. Once again, there was no mention of the fact that 762 or 76% of the 1,000 screened papers took no position on man-made climate change. This is the new "greater than 99% scientific consensus" number now making the rounds. Perhaps the biggest takeaway from the Cornell consensus study, though, was just how big a business climate change has become. Do the math, and 88,125 climate research papers published over nine years works out to slightly more than one new climate paper per hour of every day.[39]

Despite all the talk about scientific consensus and the science being settled, the climate change argument has devolved into more of a religion and an article of liberal faith rather than actual science. As a belief system, climate theory is both internally inconsistent and impervious to logic. For example, why is climate change always presented in racial terms, with demands for justice for disaffected population groups and developing nations? How does anthropogenic global warming specifically target people of color – particularly women and children – living in impoverished countries located in the Southern Hemisphere when it is purportedly a global phenomenon? Why are we focusing so much on the industrialized countries of Europe and North America, where emissions per capita have been declining for years, rather than the developing world where carbon emissions continue to rise rapidly in line with living standards? If the environmental goal is to reduce greenhouse gases in the atmosphere, then why is zero-emitting nuclear power also a nonstarter for climate activists? Why has natural gas, with its much smaller carbon footprint than crude oil or coal, become the shortest bridge fuel ever? Why is there never any meaningful discussion of human adaptation or other mitigation methods beyond just shutting down the oil, gas, and coal industries? The 1965 White House report on carbon dioxide offered up the solution of "spreading small reflective particles over large oceanic areas" to help offset the effect of atmospheric carbon dioxide and change the radiation balance in the opposite direction. Geoengineering technology has existed for decades, so why is it never talked about in climate circles? Why aren't we just planting more trees around the world? Why does every IPCC report read like a passage from the Book of Revelation?

However, anyone asking these or any other questions about the data or the science or challenging the so-called climate experts is either dismissed as lacking authority, deemed to be acting in bad faith because of some connection to the fossil fuels industry, or simply labeled a skeptic and denier, much like heretics were treated by the Catholic Church during the 12th and 13th centuries. Like the Inquisitors who roamed the Spanish countryside a thousand years ago, an army of liberal fact-checkers now police social media to denounce and discredit any publication or post questioning the climate science. A modern-day Children's Crusade has also been formed – with UN funding and logistical support – around youth activists such as Greta Thunberg and Haven Coleman and groups such as the Sunrise Movement and Zero Hour to serve as the standard-bearers for the climate movement, which further helps to shut down discussion and cut off debate since children can't be reasoned with. During the 17th century, the Catholic Church under Pope Urban VIII persecuted Galileo for his scientific belief that the Earth revolved around the sun and, therefore, was not the center of the universe. Nearly 400 years later, Pope Francis issued an encyclical in 2015 calling on the world's 1.2 billion Catholics to trust in the "very solid scientific consensus" and join the fight against climate change because the faithful must protect "Mother Earth" from "the harm we have inflicted on her."[40]

Since the 1980s, the primary objective of the UN-led climate movement has been to gain control of the fossil fuels sector, which progressives the world over view as the "terrible, horrible, no good, very bad" industry. Placing limits on carbon dioxide and other greenhouse gas emissions is just a means to this end. Up until recently, it appeared that the implementation of a permanent carbon tax on the industry – effectively, a tax on air that would never go away and only continue to rise over time – was the climate endgame, to be used to fund green energy initiatives and other government spending in perpetuity. However, it has become clear of late that many of the true climate believers, including the UN, won't be satisfied until and unless there is a complete shutdown of the industry. As the IPCC noted in its 2022 AR6 update, "Limiting global warming will require major transitions in the energy sector." Per the IPCC, keeping global temperatures below the 1.5°C Paris target will require global coal use to drop by 75% compared to 2019, crude oil by 10%, and natural gas by 10% by 2030. By 2050, all three hydrocarbons will need to be largely phased out of the primary energy supply mix – including forced cumulative reductions of 95%, 60%, and 45%, respectively – to achieve a decarbonized, net-zero world.[41]

Climate change is just the latest – although arguably the most elegant and effective – in a long line of progressive offensives against the deplorable and irredeemable fossil fuels industry. Like a multigenerational blood feud, these attacks date back almost to the day when Edwin Drake first struck oil in Titusville, Pennsylvania, in 1859. Through the mid-20th century, most of these salvoes were economic in nature. The federal breakup of the Standard Oil Company and Trust in 1911 at the height of the trust-busting era was driven by concerns about monopoly power and the immense economic wealth accumulating in the hands of John D. Rockefeller and his associates – even though the dividend payments and capital returned from Standard Oil were reinvested in other industrial firms and charitable foundations. Ultimately, this progressive government move backfired since the 34 successor companies of the energy conglomerate all experienced significant run-ups in market value post-breakup, resulting in a massive payday for all the Standard Oil owners and making the long-since-retired Rockefeller the richest man in the world. Despite industry consolidation, many of these original Standard Oil successor firms still operate to this day, including ExxonMobil Corporation (formerly the New York and New Jersey operations) and Chevron Corporation (formerly the California operations).

In the 1930s when American industries were failing across the board during the Great Depression, the federal government attempted to catch oil and gas companies in a regulatory noose, just as it had done to the power sector with the passage of the Federal Power Act and the Public Utility Holding Company Act in 1935. Thankfully, the energy industry opted not to save itself from historically low oil prices by agreeing to federal oversight, even as the nation's electric utilities submitted to regulatory approval for both capital spending projects and allowable rates of return. That choice has made all the difference in recent years as federal regulators have forced coal-fired power out of the US generation mix due to climate change concerns, while the US oil and gas shale industry has flourished on private lands under state law.

During the postwar period when the center of the oil business shifted overseas to the Middle East, the criticism of the industry became more political in nature. Given the instability in the oil-producing Middle East region during the 1960s and 1970s – including multiple wars and regular regime change – there was increased grumbling about national security and economic dependence on foreign oil. Such concerns only grew in the wake of the formation of the OPEC oil cartel in 1960 and the two major oil supply and price shocks that resulted from the 1973 Yom Kippur War and the 1979 Iranian Revolution. It was during this period that the canard about fossil fuels being a leading cause of war first started to make the rounds in progressive circles. This false claim – which ignores all the wars fought by mankind prior to the development of fossil fuels in 1880 – continues to be repeated to this day. After being used extensively during the Gulf War of 1991 and the Iraq War between 2003 and 2011, this stock line was recently dusted off around the Russia–Ukraine conflict in 2022.

For the past 50 years, though, the criticism of fossil fuels has been largely framed in environmental terms, although the narrative has changed over time. Initially, the industry was mainly faulted for periodic oil spills such as the 1969 Union Oil Company of California offshore drilling rig blowout near Santa Barbara County, which spilled three million gallons of heavy crude oil into the water and onto the Southern California coast. The industry was also blamed for the air pollution caused by automotive emissions, which was exacerbated by the addition of lead as an octane enhancer for gasoline and the use of sour crude feedstocks with a high sulfur content. By reflecting the sun's radiation, such tailpipe particulate pollution was also thought to contribute to global cooling, which was the greater climate concern during the 1970s.

During the early days of the environmental movement, the fear that human population growth would soon outstrip all of the world's natural resources gave rise to the theory of peak oil supply. It was this belief that the world would eventually run out of hydrocarbons that earned the industry the original label of "unsustainable." When huge new deposits of oil were found in Alaska, the North Sea, and offshore Mexico and technological advancements such as seismic imaging, horizontal drilling, and hydraulic fracturing put the lie to peak oil theory, the focus shifted to climate change and the amount of carbon pollution generated by the industry, which was finally a criminal charge that progressives could make stick.

Arguably the most brilliant aspect of the climate movement's protracted Madison Avenue marketing campaign has been the rebranding of carbon dioxide – a clear, odorless gas respired by humans, animals, and plants alike – as "carbon pollution." Such a description wrongly implies that carbon dioxide is a particulate pollutant like soot or smoke that causes respiratory problems such as asthma. This clever labeling is doubly efficient since it both reinforces the "dirty" image of carbon-dioxide-emitting fossil fuels and the "clean" reputation of renewable energy sources such as wind and solar power. The term is now ubiquitous across society and firmly embedded in the vocabulary of the oil and gas industry – yet another example of the progressive penchant for co-opting the meaning of words and effectively weaponizing language.

Since the 1980s, the spin has been that fossil fuels are unsustainable because there needs to be a global energy transition away from hydrocarbons to save the planet from a climate crisis. This is why almost every climate change hockey stick chart dates back to 1880 or roughly the start of the Second Industrial Revolution – to reinforce the perception that fossil fuels are causing man-made climate change, which has always been the foregone conclusion. By combining climate change theory with sustainability doctrine, the energy industry's problem has now been flipped to a theoretical one of peak demand in the future. By the time of the climate rapture in 2030 – or 2050 at the latest – all oil, gas, and coal companies will need to simply disappear.

For good measure, though, liberals have continued to attack the fossil fuels industry on other environmental fronts. Hydraulic fracturing or fracking is said to pose a danger to drinking water, even though the oil and gas shale plays being fracked are located thousands of feet below the surface where most aquifers sit. Fracking operations are criticized for the amount of water used in pressure pumping, even though the upstream industry is a major water recycler and golf courses and farms use far more water than oil and gas companies. Transporting crude oil from Canadian oil-sands projects through pipelines is deemed environmentally unsound because "tar sands" are uniquely corrosive to steel pipeline casing. Ditto for "fracked gas" pipelines given the risk of leaking methane, which is increasingly described as a "more potent" greenhouse gas than carbon dioxide. Obscure insects, bats, birds, and fish are regularly proposed for endangered-species status to shut down proposed pipeline projects and curtail oil and gas drilling on private land.

Climate change is the means of controlling the energy sector and, with it, the entire global economy. It serves as the anchor for the sustainability movement, providing both moral cover and overall structure for the sustainability argument – which, like climate change theory, also includes an ever-changing agenda, weak data, circular reasoning, faith-based trust, and a futuristic focus. As noted in the latest IPCC report, climate action moves us toward "a fairer, more sustainable world." Under the two-tiered approach of the Paris Agreement, industrialized nations must start cutting emissions immediately, while developing countries (including China and India) are given more time (often decades) before their obligations kick in, along with financial aid and technology transfers from the developed world. Such a "fair and equitable" approach to climate action is consistent with the UN's parallel sustainable development program, which is also a wealth redistribution exercise.

Most importantly, sustainability pushes the responsibility for climate action onto the corporate sector and investment community, with the energy sector standing at the top of the Most Wanted Lists for both climate and sustainability activists. Simply conceding the point on climate change also forces buy-in for the rest of the sustainability menu, which companies and investors alike will soon discover is not buffet-style.

CHAPTER 3

THE UN WANTS TO BE YOUR INVESTMENT ADVISER

An invisible empire has been set up above the forms of democracy.
Woodrow Wilson

The urge to save humanity is almost always only a false-face for the urge to rule it.
H. L. Mencken, *Minority Report*

When it was first established in October 1945 shortly after the conclusion of World War II, the original mission of the UN was simply to "save succeeding generations from the scourge of war." Or as Henry Cabot Lodge Jr., the US ambassador to the United Nations during the Eisenhower administration, put it, "This organization is created to prevent you from going to hell. It isn't created to take you to heaven."[1] While World War III did not occur during the first 40 years of the UN's existence, it was clear by the 1980s that the organization had not lived up to its postwar promise. The Brundtland Report released in 1987 admitted as much when it highlighted the "urgent task of persuading nations of the need to return to multilateralism."[2] In 1988, Paul Johnson put a sharper point on it in *Commentary* magazine: "We all of us, liberals included, know in our hearts that the United Nations has failed."[3] But even as Johnson was making this passing but obvious observation, the UN was already hard at work reinventing itself and shifting its organizational mandate. Since the late 1980s, the UN has completely disregarded the advice of Eisenhower's ambassador and mainly focused on trying to create heaven on earth – using soft rather than hard power to implement a progressive international agenda chock-full of environmental and social issues and structured around climate change and sustainable development.

Given that the UN has been leading the charge on global climate change and was the original architect of the related sustainability doctrine, it is not surprising that the supranational agency has also been the main proponent of sustainable investing – this despite having no financial qualifications in the area. Of course, doling out unsolicited investment advice is much easier than actually trying to solve all of the world's military conflicts, health pandemics, and humanitarian crises. Still, the agency's foray into the financial markets has been the worst example of the strategy drift at the UN over the past 40 years.

Once sustainability became a prerequisite of strategic planning and operational management for individual companies, it was only a matter of time before it also became a discriminant factor in the investment process when allocating capital to these same companies. If all corporations are subject to the strictures of sustainability, including financial institutions such as banks, insurance companies, pension funds, and asset management firms, then the next step was to argue that sustainable criteria should also be used as core investment parameters for any investing business looking to label itself as sustainable. If corporations have a social responsibility, then it held that investors also had an obligation to society. This was the last piece of the sustainability puzzle to be put in place, and frankly the whole point of the plan to begin with: directing investment away from politically incorrect industries – starting with fossil fuels – and toward government-favored sectors such as green and renewable energy. With capital the choke point, Wall Street is now the cop on the beat and asset managers and investors have been moved to the front line of the sustainability fight. These financial firms are now responsible for spreading and reinforcing the need for a sustainable business approach across the corporate world, regularly pressuring their portfolio companies and borrowing clients to align with the UN's SDGs and run their businesses with a stakeholder mindset by using the implicit threat of disinvestment.

As with sustainability and climate change, the concept of sustainable investing also traces its origins back to the historical and cultural threads of the 1980s. At that time, socially responsible or ethical investment styles were just making the scene on Wall Street. The first bespoke stock mutual funds were being constructed by firms such as Calvert Investment Management to filter out sin industries like tobacco, alcohol, gambling, and nuclear weapons, and satisfy the demand of faith-based investors like the Methodist Church and like-minded university endowments and public state and local pension funds. Highlighting this new morally driven investment approach was the divestment campaign against South Africa and its racist apartheid government system, which played out over the course of the decade. Despite the market hype, the South Africa divestment movement was mainly a college campus phenomenon and only 155 US and Canadian educational institutions had agreed to cease investing in the country by 1988,[4] which equated to only 5% of total post-secondary schools in North America at the time. Moreover, federal legislation in the form of the Comprehensive Anti-Apartheid Act of 1986, which banned new US investment in South Africa and prohibited the import of natural resources and agricultural commodities from the country, arguably had more of a political impact on the South African government than anything going on in the financial markets.

However, all of this was lost in the popular mythology of the period when much of the world's gaze was directed at the African continent. Even as Steven Van Zandt was promising that he was "not gonna play Sun City" in his 1985 apartheid protest song, scores of other musicians were banding together to raise money for Ethiopian famine relief and performing for free in charity concerts such as the iconic globally televised Live Aid events in 1985. Against this altruistic backdrop, the main takeaway was that the divestment campaign against South Africa had succeeded in demonstrating that capital could be choked off for social and political purposes, providing the template for sustainable investing. While ostracizing a small, developing, tourism- and export-commodity-dependent country and pariah state such as South Africa is a much different proposition from restricting capital flows to a global industry such as oil and gas, the sustainability movement has never been one to let facts get in the way of a good story.

The UN first started diversifying into the world of stock and bond picking when the agency founded its sustainable investment group, Principles for Responsible Investment (PRI), in 2006, the same year that Milton Friedman passed away at the age of 94. The moral-sounding PRI was the brainchild of then–UN Secretary-General Kofi Annan and came together over the 2004–2005 period even as war was raging in both Iraq and Afghanistan and Annan himself was under ethical scrutiny for the corruption uncovered around the UN-administered Oil for Food program for Iraq.

While billed as an investor-led initiative, the PRI is an advocacy group sponsored and supported by the UN through its affiliates, the United Nations Environment Programme Finance Initiative (UNEP FI) and the United Nations Global Compact (UNGC). The UNEP FI was founded in 1992 on the back of the Rio Earth Summit to start engaging the finance sector on sustainability, while the UNGC was formed in 2000 to encourage corporate CEOs to implement universal sustainability principles and elicit business support for the goals of the UN. The UNEP FI has rolled out principles for both responsible banking and sustainable insurance, while the UNGC, which describes itself as the world's largest corporate sustainability initiative, has introduced its own Ten Principles for responsible business covering human rights, labor, the environment, and anticorruption. Currently, the UNEP FI membership includes 500 financial institutions across 120 countries with an aggregate $170 trillion in assets,[5] while the UNGC has more than 23,000 corporate and other participants from 166 countries.[6]

The PRI represented the next tentacle to be extended into the financial industry – this one directly into the global markets to touch every financial asset owner and investment manager. The main objective of the PRI is to institutionalize an ESG investment approach across Wall Street and the global financial markets. In deliberate UN fashion, the ESG acronym was first floated by the UNEP FI and the UNGC back in 2005 – the former in a UNEP FI–commissioned report prepared by the law firm Freshfields Bruckhaus Deringer, and the latter in a conference report from the UNGC's "Who Cares Wins" initiative – and then the PRI was spun out to execute on the concept.

As with everything else sustainability related with the UN, the PRI hook was climate change, with the launch of the new organization in 2006 seemingly timed to coincide with the upcoming splashy release of the IPCC's AR4 in 2007. While the UN's millenarian timetable was subsequently delayed by the global financial crisis that hit in 2008 and the global warming hiatus controversy that surrounded the AR5 release in

2013, things got back on track in 2015 with the rollout of the 17 SDGs alongside the signing of the Paris Agreement. Now all three interlocking UN initiatives – climate change, sustainable development, and sustainable finance – are perfectly synchronized and set for the same 2030 denouement. Like Russian Matryoshka dolls, climate change is wrapped up inside sustainability and then spread through ESG across the corporate sector and financial markets.

Echoing the Brundtland formulation, the stated goal of the PRI is to reconfigure the global corporate sector to "benefit the environment and society as a whole" and to build a "sustainable global financial system,"[7] which will lead to long-term value creation that will reward long-term, responsible investment and benefit the environment and society as a whole. Displaying the trademark facility of the UN around language manipulation, the PRI went with the "responsible investing" label, rather than "sustainable" or "social impact" or any of the other interchangeable ethical investing terms, to appear noncontroversial and appeal to the broadest group of investors possible – those exclusively focused on performance and returns. To get maximum buy-in, the PRI finessed the inherent tension in its doublethink about generating financial value and achieving social values – which was reportedly a source of contention among the founding investor signatories – by emphasizing the former over the latter, qualifying many of its statements with conditional language and papering over any cognitive dissonance. Initially, PRI members were promised the discretion to focus on financially material ESG factors, consistent with the specific fiduciary responsibilities of each individual investor. The PRI took great pains to stress that responsible investing did not require the same exclusionary, results-driven approach as social impact strategies, which typically screened out specific sin sectors such as alcohol, tobacco, and defense. To further allay any lingering investor concerns, the PRI reassuringly described itself as a voluntary initiative with a neutral agenda built around aspirational goals – its sole mission being to encourage and support the uptake of best practices for responsible investing. It is only after joining that PRI members discover that they have made an open-ended commitment to an ever-changing progressive agenda.

The 63 founding signatories of the PRI back in 2006 were mainly comprised of European financial institutions, public pension funds (including the United Nations Joint Staff Pension Fund), and faith-based investors (such as the Calvert Group, Mennonite Mutual Aid, and Westpath Investment Management, the pension arm of the United Methodist Church). In total, the founding bloc members were drawn from 15 countries and managed approximately $6.5 trillion in assets at the time. Since then, the group's membership has grown dramatically, steadily adding converts in the wake of the 2008 global financial crisis, which severely tarnished Wall Street's ethical image. Many virtue-signaling accounts have answered the call of responsibility and jumped on board the PRI bandwagon in recent years. Since 2015, the organization has stepped up its outreach program – much like an Amway distributorship, the PRI has a network of relationship managers and regular membership sales quotas to hit – to build on the momentum from the Paris Agreement signing and the SDG release over the second half of that year. Since March 31, 2014, the number of PRI signatories and their collective assets under management (AUM) have both more than tripled. As of March 31, 2023, the PRI membership included 5,381 signatories from over 90 countries with an aggregate $121.3 trillion in 2021 AUM.[8] The core membership of the London-headquartered PRI remains concentrated in Europe, where more than half of the group's signatories reside and where the commitment to climate change, sustainability, stakeholder capitalism, and collectivism in general runs deep.

The PRI has taken the lead in compiling and maintaining the ever-shifting list of ESG factors to be used by investors. Over time, the ESG focus list has changed, as has the tone of the motivational message. In addition to highlighting how ESG factors can potentially affect the performance of investment portfolios, the PRI also now warns that market demand for sustainable finance is growing from beneficiaries and clients and ESG regulations are coming, so best to be on the right side of financial market history. As the PRI notes cryptically in its current marketing pitch, "Including environmental, social and governance factors in investment decision-making and ownership is no longer seen as a nice-to-do but a must-do."[9] As with climate change and sustainable development, conformity based on coercion is a key component of the PRI program.

Much like the Seven Commandments imposed on the livestock in George Orwell's *Animal Farm*, each PRI member pledges to implement six specific ESG investment principles. These six principles – each of which comes with a menu of action items attached – were carefully crafted by a 70-person expert working group drawn from the UN and other multilateral agencies, national governments, NGOs, and academia. First and foremost, there is ESG integration. Each member agrees to incorporate ESG issues into their investment analysis and decision-making processes by baking ESG into investment policy statements, developing ESG-related tools and metrics, integrating ESG factors into research and analysis, evaluating internal personnel based on their ESG competence, encouraging third-party service providers to integrate ESG into their operations, and promoting academic and industry research that extols the benefits of ESG integration. Notably, there is no boundary line for investors regarding PRI Principle #1. It is to be applied universally and indiscriminately to not just new accounts but also existing funds and not just active funds but also passive investment strategies, which raises a host of ex post legal and fiduciary problems.

Second, there is engagement, otherwise known as company harassment. PRI members must become active owners of financial assets and incorporate ESG issues into their ownership policies and diligence and surveillance practices. Toward this end, signatories are expected to aggressively exercise their shareholder voting rights and regularly file shareholder resolutions around ESG-related matters during the annual general meeting season, along with raising ESG issues in all of their day-to-day one-on-one and group interactions with the management teams of the companies that they are invested in. As with #1, all third-party service providers and investment counterparties are expected to toe the same line. Thus far, the primary corporate targets for engagement have been publicly listed companies that trade in the developed financial markets since these issuers are more vulnerable to adverse headlines and manufactured controversies, which are the stock-in-trade of the ESG movement. Such a topsy-turvy focus on the industrialized world seems designed to deflect from UN member government failings – particularly across the developing world – on climate change and other policy fronts.

Third, members are required to push for ever-greater ESG disclosure by their portfolio companies – both public and private, including for debt investments where there is no voting ownership stake involved – which creates another opportunity for still more harassment. Here members are instructed to ask for an increasing number of standardized ESG metrics – ideally integrated within annual financial reports to normalize this esoteric nonfinancial disclosure – and question companies on their compliance with international reporting standards, particularly those set by the PRI, UNEP FI, UNGC, and other UN affiliates.

Fourth, PRI members are expected to proselytize and use every chance they get to promote broad acceptance and full implementation of the PRI principles across the investment community. Rather than walking up and down Wall Street wearing a sandwich board and ringing a bell, though, signatories are asked to do something even more disturbing: retroactively rewrite and revise their investment mandates, monitoring procedures, benchmarking tools, performance indicators, and incentive structures to align with all of the PRI principles, while embedding these same ESG requirements into all requests for proposals around new business mandates. Such activity would also include public support for any financial regulation or government policy that facilitated implementation of the PRI's agenda.

Fifth, since sustainability and its sustainable investment corollary are basically collectivist movements at heart, PRI members also promise to collaborate on ESG-related topics and work together with other investors to enhance the effectiveness of the PRI's principles and overall program, while agreeing to share information, pool resources, and collectively solve any emerging ESG issues. Such a principle obviously flies in the face of the legendary competitive dynamic of Wall Street, with sell-side firms obsessed with league table rankings, buy-side accounts keenly focused on portfolio performance versus peers, and everyone scrambling to win new business and outhustle the other guy. It also violates the basic protections of intellectual property and proprietary technology enjoyed by every industry. Only in the alternate investing universe of the PRI do asset owners not compete with each other.

Lastly, the sixth principle enshrines a surveillance function into the overall program by requiring each member to report on their activities and progress toward implementing all six principles – further proof that there is nothing optional or aspirational about the PRI's agenda. Signatories must provide regular updates on ESG integration, company engagement activities, and counterparty relationships, along with progress reports structured around an ominous-sounding comply-or-explain approach.

Since 2015, the PRI program has become more prescriptive with the synching up of its sustainable finance efforts with the UN's climate change and sustainable development verticals, with everyone involved now starting to say the quiet parts out loud. The initial PRI pitch to investors was that ESG analysis can better inform investment decision-making through a focus on financially material ESG factors and a nonexclusionary approach to investing. Now, the main objective is to mobilize the private sector and use its financial resources to achieve the goals of the Paris Agreement on climate change and implement the SDGs of the UN, which is not what many PRI members originally signed up for.

The United Nations Conference on Trade and Development (UNCTAD) has estimated that meeting the SDGs by 2030 will require $5–7 trillion per year, mainly from the private sector.[10] For perspective, this annual investment figure would be roughly equivalent to the size of the entire outstanding US corporate bond market, as measured by the S&P 500 Bond Index ($5.4 trillion market value as of April 28, 2023).[11] It took nearly three decades, but finally the Brundtland sustainability bill has come due for the corporate sector, apparently with accrued interest. The need for private sector funding has become more acute in the wake of the 2008 global financial crisis, the government policy response to which continues to stretch sovereign balance sheets around the world. Moreover, the UNCTAD has noted that the financial system's role in shaping outcomes in line with the SDGs cannot only involve new capital; it also requires investors to redirect existing capital and be good stewards of the entities they invest in. This, of course, would be another way of saying an exclusionary approach based on social values rather than financial value, which is what the PRI initially promised it would never do.

In its updated manifesto "The SDG Investment Case," which was released in 2017 and translated into multiple languages, the PRI decreed, "The SDGs set the global agenda for society and all of its stakeholders – including investors." As the PRI now sees it, the SDGs are the "globally-agreed sustainability framework" that will necessarily "drive global economic growth" going forward. As such, they represent an "unavoidable consideration" for large institutional investors with longer-term horizons and broad exposure to the overall market – the group of so-called universal owners that includes insurance companies, pension funds, foundations, endowments, and sovereign wealth funds, which the PRI has specifically targeted with its strategic initiatives and membership drives. As the PRI now warns, "A failure to meet the challenges of the SDGs could significantly affect the value of capital markets or their potential for growth, and with that, the value of diversified portfolios."[12]

Moreover, the PRI has now recast the 17 SDGs as both a risk framework and a capital allocation model for investors. Companies that do not align their business practices with the SDGs and investors that do not adjust their return expectations and steer capital based on the SDGs are now viewed as inherently riskier, both from a reputational as well as a financial perspective. To justify such an SDG-driven risk approach, the PRI points to the potential for a shift in government policy and regulations down the road that could place external environmental and social costs on corporate balance sheets, which is both a hollow threat and a highly circular argument given that one of the main reasons for the entire sustainable business push to begin with is the failure to act on the part of the public sector. Nonetheless, the PRI views the SDGs as "a different lens through which to filter future investment decisions,"[13] arguing that a focus on SDG-aligned investments can create a positive impact on society and the environment. As a result, the colorful SDG icons are now included in most corporate presentations – mainly as a protective talisman to ward off ESG controversy – and regularly reported against through the SDG compliance system established by the UNGC and the Global Reporting Initiative (GRI), an international, independent ESG reporting standards organization. The PRI has also adapted its own reporting system to track member alignment with the SDGs.

The PRI version of ESG is basically a translation for the UN periodic table of 17 SDGs, with its 169 specific targets and 232 indicators against which progress will be measured as part of the UN's 2030 agenda. While including many goals that properly fall within the purview of the government sector and being overly skewed toward environmental and social issues, the current inventory of SDG-derived ESG factors reads like a progressive policy wish list. Among other topics, the environmental pillar includes climate change, resource depletion, waste, plastics, methane, fracking, water usage, deforestation, and biodiversity. The social column includes human rights, modern slavery, child labor, working conditions, diversity and inclusion, gender-pay equality, union power, and employee relations. The governance pillar includes bribery and corruption, executive compensation, board diversity and structure, political lobbying and donations, and corporate tax fairness. This is just the short list. Moreover, for each ESG factor, investors need to work with a different set of stakeholders including businesses, governments, academia, NGOs, consumers, citizens, and the media.

For the PRI, climate change remains the "highest-priority ESG issue," the more equal of all the ESG factors. Parroting the hysterical language of the IPCC and the UNFCCC, the PRI also refers to climate change as "humanity's most pressing challenge" and an existential threat to both the planet and the financial markets. When it comes to climate change, the PRI's agenda is anything but neutral, highlighting how ESG investing is basically just a repackaging of the core climate change movement designed to co-opt the corporate sector and the investment community into the decades-long fight against man-made climate change. Staking out its position in line with the rest of the UN complex, the PRI has stated that achieving decarbonization of the world economy will require an immediate end to the exploration for new oil and gas resources, a rapid increase in carbon-free sources of electricity, and a host of related shifts in production methods and consumption patterns. Moreover, these shifts will also require "a redeployment of capital in support of the transition."[14]

The PRI's obsession with climate change can be seen in all the special programs and initiatives targeting climate change sponsored and supported by the group. These include the Climate Action 100+, an investor consortium focused on engagement with the 171 largest corporate emitters of greenhouse gas emissions; the Net-Zero Asset Managers (NZAM) initiative, an international group of asset managers committed to supporting the goal of net-zero greenhouse gas emissions for their investment holdings by 2050 or sooner; the Net-Zero Asset Owner Alliance (NZAOA), a group of institutional investors (mainly insurance companies) with the same 2050 portfolio decarbonization goal; the Net-Zero Banking Alliance, which speaks for roughly 40% of global banking assets and targets net-zero bank lending by 2050; the Net-Zero Financial Service Providers Alliance, whose members have committed to aligning their relevant services and products to improve consistency in financial decision-making with achieving a net-zero economy by 2050 at the latest; the Net-Zero Insurance Alliance (NZIA), a group of leading insurers that have committed to transition their insurance and reinsurance underwriting portfolios to net-zero greenhouse gas (GHG) emissions by 2050; the Initiative Climat International, a global community of private market investors focused on achieving the objectives of the Paris Agreement and limiting global warming to 1.5°C or below; the Glasgow Financial Alliance for Net-Zero (GFANZ), which focuses on raising net-zero ambitions across the global financial system, in line with the UN's Race to Zero global campaign focused on nonstate actors; the Task Force on Climate-related Financial Disclosures (TCFD), a mandatory climate risk disclosure framework created by the Financial Stability Board (FSB) of the G20; and the Inevitable Policy Response project, which is a PRI simulator showing how an acceleration of climate policy between now and 2030 would impact investment portfolios.

To promote ESG integration, the PRI offers an array of informational primers, case studies, and background reading materials, both to its members and to any and all potential sustainable investing converts. These educational resources cover every corner of the financial markets – equity and fixed income, public and private, securities and real assets – and are customized for every type of investor – both investment managers and asset owners, including active and passive strategies and alternative players such as hedge funds and private equity shops. Most of the content produced by the PRI includes ESG instruction manuals, albeit with few how-to guides showing how ESG factors can actually drive improved investment returns. The group also provides a centralized ESG data portal and a PRI Collaboration Platform allowing for the sharing of information between PRI members and interested parties. Its PRI Academy offers accreditation services and online training modules in a variety of topics related to responsible investment.

In addition, the PRI also collaborates with third-party affinity groups – including other activist nonprofits such as The Shareholder Commons, Bloomberg Philanthropies, and Al Gore's Generation Foundation, along with a PRI Academic Network comprised of nearly 12,000 academics and investment practitioners – to ensure a steady stream of supportive research touting the benefits of sustainable investing. The PRI has also closely coordinated and synchronized its work with other like-minded and 2030-focused international organizations such as the WEF, whose affiliated International Business Council released its own set of 34 ESG-related stakeholder capitalism reporting metrics in 2020. As with climate change, an institutional echo chamber has now been constructed for consistent messaging about sustainable investing, with the PRI sitting at the nexus of industry, finance, academia, and the government and supranational spheres, where it largely sets the agenda and controls the narrative. To cheer itself on, the PRI has also assembled a worldwide fan club through its PRI Network Supporters initiative, which presently includes 71 nonprofit peer organizations that publicly express support for the PRI and its moral cause of responsible investing.

Besides its reliance on propaganda, the PRI has also shown a penchant for Soviet-style centralized multiyear planning. In 2016, 10 years after its founding and in the immediate wake of the UN's big 2015 reveal around climate and sustainability, the organization released a 10-year "Blueprint for Responsible Investment for 2017–2027," supplemented by three-year strategic plans and annual work programs. Notably, by 2027, the PRI hopes to change the pricing function of the financial markets to make sure that ESG risk is the main discriminant factor in determining the cost and availability of capital for specific industries and issuers. To achieve this goal, the group also wants to remove all of the obstacles – regulatory, market, and otherwise – currently standing in the way of achieving a sustainable global financial system, starting with the fiduciary rule. The PRI is intent on redefining an investor's fiduciary responsibility to require – not just consider or allow for – a sustainable, ESG-driven approach to investing and allocating capital, mainly through the imposition of regulatory mandates, which the group openly supports and tracks with an in-house database. Lastly, the PRI wants to start seeing actual results from investor alignment with the SDGs, including the redirection of capital toward "projects with positive, real-world impact."[15] The current 2021–2024 strategic plan ratchets up the pressure on PRI members to achieve these longer-term goals – which are now less than five years away – including more regular training, onerous reporting, and mandatory collaboration.

By now, many signatories have discovered that there is only the illusion of choice when it comes to the PRI's ESG matrix and its brand of responsible investing. Instead of aspirational goals and a discretionary approach based on financially material ESG factors, members are now being asked to hard-code their ESG analysis using the 17 SDGs and redeploy capital to support the environmental and social agenda of the

UN. They are being pressured to lengthen their investment horizons to align with the multidecadal time periods being used for climate change, while also committing to decarbonize their portfolios by screening out fossil fuel companies as part of a broader program to drive unsustainable businesses from the capital markets. Financial return is now taking a back seat to environmental and social impact. And members can't hide behind fiduciary responsibility for long since the PRI is actively working to pass ESG regulations that will redefine the role of fiduciary to require an ESG approach. And finally, investment decisions are now being evaluated more for their real-world impact and societal outcomes than their financial returns.

In contrast to the optional ESG program originally promised, all of the PRI's recommendations are now expected to be acted upon. And yes, there will be a test. To increase accountability, the PRI has increased minimum membership requirements and started grading the ESG performance of each of its signatories. Under the new house rules, PRI investor signatories must now make their ESG policies public and apply them to more than 90% of their AUM – up from 50% previously – including any asset class comprising 10% or more of overall AUM. Each member's performance is assessed and rated on a Michelin-like scale of 1 through 5 stars (previously, an A+ to E letter-grading system), both by module (such as strategy and governance and selection, appointment and monitoring) and by asset class (including listed equity, fixed income, private equity, real estate, and infrastructure). To provide encouragement, the PRI recognizes outstanding ESG performance and excellence in responsible investing by individual members through its PRI Leaders Group and annual PRI Awards, although the group's incentive structure remains more heavily weighted toward sticks rather than carrots.

To cut down on free riders, PRI members are now given a shorter two-year timeline to bring themselves into compliance, with laggards seeing their PRI-club memberships canceled fairly quickly if intervention fails. Given that the PRI has set itself up as the global stamp of approval when it comes to ESG, the threat of excommunication from the Church of Sustainability is a strong motivator given the stigma attached, which tends to spur compliance. This is the problem with joining an organization to signal your virtue: the bad signal that it sends when you decide to exit, whether voluntarily or not. Like staying at the Hotel California, once you check in at the PRI, it is not so easy to leave, even if you are not happy with the program and the accommodations. To illustrate: Of the 165 problematic members identified in 2018 when the PRI started tightening up its membership requirements, only five were ultimately kicked out in 2020 when their two-year probationary period ended. To date, no major investor has decided to voluntarily drop from the PRI despite the group's changing ESG agenda and increasingly burdensome reporting and other requirements, which speaks to the moral authority that the group has been able to accrue in a fairly short period of time. Many people on Wall Street would sooner turn back a coveted membership at Winged Foot Golf Club than have to explain why they are leaving the PRI.

To get an idea of the ESG market reach of the PRI, here are a few back-of-the-envelope numbers. Based on the group's fiscal year-end membership rolls of March 31, 2023, and assuming universal compliance with the group's recent requirement for ESG integration across at least 90% of member AUM, a minimum of roughly $109.2 trillion of financial assets in the global system as of 2021 are currently being invested using a sustainable approach. While the devil is in the ESG definitional details and there is probably some double counting in the PRI's reported AUM figures for asset owners and investment managers, this is still a significant following, on par with the popularity of the Unification Church of Reverend Sun Myung Moon back during its heyday in the 1980s. For perspective, in 2021, global GDP totaled $96.9 trillion based on World Bank data,[16] while the Securities Industry and Financial Markets Association (SIFMA) estimates that the global equity market capitalization stood at $124.4 trillion and total global bonds outstanding amounted to $126.9 trillion that same year.[17]

Moreover, the ESG influence of the PRI extends far beyond the ranks of its sizable membership rolls. By design, its principles and policies are meant to catch up as many market participants as possible within its sticky ESG web, including nonsignatories and other innocent bystanders. To spread the ESG gospel, the group disguises activism as active ownership and compels its members to be good stewards by using their influence to pressure every financial counterparty into ESG compliance, which is a fairly perverse interpretation of the term "stewardship." By integrating backward and specifically targeting universal owners – the large institutional investors that hold title to most of the investable capital in the markets – the PRI is able to maximize its leverage over the entire system through "the top of the investment chain." These asset owners are the ESG market fulcrum since they hold sway with investment managers – including the Big 3 index-driven shops of BlackRock Inc., The Vanguard Group Inc., and State Street Global Advisors – as well as consultants, rating agencies, and other third-party service providers and can help drive a reengineering of requests for proposals, due diligence questionnaires, and the other workings of the financial markets. Their ESG asks are basically offers that cannot be refused. The threat by a major buy-side client to "pull the wire" and stop doing business altogether tends to cut down on ESG dissent among the investment banks.

In many ways, the tactics being used by the PRI to drive a deep, systemic incorporation of ESG across the financial markets are like those used historically by the Mafia to push its way into the carting, construction, restaurant, and gambling industries. Like the Five Families, the PRI uses a combination of pressure (peer and financial), public intimidation, and regular surveillance to shake down companies and investment firms and enforce across-the-board ESG conformity. The PRI's warning that ESG investing is now a must-do for Wall Street can basically be paraphrased as follows: "Nice asset management business you got here. Be a shame if anything happened to it." Few market participants are willing to get into a public fight with the PRI or any other ESG advocacy group since this would necessarily require a challenge to the core sustainability tenet of climate change, which is a first punch that no one on Wall Street appears willing to throw. Climate change provides the protection for the entire ESG racket, and the PRI uses this fact to its advantage.

As the leading proponent of responsible investing, the PRI is the body most responsible for the ESG bureaucratic superstructure that has gone up all around Wall Street in recent years. Its extrusive policies have created a pernicious system of ESG thought across the financial markets that pits everyone against each other, with every market player now looking over its shoulders for fear of being brought up on charges of ESG thoughtcrime. This mental scaffolding will now become more rigid and reinforced as the PRI works to complete its market renovation work by the hard delivery date of 2030. It is ironic that the current Hobbesian ESG world being formed by the PRI and its various UN affiliates is meant to usher in the group's utopian goals of a "sustainable global financial system" and a "more prosperous world for all."

CHAPTER 4

WALL STREET: IN THE SHADOW OF THE MUSHROOM CLOUD

Come, the New Jerusalem.
Carly Simon, "Let the River Run"

It's no use going back to yesterday, because I was a different person then.
Lewis Carroll, *Alice in Wonderland*

When Lehman Brothers Holdings Inc., the fourth largest US investment bank, hurriedly filed for bankruptcy protection early on the Monday morning of September 15, 2008, it triggered a global financial crisis that nearly brought down all of Wall Street. Credit markets seized up, liquidity vanished, and trading stopped. Absent extraordinary government intervention by suddenly emboldened US regulators, American International Group Inc. (AIG), Goldman Sachs, and Morgan Stanley would likely have met the same fate as Lehman Brothers by week's end, with more firms falling like dominoes thereafter. It is not hyperbole to state that the world's financial system was at risk of collapse that fateful week when the markets stood still. To this day, many on Wall Street still refer to modern financial history in pre- and post-Lehman terms, much as the Gregorian calendar uses the BC and AD designations to organize human civilization.

For more than two centuries prior, though, Wall Street had repeatedly shown its ability to weather periodic financial and economic shocks – including the deep stock market crashes of 1929 and 1987, the protracted Great Depression, and two world wars – and move on from the regular loss of financial firms in its midst, always bouncing back with renewed vigor. In fact, in the previous two decades alone, Wall Street had successfully navigated through a series of crises emanating from multiple geographies (Latin America, Asia, and Russia), sectors (commercial real estate, savings and loan, technology, telecommunications, and merchant energy), and markets (Nasdaq Composite, high-yield bond, and emerging markets). Along the way, benchmark industry names such as Drexel Burnham Lambert Incorporated, Kidder Peabody & Company, and Long-Term Capital Management (LTCM) all disappeared suddenly, mostly due to self-inflicted wounds. In each of these cases, the government and financial regulators made sure that there was limited systemic spillover and the Street was able to quickly close ranks.

However, the 2008 global financial crisis was different. When Lehman Brothers failed, it was a unique type of seismic event for the industry. In geological terms, it was the equivalent of earthquake-induced soil liquefaction, as is often seen in the San Francisco Bay area and the Mexico City capital region. Metaphorically speaking, the Lehman bankruptcy in 2008 had the same effect on the financial markets. While Lehman's asset quality, leverage, and liquidity problems were of its own making, its sudden bankruptcy filing amplified these company-specific risks across the financial system through the interlocking risk between firms – mainly through credit default swaps and other structured credit products, compounded by the lack of financial transparency. Ultimately, though, it was regulatory uncertainty – whether through sheer incompetence or by willful design – that caused the market's foundation to shift and nearly bring down the entire system, leaving many institutions teetering on the edge.

Over the previous quarter century, Lehman Brothers had been the little engine that could on Wall Street. The scrappy fighter perpetually punching above its weight as it tried to break into the ranks of the top investment banks – always with a chip on its shoulder. After being forced to sell itself to Shearson/American Express Inc. in 1984, it took 10 long years before the company regained its independence in 1994 when it went public through a spinout to shareholders. It was during this decade of occupation that the firm's fixed income division, led by Richard (Dick) Fuld Jr., solidified its hold on the management reins – the bankers may have won the battle to sell the private partnership in 1984, but they had lost the war for control of the firm with the traders – and built up a strong but insular culture to preserve a kind of virtual partnership within its retail-oriented financial services parent conglomerate – much like Jonah biding his time in the belly of the whale. Post-emancipation, the company expanded, diversified, and succeeded in transforming itself from a fixed income shop primarily focused on secondary US trading during the 1980s to a global investment bank, equally strong in debt and equity, with an asset management arm and the leading research and bond index franchise on Wall Street.

But along the way, risk management and politics, the combination of which had toppled the firm in 1984, remained persistent problems and chronic weaknesses of the company. Shortly after going public in 1994 – a year marked by six rate hikes by the Federal Reserve and heightened volatility across the emerging markets – the firm became one of the largest holders of Mexican-government-issued dollar-denominated debt known as *Tesobonos* right before the peso was devalued at year-end, touching off a currency and external liquidity crisis for the country. Lehman Brothers was bailed out of its multibillion-dollar *Tesobonos* position when the US government led a $50 billion International Monetary Fund rescue package for Mexico in early 1995, but not before the firm was downgraded by Moody's Investors Service Inc. and lost its all-important A3 long-term rating, which raised the company's annual funding costs by approximately $50 million.

Three years later, the firm had another near-death experience when, on the heels of the 1997 Asian financial crisis, the Russian government unexpectedly defaulted on its domestic debt in August 1998. This black swan event, in turn, led to an across-the-board flight to quality and caused severe financial market dislocations that triggered the sudden collapse of LTCM, the highly leveraged quantitative hedge fund run by John Meriwether of Salomon Inc. fame, only a few weeks later. Rumors swirled for months thereafter that Lehman Brothers had substantial exposure to both Russian ruble bonds and LTCM, causing its share price to drop by roughly 70% between July and October of that year. Led by CEO Fuld, the firm responded aggressively, publicly shouting down its critics, threatening legal action against any rumormongers, and standing ready to buy back any Lehman Brothers bonds that came in for the bid. The show of bravado worked and the company's share price recovered by year-end. The episode fed the mythology around the pitchman Fuld and the unsinkable Lehman Brothers, but the incident was yet another reminder that the company was perceived as small and thinly capitalized. Moreover, it had been a close call. For a publicly listed broker-dealer, a single-digit share price is often enough reason for trading counterparties to stop doing business with a firm, precipitating a liquidity crisis and a run on the investment bank. In the fall of 1998, the company's share price had dipped down as low as the teens. The next time that Lehman Brothers' share price revisited the teens was the summer of 2008, when there would be no bounce and no stopping before the stock hit single digits on September 9, 2008, just days before the end.

In 2006, the firm aggressively ramped up its risk tolerance and principal positions across all of its business segments. The directive came down explicitly from the corporate suite on the 31st floor of the company's Midtown office tower, almost like the ringing of a bell. Between 2006 and 2007, the firm added outsized commercial and residential real estate exposure (much of it subprime), wrote millions of credit derivative contracts, scaled up three large internal hedge funds, built out its commodity trading business from scratch, added proprietary positions across all of its liquid market-making operations, provided billions of dollars of largely unsecured lending commitments, and wrote equity checks for large LBOs such as the take-private of Archstone-Smith Trust, which closed in October 2007 at the top of the market. For years, the firm had prided itself on the motto of being in the moving, not the warehousing, business when it came to risk exposure. Yet, over fiscal years 2006–2007, the firm expanded its balance sheet by 69%, increased its gross leverage ratio from 24.4x to 30.7x, and more than tripled its value-at-risk (VAR) – the model-projected maximum amount of money that could be lost in one day of trading – from $38 million to $124 million. Moreover, its balance sheet grew more illiquid, with net Level III assets – those financial instruments without a discernible market value that must be hand-priced – totaling $38.9 billion as of November 30, 2007, almost double the size of the company's stockholders' equity.

The timing for this across-the-board risk-on trade was stupefying. It was already late in the credit cycle, interest rates were ticking up, and the red-hot, debt-fueled residential real estate market was starting to show signs of cracking. But by 2006, there were few within the Lehman management ranks willing or able to push back and challenge the two men at the top, CEO Fuld and his second-in-command, President and COO Joseph Gregory.

Even by Wall Street standards, Lehman Brothers had always been a hyperpolitical firm. The legendary animosity between traders and bankers described in Ken Auletta's 1986 book *Greed and Glory on Wall Street: The Fall of the House of Lehman* improved somewhat after the company regained its independence, but never quite went away. The insularity also remained. Outside hires, even top producers from Wall Street competitors, were always viewed suspiciously and placed on long probationary periods. Some were able to carve out niches and business fiefdoms, but many did not last long and none was ever a candidate to run the company. After going public in 1994, Lehman Brothers continued to be run by the same people from its core fixed income trading business who had held the firm together during the 1980s, with one poignant exception. In 1996, a management putsch led by Gregory, who was then cohead of fixed income, removed the last remaining threat to the Fuld–Gregory leadership tag team with the ouster of T. Christopher Pettit, the president and COO and long-standing #2 partner to Fuld during the occupation years. A decorated Vietnam War veteran and West Point graduate, Pettit was an inspirational and natural leader of the Lehman troops, as well as a solid business and risk manager. After one of his rousing town halls at the end of the trading day, employees would often march back to their desks and go back to work. Shortly after he was forced out, Pettit died tragically in a snowmobiling accident, eliminating any chance for a comeback and leaving only sad thoughts of what might have been for the firm.

For the next 12 years, it was Fuld and Gregory running the firm – ultimately into the ground – with little serious challenge from below. The next generation of firm leaders was never allowed to move up and take over because any business manager who worked his way up through the ranks – even those from its favored fixed income franchise – was inevitably sidelined or pushed out by Gregory. The company's board of directors was also duly compliant, being comprised mainly of ex-CEOs with non-financial backgrounds – along with one Broadway producer – and basically functioning as a rubber stamp. Over time, decision-making became more sclerotic as the top management of the firm became increasingly isolated and removed from the firm's underlying businesses and the financial markets because of its attitude of "Don't nobody bring me no bad news." Investment banks, like fish, also rot from the head down.

The one-firm cultural mandate that had been in place since 1994 began to fray. Annual bonus pools became more skewed toward the upper echelons of the firm, as kleptocracy replaced meritocracy and the unwritten compensation code of insulating junior staff from market volatility was increasingly ignored. In the last two years of the firm's existence, a handful of line managers did start to speak up and disagree, but it was too little too late. Moreover, for some of these conscientious objectors, the primary goal seemed to be getting fired and allowed to "retire" as a means of vesting five years' worth of accumulated stock compensation – the Wall Street version of rats jumping from a sinking ship.

In hindsight, there were many eerie parallels between the 1984 and 2008 collapses of Lehman Brothers. In both cases, the firm was just coming off a record profit year – in fiscal year 2007, the company posted $4.2 billion of net income – before collapsing barely nine months later. In both instances, the problems were risk management and capital adequacy, compounded by internal politics. In his 1985 magazine article in the *New York Times* – the precursor for his 1986 book – Auletta described the events of 1984 as follows: "What happened at Lehman is a tale of political intrigue, of incompetence unmatched even in the civil service, a sordid tale of vanity, avarice, cowardice, lust for power and a polluted Lehman culture. [T]hese ingredients ... are what ultimately crushed a venerable institution."[1] The same words could be cut out and pasted in as the explanation for the firm's bankruptcy in 2008.

The fact that Fuld and much of his inner circle were at the helm both times and apparently learned nothing from the prior experience – including the value and optionality of living to fight another day – made the events of 2008 all the more tragic. Notably, Fuld was one of the few partners to vote against the 1984 sale of the company. Nearly a quarter of a century later, his position had not changed so he dusted off the same playbook. The same reluctance to sell and give up control can be seen in the firm's attempts to shore up its financial position throughout 2008 – all of which were spearheaded by Fuld – which mainly included third-party capital raises and offering minority stakes to nonthreatening financial partners such as Korea Development Bank (KDB). By the time

Fuld had his epiphany about selling outright – perhaps remembering his fiduciary responsibility to the firm's 26,200 employees, who collectively owned 30% of the firm – the company was already on its deathbed.

While Lehman Brothers' problems were self-inflicted, they were hardly unique within the financial industry. Heading into 2008, all of the top five investment banks were sporting balance sheet leverage in the 25–30x range, while Lehman was not the only firm on the Street to use repurchase agreements as a form of balance sheet window dressing at each quarter-end. The Bear Stearns Companies Inc. and the two government-sponsored mortgage lenders, Federal National Mortgage Association (Fannie Mae) and Federal Home Loan Mortgage Corporation (Freddie Mac), had already failed by the end of the summer, the former acquired by JPMorgan Chase & Co. (with $30 billion of US government support) and the latter two institutions nationalized by the federal government. Merrill Lynch & Co. Inc. arguably had a weaker balance sheet (including $81 billion of mortgage market exposure as of June 27, 2008) and would have failed the same day as Lehman Brothers had not Bank of America Corporation stepped in at the last minute to buy the firm. The next day, AIG would also have filed for bankruptcy protection had not the Federal Reserve stepped in with an $85 billion loan (in exchange for 79.9% of the company's common shares) to stabilize the insurer's $447 billion credit default swap book, a major counterparty of which was Goldman Sachs. The following week, Washington Mutual Bank was seized by the Federal Deposit Insurance Corporation (FDIC) and all of its assets and liabilities were transferred over to JPMorgan Chase.

Throughout the extraordinary 2008 year for the markets, the Federal Reserve and US Treasury repeatedly took bold and unprecedented actions to shore up the financial system and save each failing institution when its turn came, mainly by forcing a merger with a stronger commercial bank competitor, often with government financial support. After the collapse of Bear Stearns in March, the Federal Reserve created the Primary Dealer Credit Facility (PDCF) to provide overnight loans to primary dealers (including investment banks) collateralized by a broad range of investment grade securities. The day after Lehman filed, AIG was bailed out and the PDCF window was expanded to take high-yield securities and equities as collateral in addition to investment grade debt. Later that same week when money market funds started to "break the buck," the US Treasury stepped in with taxpayer-funded insurance to guarantee the value of each money market fund share at $1.00. In early October, the US Congress passed the Emergency Economic Stabilization Act of 2008, which authorized the $700 billion Troubled Asset Relief Program (TARP) to purchase toxic assets from, and preferred stock in, the country's major commercial and investment banks. Some of this TARP money was used to further bolster AIG and support the pending merger of Bank of America and Merrill Lynch, along with the just-announced distressed sale of Wachovia Corporation to Wells Fargo & Company.

Why was Lehman Brothers the only firm that was not saved by the US government and financial regulators during the rolling global financial crisis of 2008? Not only was it not saved, but the Federal Reserve and US Treasury both went out of their way to force a bankruptcy filing by the firm. Lehman Brothers experienced a liquidity run during the week of September 8, 2008, following the collapse of talks with KDB and the early release of horrible quarterly earnings – the combination of which drove the company's share price down to mid–single digits – as many of its trading and lending counterparties started to cut lines or demand more collateral. Heading into that final weekend, Lehman's main clearing bank, JPMorgan Chase, alone was holding up $17 billion of the company's cash and securities while demanding additional collateral on top of this.[2] Rather than working to alleviate the company's liquidity crisis, the Federal Reserve compounded the problem by further restricting Lehman's access to the PDCF window. That weekend, all of Lehman Brothers' Wall Street competitors were given an inside look at the company's financial accounts in what was basically a going-through-the-motions exercise with a little prebankruptcy window shopping thrown in. When a deal to sell the entire company to Barclays Bank PLC was negotiated by Sunday, the US government declined to provide any support to bridge the transaction until a shareholder vote could be held on the Barclays side, in accordance with UK Financial Services Authority (FSA) requirements. That night of September 14, the Lehman Brothers board of directors was instructed by US regulators to file for Chapter 11 bankruptcy "quickly because of the markets." Incredibly, the Federal Reserve stated that its preference was that the company "be wound down in an orderly fashion."[3]

To this day, the official explanations by the government trio in charge at the time – Ben Bernanke, chair of the Board of Governors of the

Federal Reserve System, Timothy Geithner, president of the Federal Reserve Bank of New York, and Henry Paulson, US treasury secretary and former chairman and CEO of Goldman Sachs – remain unconvincing, especially as the story has changed over time. The main arguments that have been used to justify not rescuing Lehman Brothers are that the firm was given plenty of time to save itself; it was already insolvent; it did not have adequate collateral to lend against; and the Federal Reserve and the federal government were hamstrung in their legal authority to help. These various reasons were all cited as recently as 2018 when Bernanke, Geithner, and Paulson took their 10-year victory lap to publicly reminisce about the events of 2008.

Taking each argument in turn: Lehman Brothers had been scrambling for six months, ever since the failure of Bear Stearns in March 2008, to shore up its financial position. The company succeeded in raising nearly $12 billion of common and preferred stock during the first half of 2008, but was never going to be able to self-solve for its balance sheet problems given how quickly the real estate and credit markets were deteriorating. As Professor Laurence Ball of Johns Hopkins University summarized in his 2016 working paper and then detailed in his 2018 book *The Fed and Lehman Brothers: Setting the Record Straight on a Financial Disaster*, while suffering from an immediate liquidity crisis, Lehman Brothers was not insolvent at the time of its forced bankruptcy. Even applying healthy valuation haircuts to the left side of its balance sheet, the company still had positive stockholders' equity. Moreover, based on Ball's calculations, it also had sufficient collateral against which the Federal Reserve could have safely lent upward of $88 billion through the existing PDCF had the Federal Reserve taken the time to do the collateral analysis, which it did not.[4] As for the absence of legal authority, government actions both before and immediately after September 15, 2008, contradict this argument, particularly the extraordinary measures taken to save AIG and, by extension, Goldman Sachs, the very next day. Apparently, it was only a 24-hour case of alligator arms that US regulators were suffering from. Notably, in 2015, a US Court of Federal Claims judge ruled that the Federal Reserve had overstepped its legal powers under the Federal Reserve Act with its actions around the bailout of AIG, calling the forced taking of 79.9% of the company's equity an "illegal exaction" and the terms of its $85 billion rescue loan unfair and off-market.[5] Of course, by then the legal point was moot since AIG (and its many financial counterparties) had already been saved.

In the middle of a systemic financial crisis – one brought on by bad government policy that promoted loose mortgage-lending standards – why did the US government stand on protocol and hide behind legal technicalities only when it came to Lehman Brothers? During that pivotal final week in September 2008, the Federal Reserve's stance toward Lehman Brothers was analogous to a fireman waiting for a search warrant to enter a burning building, more focused on finding an excuse not to help rather than stepping up in its role as lender of last resort. Despite the voiced concerns about where the Asian markets would open up that Monday morning, it is hard to imagine that government officials actually believed that a rushed overnight Chapter 11 filing by Lehman Brothers, the fourth largest US investment bank with more than 900,000 derivative contracts, would be therapeutic for the global financial system. The global economic fallout and financial catastrophe that were touched off by the government-allowed failure of Lehman Brothers put the lie to this view, as does the 14 years that it took to wrap up the dead company's estate.

Based on all the postmortems in the years since, politics and personality issues seem to have played a role in the rough justice meted out to Lehman Brothers. Throughout 2008, Paulson took the lead with regard to dealing with the financial crisis in general and Lehman's problems in particular, with the Federal Reserve typically deferring to Treasury officials. In the wake of the government rescues of Bear Stearns, Fannie Mae, and Freddie Mac, Paulson was reportedly worried about his public legacy and being forever labeled "Mr. Bailout." At the time, he was getting grief from both sides of the aisle for his taxpayer-funded bailouts of Wall Street in the middle of a recession. It was also a presidential election year, with the race close between Senator Barack Obama and Senator John McCain – the two were effectively tied in the polls in mid-September. Getting any supportive bipartisan financial legislation passed by Congress was problematic. If Paulson was looking for a catalyst to get the attention of US lawmakers and motivate them to action, the Lehman bankruptcy clearly provided it, as seen by the creation of TARP just two weeks later.

It is also fair to ask what role personal dynamics played in the process at the end because, in the business of Wall Street, everything is personal.

Lehman CEO Fuld was an intimidating figure, given to angry outbursts, with a menacing, monosyllabic demeanor. He fully lived up to his nickname of "The Gorilla," both internally and outside of the firm, almost to the point of caricature. He was an aggressive competitor, particularly obsessed with beating the two white-shoe investment banks, Goldman Sachs and Morgan Stanley, and generally looked down upon by the heads of the other Wall Street firms – and not just because of his small stature. Moreover, the visceral antipathy of the longtime trader Fuld toward bankers took on a whole new dimension when it came to going up against competitive firms run by investment bankers. During the last few years of Lehman's corporate life, especially strong quarterly earnings out of Goldman Sachs and Morgan Stanley would always throw Fuld into a rage, helping to drive much of the firm's excessive risk-taking at the end. None of this history helped in 2008 when Fuld was dealing with – and dependent on – Paulson, the investment banker and former adversary who had run Goldman Sachs from 1999 through 2006 and was now his regulator and ultimate savior. Was 2008 some form of competitive payback or comeuppance for Lehman Brothers for being one of the only Wall Street firms that did not participate in the bailout of LTCM in 1998? Despite strong circumstantial evidence, we will never know the answers to these questions.

Lehman Brothers was 158 years old when it filed for bankruptcy on September 15, 2008. There was no public mourning period. Almost immediately, the firm became a punch line for late-night comics. According to firm lore, the company traced its founding back to 1850 when the three Lehman brothers, Henry, Emanuel, and Mayer, all immigrants from the Bavarian region of Germany, opened up a dry goods and commodity trading store in antebellum Alabama. Notwithstanding the governance failings and personal foibles of its senior management team at the end, most people on Wall Street would still agree that the company died too young.

Because of its arbitrary and capricious nature and the consensus view that it should have been avoidable, the signal that Lehman's failure sent to the financial markets was much more than a simple moral-hazard warning. Rather, the main takeaway was that financial firms needed to stay on the good side of the US government and the financial regulators. The same day that Lehman Brothers filed for bankruptcy, Merrill Lynch was acquired at a 70% stock premium. In 2008, it was the regulators that picked the winners and the losers, and it was only government largesse that saved the Wall Street survivors. That message has not been lost on the industry. Notably, all of Wall Street – even better-capitalized commercial banks such as JPMorgan Chase – got in line and took their TARP medicine shortly after Lehman filed.

The events of 2008 fundamentally changed Wall Street in terms of risk appetite and tolerance, much as the generation that grew up during the Great Depression remained personally frugal for the rest of their lives. Further reinforcing this industry-wide risk aversion has been the government policy overreaction to the crisis on the legal and regulatory as well as monetary fronts. To reinforce obedience and further deflect government responsibility for the subprime mortgage fiasco that triggered the global financial crisis, financial firms were pilloried in the press – headlines screamed how Wall Street had ruined Main Street – and sued by the US Department of Justice (DOJ) under the Obama administration. These DOJ civil lawsuits were joined by most of the 50 states plus the federal department of Housing and Urban Development (HUD), the latter of which is rich given that it was HUD affordable housing policy, implemented through the government-sponsored enterprises Fannie Mae and Freddie Mac, that was the primary cause of the subprime mortgage crisis.

Beginning in the early 1990s, increasing affordable housing quotas set by HUD forced the loosening of underwriting standards across the mortgage market to make more credit available to lower-income and minority borrowers and meet the demands of the federal government. By 2007, 55% of the residential mortgages purchased by Fannie Mae and Freddie Mac were required to be affordable. Wall Street's role was mainly to repackage these GSE mortgage loans, which were notably insured by the Federal Housing Administration within HUD, into mortgage-backed securities to be sold to institutional investors, thereby freeing up balance sheet capacity throughout the banking and government chain for more mortgage lending. These mortgage-backed securities were simply the transmission mechanism for the toxic government-sponsored mortgage loans that infected the entire global financial system.

Despite the frivolous nature of these fraud charges, all of Wall Street opted to settle the civil suits brought by the federal government around the mortgage crisis due to the implied threat of criminal cases coming next. Since criminal charges are an effective death sentence for any bank or broker-dealer, financial firms agreed to pay out billions of dollars in damages to make the issue go away, with most banks copping only to technical infractions such as mortgage servicing and foreclosure processing problems. Through 2016, Wall Street settlement payments and fines related to the mortgage crisis totaled approximately $110 billion, based on an analysis by the *Wall Street Journal.*[6] Add on another $16 billion in dividends and capital gains from the preferred equity stakes forcibly taken through the TARP program and the US government made a fairly attractive return on the global financial crisis that it primarily caused. In the end, no Wall Street banker – including anybody from Lehman Brothers – ever went to jail for their role in the global financial crisis, mainly because stupidity and incompetence are not criminal offenses.

To further keep the industry in line, Wall Street was then hit with a wave of new regulations, even though it was not a lack of rules on the books, but bad policy compounded by regulatory uncertainty, that led to the global financial crisis. The Dodd–Frank Wall Street Reform and Consumer Protection Act, with its companion Volcker Rule, was signed into law by President Obama in 2010, mandating a total of 390 new rulemakings for the financial sector. Of this target, 274 major rules or 70% had been finalized by the end of the second term of the Obama administration in 2016. Over six years, the industry was hit with roughly $36 billion of additional regulatory costs and 73 million more man-hours of paperwork, based on numbers compiled by the American Action Forum.[7] Wall Street banks and investment firms are now consumed with legal compliance and have become the equivalent of regulated power utilities – the only difference being that finance is much more complicated than keeping the lights on.

The one lesson from Lehman Brothers that everyone can agree upon was that, in the modern age of integrated global finance, the bankruptcy of a major investment bank can never be orderly. Yet, under the Dodd–Frank Act, the game plan will be the same going forward, with any future failing financial firm to be resolved through an orderly liquidation process. All systematically important financial institutions must now have "living wills" in place to facilitate a rapid and orderly shutdown of operations, as if an investment bank were the same thing as an automotive assembly line. An entire death care industry has now gone up around Wall Street, including a permanent Financial Stability Oversight Council (with its Orderly Liquidation Fund) and the FDIC now empowered to seize any distressed financial company – not just depository institutions – on the back of an order from the US District Court for the District of Columbia. Previously, financial firms that ran into trouble were simply merged with their stronger brethren, typically a larger commercial bank and often with backstop financial support from the government. This had always been the case both prior to and during the 2008 global financial crisis, with the only exception being Lehman Brothers, which was allowed to fail. Now Lehman Brothers has become the default position, with financial regulators standing ready to block any potential rescue merger of a struggling firm in favor of a forced wind-down if they perceive "a great threat to the financial stability of the United Sates."[8]

Lehman Brothers still ranks as the largest and most complex US corporate bankruptcy to date. The company reported $613 billion of total liabilities when it filed Chapter 11 in September 2008, with the final distribution on the bankruptcy estate occurring in September 2022. Along the way, there was an incredible destruction of value across the financial system and the global economy. Even with do-not-resuscitate orders on file, there is little reason to expect different results the next go-round, especially in a repeat scenario of 2008 when a series of major bank bankruptcies would need to be orchestrated in the midst of a systemic crisis caused by a market trigger. These confidential company directives are more placebo than panacea, and do not abrogate the need for regulatory support and consistency to maintain liquid and functioning financial markets during periods of stress. While the new regulatory stance reads like the definition of insanity, Wall Street firms have reacted rationally by sharply limiting their risk tolerance to stay out of trouble, which is the natural response of anyone being measured for a coffin by the town undertaker.

Feeding the risk-averse mentality of the industry has been a sharp shift in monetary policy postcrisis. Since 2008, Federal Reserve policy has distorted the pricing of all risk assets, as interest rates have been kept too low for too long and the US central bank has regularly stepped in to prop up the financial markets and manage asset prices. The federal funds rate was kept at effectively zero throughout the eight years of the Obama administration, augmented by a policy of quantitative easing whereby the Federal Reserve purchased for its own account an increasing amount of Treasury bonds, mortgage-backed securities, and other instruments. Between 2009 and 2016, the size of the Federal Reserve's balance sheet ballooned from less than $1 trillion to more than $4 trillion, during which time the value of the S&P 500 equity index increased by 147.86%.[9] During the Obama years, bad economic data – whether anemic GDP growth or tepid employment numbers – typically translated as good news for stocks and bonds due to the Federal Reserve feedback loop. During this "Fair is foul and foul is fair" period for the markets, any hint at a change in monetary policy, whether a 25-basis-point increase in interest rates from a zero starting point or a tapering of bond market purchases, was enough to paralyze the financial markets, which helped to preserve the Federal Reserve status quo. Many CIOs, hedge fund managers, and investment strategists effectively became Fed jockeys, endlessly deciphering the latest Fed-speak like latter-day Kremlinologists.

While monetary policy started to tighten during the Trump administration, this was quickly reversed in 2018 at the first signs of equity market spillover. During the fourth quarter of that year, the S&P 500 index dropped by 13.97%.[10] When the COVID-19 pandemic hit in early 2020, the target federal funds rate reverted to zero and the central bank balance sheet ballooned to nearly $9 trillion over the next two years as the Federal Reserve restarted quantitative easing and expanded its buying program to include primary and secondary market purchases of corporate bonds and commercial paper. With inflation spiking to high single digits in 2022 on the back of outsized government spending by the Biden administration, global supply chain disruptions, and a regulatory policy-induced energy crisis, the central bank's hands were effectively tied. The prospects of rate increases without quantitative easing – the Federal Reserve stopped adding to its balance sheet in March 2022 – struck terror into the hearts of traders. Yet, despite negative interest rates, many market players still stuck with a "Buy on the dip" trading approach throughout 2022 and into 2023, convinced that the Federal Reserve would have to soon pause its rate hikes and shift once again into easing mode.

Since the 2008 global financial crisis, the financial community rarely publicly disagrees with US government policy – neither monetary nor fiscal and certainly not regulatory. No matter how shortsighted, ill-conceived, or politically motivated the initiative, Wall Street has now become a government cheerleader, often choking on its pom-poms in the process. Even though zero interest rates have severely punished savers and people on a fixed income and dampened bank lending and profitability, few analysts have called out the Federal Reserve for its perpetual easy-money stance. Unchecked US government spending has more than tripled the public sector debt burden – from $10.0 trillion or 67% of GDP as of September 30, 2008, to $31.4 trillion and 120% as of December 31, 2022[11] – and recently ignited inflation to levels not seen since the 1970s, yet few Wall Street economists and market strategists have challenged the government's profligate fiscal policy for fear of retribution. When the US posted two consecutive quarters of negative GDP growth during the first half of 2022, Wall Street analysts were hesitant even to acknowledge economic reality, mostly echoing the self-serving denials by the Biden administration that the country was in recession, with some rolling out the new economic term "technical recession" as cover.

Such analytical laziness is also the result of technical factors overwhelming fundamentals for such a protracted period. Postcrisis, the market's risk-pricing and analytical skills have slowly deteriorated over time as volatility has evaporated from the markets. Apart from a momentary spike in 2011 when the US government was downgraded by S&P Global Ratings, the Chicago Board Options Exchange Volatility Index (VIX) traded below 20 for most of the decade of the 2010s. The current generation of Wall Street players has never experienced a normally functioning market where there are true risk–reward trade-offs and risk assets are properly valued in the absence of a Federal Reserve safety net – or, more accurately, a central bank put. In a bull market, every analyst and trader is a rock star. In a zero-interest rate environment with readily available leverage to goose returns, every hedge fund manager and private equity investor is a superhero. As Marc Rowan, the CEO of Apollo Global Management LLC, has joked to his firm's employees, "You've worked for me for 10 years and I still don't know if you are a good investor."[12] Some market players have casually referred to the 2022 sell-off in both the equity and debt markets due to rising interest rates as a "Lehman moment" of extreme volatility, which highlights the inexperience of many current players in the market, along with their complete lack of historical perspective.

Over the past decade, the financial industry has lost a significant amount of market experience through repeated head-count cuts and downsizing rounds, driven by consolidation and thinner profitability on the back of less volatile trading markets. Between June 2008 and March 2010, total national employment in the securities, commodities, and financial services sector declined by 81,200, based on Bureau of Labor Statistics (BLS) data.[13] Since 2007, the number of broker-dealers registered with the Financial Industry Regulatory Authority (FINRA) has decreased by one-third from 5,002 to 3,394, while total registered representatives have declined by 57,337 or 9%.[14] In the New York City core of the securities industry, total headcount dropped by 12% between 2007 and 2010 when roughly 23,000 Wall Street jobs were eliminated.[15] As of 2022, it still had not recovered to precrisis levels.[16]

The brain drain has been particularly acute among Wall Street research departments, which were already in a weakened state due to regulatory and organizational changes made some 20 years ago in the run-up to the global financial crisis. After the dot-com stock market bubble burst over 2000–2001, a global equity research settlement agreement was reached between the Securities and Exchange Commission (SEC) and 10 leading Wall Street firms in 2003, under which $1.4 billion in aggregate penalties were paid to the government and sell-side equity research was permanently separated from investment banking, both in terms of report content and analyst compensation. A year later, the same research restrictions started to leak into the fixed income markets when The Bond Market Association rolled out its own "Guiding Principles to Promote the Integrity of Fixed Income Research" in 2004.[17] These self-imposed rules similarly walled off fixed income research groups from investment banking. Even though secondary market knowledge is more critical to the role of the fixed income analyst, fixed income research began to decouple from sales and trading as individual firms tried to outdo each other with regard to compliance in the eyes of the regulators, resulting in a race to the bottom. Fixed income research was gradually separated from sales and trading, first physically and then from a P&L perspective. The resultant loss of fixed income analysts as risk managers was an important contributing factor to the 2008 crisis, which originated in the credit markets.

The effect over time has been to convert sell-side research departments from their historical role as revenue-generating groups into cost centers and service providers. Helping to feed this trend was the passage of Regulation Fair Disclosure (FD) by the SEC in 2000. While designed to promote full and fair financial disclosure by public companies by requiring an 8-K filing for any material nonpublic information, the effect of Regulation FD has been to eliminate the information and insight edge enjoyed by the most experienced analysts on the Street. This has accelerated the shift from idea-driven research to maintenance coverage marked by quarterly elevator analysis and endless regurgitation of company press releases. Many independent publishing analysts have opted to become trading desk analysts to stay close to a revenue-generating business. Long gone are the days when industry analysts could regularly move the markets with their research calls. Now, having a differentiated research view about a company is almost frowned upon because it is taken to indicate an unfair sell-side advantage. Reinforcing this perception, investment banks continue to this day to suspend research coverage, both debt and equity, whenever a sell-side firm is involved in an M&A transaction with an issuer, even though research departments have been separated by a Chinese wall from investment banking for the past two decades.

On the buy side of the business, there has been a pronounced market shift from active to passive investment strategies postcrisis, which has further diminished research groups since passive accounts are basically computer exercises that require minimal analytical support. While some hedge fund managers like John Paulson shorted the subprime housing market and hit a home run, few investors saw the events of 2008 coming. Even David Einhorn of Greenlight Capital, who made a public show of shorting the common stock of Lehman Brothers in the spring of 2008, did so mainly because he viewed the stock as being overvalued due to the firm's undercapitalization, not because he thought the company was a candidate for bankruptcy. Otherwise, his hedge fund would not have been net long risk and lost 17.9% during the third quarter of 2008 when the investment bank failed.[18] Many sophisticated investors, including BlackRock and PIMCO, were also buyers of Lehman Brothers common shares and bonds shortly before the music stopped in September 2008.

As the dust cleared after the 2008 crisis, many investors rightly questioned why they were paying higher fees for actively managed accounts that were, in hindsight, more market beta than idiosyncratic alpha and completely unhedged to boot. This revelatory moment led to downward pressure on management fees pretty much across the board plus a general reallocation of capital between funds based on strategy expertise and manager incumbency, with the larger, more established players in each investment vertical growing larger in the process. At the same time, passively managed index and exchange-traded funds have seen dramatic net inflows as many investors have opted simply to take market risk while paying minimal fees. Since 2010, the active versus passive split of all US long-term funds, both debt and equity but excluding money market, has gone from 80–20 in 2010 to 53–47 in 2022,[19] with passive US strategies seeing $1.5 trillion of net inflows over 2021–2022 alone.[20] At year-end 2022, passive accounts comprised approximately 63% of BlackRock's $8.6 trillion of AUM, 79% of Vanguard's $7.2 trillion of AUM, and 83% of State Street's $3.5 trillion of AUM.

As fundamental research has been devalued across Wall Street and less of a premium has been placed on individual stock and bond picking, investment banks and asset management firms alike have reached for quantitative and other gimmicks to give them some research edge. Given this backdrop, it is not surprising that there has been a wave of investment fads in recent years. AI and big-data scraping methods are used to discern investment trends that are not visible to the naked analyst eye. Autonomous vehicles and smart cities are studied for their potential to revolutionize how people live, work, and move. For a brief period, special purpose acquisition companies (SPACs) became the hot new vehicle for taking private companies public, even though the multistep SPAC process is more costly and complicated than the traditional IPO route. Blockchain is touted as a new technology to streamline ledger transactions such as fund transfers and trade settlements – basically, providing a solution to a problem that does not exist. Various forms of tradable cryptocurrency are rolled out and offered up as either a transaction medium, a store of value, or an inflation hedge against fiat money, with none of these claims yet proving true. The metaverse is championed as a new activity forum for everything, with none of its advocates realizing that it is just a commercialized version of "Imaginationland" from *South Park*.[21] Viewed in this context, sustainable investing is just the latest in a recent series of shiny objects to capture the market's attention, although arguably the one with the most durable luster.

Lulled into a Fed-induced trance for the past several years, the industry's analytical defenses against the sophistry of sustainability have been weakened. Hectored by government regulators, Wall Street is more focused on legal compliance than financial innovation. The industry is struggling to attract and retain both experienced and junior talent. In the clearest sign that a job on Wall Street is no longer the career draw it used to be, investment banking analysts and associates are now revolting about compensation and working conditions at Goldman Sachs, which has always been the Willy Wonka golden ticket on Wall Street. While primary issuance has been robust as M&A activity has picked up and corporate treasurers have taken advantage of lower interest rates to regularly refinance their balance sheets, secondary trading activity, dealer inventories, and market liquidity have all declined. Risk tolerance and positioning appetite have decreased. While systemic risk is down, it has come at a steep cost as the industry has lost much of its dynamism, independence, and creativity since 2008 – even though, on the surface, Wall Street has been posting solid profits on the back of an extended bull market run.

Since the global financial crisis, Wall Street has arguably gone into a state of decline, entering what the British historian Arnold Toynbee might describe as its universal state. In his voluminous work *A Study of History*, published in serial format over the course of a quarter-century, Toynbee described how all the world's great civilizations from antiquity up until the present day – including Egyptian, Hellenic, Syriac, Babylonian, Indic, Sinic, and Mayan – have been marked by similar life cycles of genesis, growth, breakdown, and disintegration. Human societies only flourish and continue growing as long as they are being creatively challenged. Once this spark is lost, civilizations inevitably stagnate and eventually decay. Typically, the catalyst for this decline has been a period of turbulence or what Toynbee referred to as a "time of troubles."[22] For the Western Roman Empire, it was persistent wars with neighboring Germanic tribes during the fifth century AD. For the Eastern Roman Empire, it was the steady encroachment by the Ottomans nearly a millennium later. Thereafter, civilizations start to break down and move into a universal state where creativity is stifled, pride and vanity lead to decadence, and society is ruled by a dominant minority, often through force and coercion.

Applying Toynbee's historical rubric to the financial industry, 2008 was the shock that triggered a regulatory onslaught and the time of troubles for Wall Street, ushering in a universal state with ESG activists now forming the dominant minority within the industry. Having lost its spark of creativity, Wall Street has now become more of a manufacturing operation. While very efficient at raising capital for company operations and corporate acquisitions, sustainability advocates from both within and without the industry are increasingly dictating the product line. Soon, every Ford coming off the Wall Street assembly line will be available only in black – or perhaps a sustainable shade of green. Toynbee also noted that as societies slowly decay during their universal states, people often resort to futurism and religious transcendence, both of which are key elements of sustainable investing.

Lastly, ESG also plays to the virtue-signaling needs of many of the leaders of Wall Street. In 2008, the Wall Street versus Main Street argument was mainly created to deflect blame for the global financial crisis away from the political class. However, in the ensuing years, it has grown into a legitimate complaint against Wall Street as Federal Reserve policy and low interest rates have mainly buoyed the financial markets and supported financial asset prices, while hurting the vast majority of Americans not invested in the equity markets but reliant on a fixed income and dependent on bank savings. Between the low tick of March 9, 2009, and year-end 2021, the S&P 500 Index jumped more than sevenfold, translating into an annual rate of return of 16.47%.[23] Most egregiously, in 2020 when COVID-19 government lockdowns caused US real GDP to contract by 2.8% and annual unemployment to more than double to 8.1%, the S&P 500 Index posted a gain of 16.26% for the full year – thanks to the Federal Reserve. It was also during the pandemic year of 2020 that Wall Street's New York City bonus pool finally regained and surpassed the previous precrisis peak of $33.0 billion set in 2007, totaling $37.1 billion based on numbers compiled by the Office of the New York State Comptroller.[24] As of January 2023, 54 of the 500 people listed on the Bloomberg Billionaires Index hailed from the finance industry, many from private equity, hedge funds, and asset management.[25]

There is a natural tendency among highly successful people – those to whom much is given – to want to give back to society, and Wall Street is no different in this regard. People who make a lot of money over the course of their professional lives often reach a point where they want to be remembered for more than just the ability to make money, perhaps as they ponder whether a camel can really pass through the eye of a needle. The public altruism and moral messaging of sustainable investing has much appeal for Wall Street CEOs looking to further buffer public criticism of both themselves individually and the financial services industry more broadly.

Over the years, Wall Street has generated significant wealth for many of the people who have worked in the industry, particularly those at the top. This, in turn, has led to a steady flow of money to the charitable causes supported by these well-paid individuals. However, the rule has always been that first you make the money and then you donate it based on your own personal preferences. The problem with ESG is that it is an attempt to cross the streams of wealth creation and charity and reorder the normal sequencing of events, breaking the space–time continuum and replacing individual choice with a collective exercise. With ESG, Wall Street CEOs are basically converting their firms into virtual versions of personal charitable foundations and using other people's money to demonstrate their virtue.

Sustainable investing sets up as a kind of self-assembly Trojan Horse kit for the financial industry. Like the wooden gift left behind by Odysseus and the departing armies of Greece, ESG appeals to the vanity and pride of Wall Street CEOs. It also offers up a new source of profitability, both as an incentive and a distraction. Investment banks and investment firms are now jumping in with both feet without looking first and thinking through the long-term ramifications. The Achilles' heel of Wall Street has always been its keen commercial instincts and its problem-solving abilities, quick to figure out how to do something but seldom stopping to consider whether it should. The industry is approaching ESG as just another financing problem to be solved in an eerie replay of the subprime mortgage crisis of the mid-2000s. By reverting to form, Wall Street is missing the bigger ESG picture. Once fully constructed, ESG will attack the industry from the inside, much like the city of Troy.

In the long wake of the 2008 global financial crisis, Wall Street is particularly vulnerable to the sustainable investment scam. Cowed by compliance, hounded by the regulators, and unsure of itself, the industry has become more risk-averse and used to taking its business and market cues from the government. Market participants have become conditioned to think about how others will react to the latest Federal Reserve move and other economic news, rather than having an independent view and trusting their own opinion. Not surprisingly, this deferral to third-party consensus has resulted in trend following and increased flocking and herding activity in the financial markets, with traders and portfolio managers having less conviction around positioning and second-guessing themselves on their market and company calls. At the same time, Wall Street has grown more self-conscious, shrinking from defending itself and the capitalist system because the industry is embarrassed by its wealth – unlike Silicon Valley executives or professional sports athletes – which has provided implicit support for the stakeholder capitalism cause.

In her extensive writing on power, authority, and totalitarianism, the political philosopher Hannah Arendt observed that revolutionaries do not make revolutions; rather, "revolutionaries are those who know when power is lying in the street and when they can pick it up."[26] For the ESG activists now trying to gain control of the global financial system, the power has been lying in the middle of Wall Street since 2008 – there for the asking, ready to be picked up and turned against the industry. In 1920, anarchists tried the direct approach to toppling the capitalist system by detonating a horse cart full of explosives and shrapnel at the corner of Wall and Broad Streets, just down the street from Trinity Church and steps from Federal Hall and the New York Stock Exchange (NYSE) Building. The pockmarks from the terrorist attack can still be seen today on the façade of the former J. P. Morgan headquarters building at 23 Wall Street. A century later, the ESG movement is taking an indirect approach and only needs to stoop to conquer Wall Street.

CHAPTER 5

ESG: THE SOCIAL CONTROL NETWORK

In those days a decree went out from Caesar Augustus that all the world should be enrolled.
Luke 2:1, Revised Standard Version

I attempted to rise, but was not able to stir: for as I happened to lie on my back, I found my arms and legs were strongly fastened on each side to the ground; and my hair, which was long and thick, tied down in the same manner.
Jonathan Swift, *Gulliver's Travels*

Governments collapse, civilizations fall, and, in the end, we humans are all dust. Yet the companies that we patronize and invest in must be sustainable and last forever, with the secret to eternal corporate life being the acceptance of every tenet of the progressive agenda.

This is what the updated version of stakeholder capitalism looks like in the 21st century. In contrast to the long-standing Milton Friedman view that the "one and only one social responsibility of business" is "to increase its profits so long as it stays within the rules of the game,"[1] stakeholder capitalism posits that corporations are the trustees of society, responsible for looking after the interests of all stakeholders – both within and without a company – not just shareholders (if at all). Companies are not only responsible to their business constituencies – including employees, suppliers, customers, government regulators, and capital providers – but also to the ethereal concepts of civil society, the state, and the international community. Stakeholder capitalism is now comprehensive in form and global in nature, while also setting an impossible standard. Channeling the words of the Brundtland Report, stakeholder capitalism is built around the gauzy concept that "the well-being of people and planet are at the center of business."[2]

For the past 50 years, the UN and the WEF – working in tandem – have been the main proponents of this novel financial theory that companies should focus on values and society rather than value creation and financial returns and be judged based on a whole new set of nonfinancial metrics or ESG factors. It is marketed as a new form of capitalism – capitalism reimagined – even though it closely resembles 1930s fascism and is more accurately described as reworked socialism. It seeks to build a more sustainable global economy and financial system by the year 2030 – the coordinated target date for both the UN's climate change and sustainable development programs and the WEF's Great Reset Initiative – but it is mainly designed to choke off capital to politically incorrect industries and companies and redirect investment toward favored progressive sectors and projects, starting with green, clean, and renewable energy.

ESG is the viral delivery mechanism that is being used to spread stakeholder capitalism throughout the business world and the financial markets. Wall Street firms, both investment banks and investment managers, have been enlisted as the agents of the movement, forced to spread the ESG gospel and enforce the rules of the system – the latter of which are set not by market practitioners but by corporate sustainability advocacy groups such as the PRI, the UNEP FI, and the UNGC. Virtue-signaling "corporate wokeness" is the outward symptom, but the real damage being done by ESG is occurring behind the scenes in the financial markets where it is slowly changing the DNA of Wall Street.

Stakeholder capitalism is now seeping into the global financial system through the pincer movement of ESG integration and engagement being executed primarily by buy-side investors and asset owners and belatedly by sell-side analysts and investment bankers. ESG integration is a process that is internal to Wall Street. It requires a comprehensive reworking of fundamental research, investment analysis, asset allocation, and security selection to incorporate ESG into every step of the process of trading securities and deploying capital. Integration typically starts with the translation of the 17 SDGs of the UN into specific themes or ESG factors across each of the core environmental, social, and governance pillars. Typically, the E column would include carbon emissions, biodiversity, energy consumption, water usage, waste generation, and environmental justice; the S column would include human rights (Indigenous, minority, women, and children), local community spending, supplier policy, unionization rates, employee safety, workforce diversity and training, average compensation levels, and employee turnover; and the G column would include board independence and diversity, management compensation, and ESG disclosure, goal-setting, and performance measurement. While generally tracking the PRI-promoted SDG taxonomy of the UN, financial firms have enjoyed some discretion – at least thus far – around ESG factor selection, with some relying on the PRI (169 targets and 232 indicators), the WEF's International Business Council (34 stakeholder capitalism metrics), and other third-party sources, and others compiling their own bespoke lists in-house. No matter who you talk to, ESG factors and reporting metrics number in the hundreds for most Wall Street firms.

Needless to say, ESG integration has made investing incredibly more complicated, with every issuer discussion now requiring multidimensional company analyses and supporting data on a par with the 3D hologram design plans for the Death Star in *Star Wars: Return of the Jedi*. Now, every operating and financial facet of an issuer's business must be evaluated from a sustainability perspective, along with every firm counterparty to make sure they are also living up to the same standards. This list of ESG factors is then customized by industry, calibrated with different weightings for scoring purposes, and then spread across a matrix of relevant company stakeholders – including employees, suppliers, customers, communities, government regulators, and the environment – to gauge a company's net impact on society as whole. Last – and, most decidedly, least – in the stakeholder pecking order would be the providers of capital – shareholders, bondholders, and bank lenders – that facilitate business expansion and growth, which is ironic given that this constituency is the one chiefly responsible for implementing and enforcing the new sustainable investment protocol. It is quite remarkable how easily Wall Street has fallen for the Jedi mind trick of sustainability, with its specious argument that running a company for the benefit of every constituency in society except for capital providers such as shareholders and creditors somehow leads to improved pricing for financial assets such as stocks, bonds, and bank loans.

Despite the extra work, time, and cost associated with ESG integration, many financial firms have submitted willingly – some to make a moral statement, some to stake out a new business activity. Most have done so because their PRI membership card requires it. Many have adopted a defensive posture, arguing that ESG has always been part of their investment approach. Technically speaking, this is a partially true statement for most market participants, given that environmental, social, and governance issues are always factored into the investment decision-making process. A standard due diligence checklist would already include a review of company compliance with health, safety, and environment (HSE) regulations and Equal Employment Opportunity Commission (EEOC) programs and an evaluation of the potential for contingent legal liabilities in both areas. Moreover, since governance or management quality is central to any corporate investment, it is tautological that the G is always included in the mix, which is the foot in the door that the ESG movement needs. By touting their intrinsic ESG credentials, these Wall Street firms have now bought into the system of stakeholder capitalism and are just asking for trouble. Basically, it is the corporate equivalent of inviting a vampire into your house. Much as the entomophagous mental patient Renfield discovered after he invited Count Dracula into the asylum, welcoming and embracing ESG will have unintended consequences and lead to bad things happening down the road. It will also prove a very difficult invitation to revoke.

Once buy-side and sell-side firms have gotten their ESG houses into some semblance of order and integrated sustainability into their respective investment and market-making operations, Wall Street then pushes these same requirements onto the corporate sector through the process of engagement. While deceptively neutral-sounding, engagement is passive-aggressive analyst behavior that mainly entails harassing and haranguing corporate management teams, which is what passes for active ownership these days in the ESG investment world.

The first goal of engagement is for companies to increase their disclosure and standardize their reporting on a range of ESG metrics, starting with greenhouse gas emissions given the primacy of the climate emergency. Once there is greater transparency and more consistent ESG disclosure across industries, individual companies can be targeted for reporting noncompliance using peer pressure and forced rankings and holding out best-in-class ribbons as an incentive. The next phase of engagement involves pressuring companies to set and hit sustainability targets for their businesses, starting with net-zero emissions goals and green energy transition commitments. Whether explicitly or implicitly, all companies are pushed to align their businesses with the stated goals of the climate change and sustainable development programs of the UN, even though neither initiative is legally binding on its member states or the companies operating therein.

For obvious reasons, oil and gas companies have been slow to ramp up emissions reporting and to sign up for carbon reduction plans that would place these businesses into runoff mode. For energy issuers, ESG engagement is a no-win situation since providing emissions figures just gives sustainable activists a clear target to shoot at. Essentially, the ESG movement is offering the fossil fuels industry the same deal that accused witches were given during the 16th century. Back then, either you confessed that you were a witch or someone would tie a millstone to your neck and throw you in the river. However, if you confessed that you were a witch to save yourself from drowning, then you would be burned at the stake to save your soul. It's kind of like that for energy companies when it comes to ESG investing.

ESG engagement is now a daily phenomenon on Wall Street. It is occurring whenever company management teams interact with buy-side investors and portfolio managers and with sell-side analysts and investment bankers. It comes up in both one-on-one settings and group meetings, including industry conferences, roadshow presentations, and quarterly earnings calls. Every corporate meeting is now an opportunity to air an ESG grievance. Based on data tracked by FactSet, the number of ESG mentions on quarterly earnings calls for the S&P 500 Index universe of companies has skyrocketed from two in the first quarter of 2017 to 155 in the fourth quarter of 2021.[3] Whenever two or more people working in finance are gathered to discuss an investment or trade idea, ESG is a topic of conversation. It is the 800-pound gorilla in every room on Wall Street.

As with climate change and sustainable development, ESG engagement activity is also primarily focused on the industrialized world – in particular, publicly listed companies headquartered in North America and Europe, where the goal is to break down the agency of corporate executives and board members. Even though this group of large-cap, transnational firms is, on average, very highly rated from a credit perspective, with few glaring environmental, social, or governance weaknesses, these companies are also vulnerable to pressure from customers, employees, public shareholders, and the media, while also having deep financial pockets. In a sign of the sustainable times, the Business Roundtable, an association of America's leading CEOs, issued a policy statement in 2019 wherein the group redefined the purpose of a corporation to include improving society and meeting the needs of all stakeholders.[4] Also, since many of the large US private equity shops are now publicly listed – including Apollo, Blackstone Inc., The Carlyle Group Inc., and KKR & Co. Inc. – this extends the reach of sustainability into the private markets through the portfolio companies of these dominant investors, the majority of which will be monetized through a public market exit. ESG engagement is more about messaging and crowd control, so targets are chosen for maximum publicity effect. Based on data tracked by Insightia, of the 700 companies worldwide that were subjected to ESG activist demands in 2022, 63% were headquartered in the United States, 79% in Europe and North America, and greater than 95% in developed countries. Only 10% of the companies targeted were located in emerging markets, even though this cohort is, on average, lower rated with weaker environmental track records and subpar governance standards due to either private family control or government ownership.[5]

Thus far, most corporate CEOs operating in the developed markets have gotten the message about ESG engagement, both in terms of improving disclosure and setting actionable targets. Based on data tracked by the Governance & Accountability Institute, in 2020, approximately 92% of the companies in the S&P 500 Index published a Corporate Sustainability Report or the equivalent.[6] This compares to 20% in 2011, showing the sharp uptake over the past decade as both climate change and sustainability have become in vogue. Since most company sustainability reports average about 100 pages, this new annual disclosure requirement essentially duplicates the yearly report and public company SEC 10-K filing process, both from a time and cost perspective. Corporate Register, an online directory of corporate responsibility reports, currently holds more than 190,000 reports published to date by more than 27,000 organizations worldwide.[7]

Similarly, more than 8,900 companies have joined the Race to Zero global campaign sponsored by the UN and pledged to reduce the full-scope greenhouse gas emissions of their businesses by roughly one-half by 2030 and reach net zero by 2050 at the latest – all in line with the stated goals of the Paris Agreement.[8] Roughly 2,300 corporations and financial institutions have made a similar net-zero pledge to the Science Based Targets initiative (SBTi), a climate action outfit backed by the UNGC and several environmental groups that pushes the private sector to take the lead on reducing carbon emissions.[9] A total of 424 companies have signed The Climate Pledge, which commits them to achieving net-zero carbon by 2040.[10] Again, the majority of the virtue-signaling corporate signatories to these climate pacts hail from North America and Europe.

For energy and other companies that do not respond appropriately to behind-the-scenes ESG engagement activities, there is an escalation process to get management's attention, as laid out in the primer published by the PRI on "Active Ownership 2.0."[11] Typically, this means publicly embarrassing companies by hijacking the annual general meeting process. April, May, and June are now the cruelest months for corporate management teams as they spend the shareholder meeting and proxy reporting season fending off growing demands for ESG policy commitments.

As part of this now-annual ritual, public companies are presented with a list of ESG demands in the form of shareholder resolutions, much like the 95 theses nailed to the church door in Wittenberg, Germany, by Martin Luther back in 1517. Five hundred years later, ESG advocates believe that the way to reform the capitalist system is by scaring private sector businesses into compliance and branding outliers as sustainability heretics. In 2022, based on data compiled by Proxy Preview, US companies were presented with a total of 628 shareholder resolutions related to environmental, social, and governance matters. This represented a roughly 26% increase over 2021 and a more than 50% jump since 2013. The recent increase in climate- and sustainability-related proposals is owing to the spread of ESG integration across the markets since 2015, as well as recent revised guidance issued by the SEC that limits the ability of public companies to omit certain demonstrably frivolous shareholder resolutions, effectively lowering the bar for ESG activists. Of the total 628 shareholder proposals received in 2022, 316 were voted on, with only 12% of these passing with majority support. However, 273 were voluntarily withdrawn based on discussions with company management. Effectively, these negotiated withdrawals functioned as consent decrees that allowed many of these 273 proposals to go quietly into effect while avoiding a public scene.[12]

For those companies needing even more of a public slap, sustainable investors are now copying the playbook of hedge fund shareholder activists such as Carl Icahn and Elliott Management and launching ESG-related proxy fights to gain more board control and influence. While messy, such a legal maneuver is consistent with the argument made by sustainable activists that board directors need to have "ESG experience" because ESG is a risk framework that, if ignored, would indicate a governance weakness in the self-serving circular logic of ESG. To further ensure management control, executive and board compensation levels are increasingly being tied to ESG performance metrics. Based on data tracked by the ESG Center at The Conference Board, as of year-end 2021, approximately 73% of S&P 500 companies tied executive compensation to some measure of ESG performance – in the main, climate- and diversity-related goals.[13]

In 2021, the concept of an ESG proxy fight was test-run on ExxonMobil when Engine No. 1, a small start-up activist sustainability fund with a 0.02% stake in the company's shares, offered up a slate of four board directors to help accelerate the company's energy transition plans and bring its business model in line with the goals of the Paris Agreement. Specifically, the tiny investor demanded that ExxonMobil set a goal of achieving net-zero emissions – including Scope 1, 2, and 3 – by 2050, even though such an objective is not currently feasible from a technological perspective in the absence of the company ceasing all oil and gas production – which, of course, is the ESG goal when it comes to energy companies. Moreover, the four independent directors proposed for the 12-member ExxonMobil board mainly hailed from the fossil fuels industry and did not have the renewable energy resumes that would suggest a radical new strategic plan for the company. Nonetheless, three out of the four directors put up by little Engine No. 1 were voted in, mainly due to support from large public pension funds from blue states like California and New York and the three large index fund managers, BlackRock, Vanguard, and State Street, all of which have come out as strong supporters of ESG.

While touted as a huge victory for the sustainability side and an ESG wake-up call for management, not much has changed at ExxonMobil in the wake of the 2021 board skirmish. In January 2022, the company announced an "ambition" to achieve net-zero emissions for its Scope 1 and 2 operated activities by 2050, subject to technology improvements and government support. During the 2022 annual meeting season, ExxonMobil's board (with its three new directors from 2021) recommended against a shareholder resolution requiring a reduction in the company's Scope 3 emissions and hydrocarbon sales, which was ultimately voted down with only 27% support from shareholders. And while the company is now allocating a slightly larger token amount of its capital spending – a total of $15 billion or approximately $2.5 billion per year over 2022–2027 – on clean energy and low-emission initiatives such as carbon capture and sequestration, hydrogen, and biofuels, ExxonMobil continues to spend roughly $1–2 billion per year on upstream exploration projects looking for the next big oil play as it increases its oil production out of the Permian Basin and offshore Guyana, both of which are multidecade oil manufacturing facilities. This biting reality has not stopped the Engine No. 1 founder Christopher James from using his ExxonMobil "victory" as a fundraising tool for his nascent impact investing business, much in the sustainable marketing mold of Al Gore.

The 2021 ESG proxy fight at ExxonMobil also exposed a market anomaly – ironically, a G-for-governance shortcoming – around the active voting of shares held by passive investment management firms. Given the rise of passive investing postcrisis, as a group, BlackRock, Vanguard, and State Street now hold significant equity stakes in almost every publicly listed company – 20.6% in aggregate in the case of ExxonMobil in 2021. At the same time, all three asset managers have become active on the ESG front when it comes to matters related to climate change and sustainable development – consistent with the PRI stewardship code, which states that even passive investors must now be active owners to demonstrate good stewardship in the new upside-down world of ESG investing. The ExxonMobil incident highlighted just how significant a voting bloc the Big 3 index houses now control and how these stakes can be leveraged by ESG advocates to pressure company boards. The strategy has backfired somewhat, as increased scrutiny has led to pushback from red-state pension funds and Republican government officials. Not surprisingly, all three passive fund managers kept a lower profile during the 2022 and 2023 proxy seasons, with BlackRock announcing plans to delegate voting choice back to the institutional and retail investors in its managed index funds.

Supplementing the annual spring outbreak of board confrontations, there is also the year-round sport of raising ESG controversies to publicly shame management teams and further spur compliance. By regularly airing ESG concerns that isolate specific issuers – especially energy and other industrial companies – this provides negative reinforcement for the entire corporate sector, while keeping the entire system off-balance and on-guard.

Mostly, the controversies highlighted by ESG activists are one-off, nonrecurring operating accidents – often caused by human error – that are blown way out of proportion and used to indict a company's culture and ethical character. Energy and other industrial sectors are the main targets due to their large asset footprints and significant carbon emission profiles, with climate, environmental justice, and human rights being the main angles of attack. In general, the Ten Principles of the UNGC are used as the universal framework for determining a corporate ESG infraction and a violation of so-called international norms, even though the UNGC is a voluntary nonbinding pact whose platitudinal principles would only apply to its signatories. Often, the controversies are inherited through mergers or corporate acquisitions. Moreover, because sustainability is basically a crowd-sourced system, no formal process or court of arbitration exists for appealing an ESG controversy, either on the facts or the law. Even the passage of time is not sufficient to restore a company's reputation since ESG controversies have a very long tail with no apparent sunset. Given the puritanical streak of the sustainability movement, E, S, and G are often like scarlet letters carved into the soul of offending companies.

It is an ever-growing list of energy companies caught in the catch-22 of ESG controversies. Oil spills, however infrequent, are viewed as the original ESG sin of the energy industry, consistent with the 1969 Santa Barbara offshore spill that served to galvanize the environmental movement. ExxonMobil is still being pilloried for the March 1989 Exxon Valdez spill of 11 million gallons of crude oil into Prince William Sound, Alaska, even though the tanker grounding was due to pilot and crew error and the company paid more than $1 billion in punitive damages and cleanup costs to remediate the environment and compensate affected property owners and Indigenous groups. According to the Exxon Valdez Oil Spill Trustee Council, most of the 28 types of plants, animals, and marine habitats affected by the oil spill in Prince William Sound had fully recovered by – most well before – the 25-year anniversary in 2014, when the joint state and federal organization started to wind down its operations.[14] In response to the Exxon Valdez spill, the Coalition for Environmentally Responsible Economies (CERES) was founded that same year, offering a set of new environmental guidelines – initially dubbed the Valdez Principles – to guide investment decision-making, modeled on the Sullivan Principles that were used to discourage investment in South Africa as a protest against apartheid. The Exxon Valdez accident served as the catalyst for the formation of several other corporate sustainability groups, including the GRI in 1997 and the UNGC in 2000.

Similarly, the ESG reputation of BP PLC, which started going green more than 20 years ago when it rebranded itself under CEO Lord John Browne with the "Beyond Petroleum" slogan, is still being tarnished to this day by the catastrophic blowout of its Macondo well on Block 252 of the deep-water Mississippi Canyon back in April 2010, which spewed an EPA-reported 168 million gallons of crude oil into the Gulf of Mexico offshore Louisiana before finally being capped months later. The cause of the accident was a defective cement job used to temporarily cap the well, compounded by a malfunctioning blowout preventer, the combination of which allowed natural gas to escape, triggering an explosion and fireball that destroyed the Deepwater Horizon drillship and killed 11 workers. The cementing work was done by Halliburton Company and the blowout preventer was part of the drillship owned and operated by Transocean Inc., but as the leaseholder, oil field services lessee, and strongest financial party in the room, BP shouldered the lion's share of the environmental and legal liability for the accident – often declining to contest many of the dubious pile-on claims that surfaced for the rapidly expanding BP slush fund. Over the next eight years, BP paid out more than $65 billion in legal penalties and cleanup costs to federal and state governments and local Gulf Coast communities.[15] Louisiana's fishing and tourism industries both recovered within three to four years following the 2010 spill.[16]

Many times, ESG controversies are simply fabricated out of whole cloth based on allegations or media-curated public narratives. Consider the Kafkaesque experience of Energy Transfer LP, one of the largest midstream energy companies in the US, around its now-infamous Dakota Access Pipeline (DAPL) project. The 1,172-mile DAPL pipeline currently transports an average of 570,000 barrels per day of crude oil from the Bakken resource play in North Dakota down to the Midwest and Gulf Coast refined product markets. First announced in 2014, construction work began in June 2016 but was stalled in the waning days of the Obama administration because of last-minute protests by Native American groups and environmentalists. Shortly after taking office, President Trump greenlighted the project, and the pipeline was completed and placed into service in mid-2017.

For all the breathless press coverage about the company bulldozing sacred burial sites and encroaching on native territory and the pipeline endangering the environment and the water supply of the Standing Rock Sioux (SRS) tribe, none of these allegations are true. DAPL does not touch SRS land, and it sits in the right-of-way of an existing natural gas pipeline system, the Northern Border Pipeline (NBP), which has been operating since 1982 without any complaints from the neighboring SRS – even though NBP crosses the Missouri River, or Lake Oahe as the tribe refers to it, just upstream from their reservation. DAPL crosses the Missouri River at the same narrow point as NBP, the only difference being that the legacy natural gas pipeline sits on the bottom of the riverbed while DAPL crosses under the river by a minimum depth of 95 feet below, making it nearly impossible for the oil pipeline to leak into the water above. Moreover, the water supply source for the SRS reservation is located some 75 miles away from where DAPL crosses under the Missouri River. Further weakening the Indigenous environmental argument against DAPL is the fact that other Native American groups – chiefly, the Mandan, Hidatsa, and Arikara Nation, known as the Three Affiliated Tribes – are currently producing oil from the Fort Berthold reservation roughly 100 miles upstream, with most of these oil volumes either flowing through DAPL or being carried to market in railcars that traverse the SRS reservation. Moreover, the Biden Interior Department recently ruled that there is no environmental issue preventing the Three Affiliated Tribes from drilling for hydrocarbons below the Missouri River.

DAPL received all the environmental and safety approvals required by state regulators along the route and the Army Corps of Engineers, which issued the CWA permit for the 1,100-foot crossing of the Missouri River and took the federal lead on negotiations with the SRS and other native groups due to their sovereign status. This fact pattern has not stopped the SRS from trying to shut down the pipeline retroactively through legal action and a "Water is Life" marketing and fundraising campaign coordinated with environmental activists who are more than happy to use the moral authority of native groups and the cover of climate justice to push their anti–fossil fuel agenda.

The SRS opposition to DAPL has always been more about economic than environmental concerns. At an infrastructure symposium held at New York University's Stern School of Business in 2018, two members of the SRS tribe, the former chairman David Archambault and the Housing Authority executive Chad Harrison, participated in a panel discussion on DAPL and went on at length about the tribe's opposition to the project. After a litany of complaints about broken federal treaties from the 19th century and the US government's decision to dam the Missouri River during the mid-20th century, Archambault cut to the heart of the matter for the audience by stating that opposing DAPL was about the SRS using its leverage to get "a piece of the economic pie."[17]

Energy Transfer management has confirmed as much to Wall Street analysts, noting that there was a financial request made by the SRS prior to the native group cutting off discussions with the company during 2016 and coming out publicly against the pipeline project. Even though gaining the support of the SRS and other native groups would have undercut much of the environmental criticism of DAPL and the reported ask of $16 million was a rounding error relative to the overall project cost of $3.9 billion,[18] Energy Transfer rebuffed the tribe's monetary demand for obvious reasons. Besides setting a terrible holdup precedent around energy infrastructure development in the US, making such a payment to the sovereign nation of the SRS would have been little different than paying a government bribe to an emerging market country and likely a violation of the Foreign Corrupt Practices Act of 1977.

These facts have been lost in all the misinformation about the DAPL project. Over the past six years of operations, DAPL and its corporate sponsor and operator, Energy Transfer, have been dogged by lawsuits from the same set of original protestors, even though the pipeline system was fully permitted and has had no reported environmental or safety issues to date. Because of this continuing legal opposition, though, the project has been flagged as an ESG controversy for the company both in terms of human rights and environmental safety, resulting in Energy Transfer being labeled a violator of the UNGC's Ten Principles – chiefly those related to human rights (#1 and #2) and the environment (#7–9). In 2020, these opposition groups finally received a favorable legal decision from US District Judge James Boasberg, an Obama appointee, who ruled that a detailed Environmental Impact Statement (EIS) should have been prepared by the Army Corps for DAPL's quarter-mile crossing of the Missouri River – rather than the streamlined environmental assessment used – due to the "highly controversial" nature of the project. Now, Energy Transfer remains in ESG legal limbo as it awaits a final EIS ruling around DAPL from the Army Corps and the Biden DOJ due to the project's climate and social justice implications.

And then there is the ESG case of Shell plc, the European integrated oil and gas company. Unlike most of its US peers, Shell has bent over backwards to try to appease ESG activists, for all the good it has done the company. In addition to spending significant capital to build out its renewable business activities and slowly morph the company into a regulated power utility, Shell was one of the first of the oil majors to set a net-zero 2050 target for Scope 1 and 2 emissions. Toward this goal, it has been shifting the commodity mix of its upstream operations from oil to natural gas over the past few years to help reduce the size of its carbon footprint. Since purchasing the natural-gas-leveraged BG Group plc in 2016, the company has exited the Canadian oil sands, downsized its North Sea operations, unloaded producing properties in the US Gulf of Mexico, and sold off core acreage in the Delaware side of the Permian Basin.

Not satisfied with the energy company's progress to date at self-destruction, the beleaguered Shell was successfully sued in the Netherlands by the Friends of the Earth and other NGOs plus 17,000 Dutch citizens, with the District Court at The Hague ruling in May 2021 that the company had to reduce its worldwide Scope 1 and 2 greenhouse gas emissions by 45% by 2030 – more than double the 20% reduction previously targeted by the company – in order to bring Shell in alignment with the nonbinding government commitments under the Paris Agreement. The company filed an appeal of the Hague ruling in March 2022. In February 2023, the environmental law firm ClientEarth upped the ante by bringing a climate lawsuit against the board of directors of Shell, suing each of them individually in the High Court of England and Wales. The shareholder suit alleges that Shell's 11 directors have mismanaged the company's exposure to climate risk by "failing to move away from fossil fuels fast enough." The plaintiffs argue that Shell's energy transition strategy does not align with the Paris Agreement. As such, the Shell board stands in breach of its company duties under English law. Under the UK Companies Act of 2006, directors have a legal duty to promote the success of their companies and, for any board decision, are required to consider the long-term consequences (including reputational) and the impact on the community and environment. UK directors must also avoid conflicts of interest. While the claim was dismissed by the UK High Court in May 2023, the plaintiffs have promised to appeal. If the case ever goes to trial, it would be interesting to see if ClientEarth tries to argue that a continued focus on more profitable fossil fuels somehow represents a conflict for Shell's directors since such a strategy would translate into higher performance-based remuneration for them personally. Such an insane claim would be logically consistent in the inverted world of ESG.[19]

Apart from its climate transgressions, Shell continues to be dogged by ESG controversy around its Nigerian operations. Specifically, the company stands accused of causing catastrophic environmental damage to the Niger Delta region of the country because of the frequent leaks from its pipeline system in the oil-producing region, where it also owns 19 oil mining leases. Almost all of these oil leaks have been owing to pipeline ruptures caused by product thieves, illegal refiners, and local saboteurs. There are hundreds of oil-pipeline attacks in Nigeria each year due to such criminal behavior, which often leads to mass casualty events caused by the resultant fires and explosions.

Even though Shell is the operator, its onshore pipelines and producing properties are owned through a joint venture company majority owned (55%) by the Nigerian government, with Shell holding only a minority stake (30%). Shell's Nigerian government partner is primarily responsible for pipeline security and has often responded to such attacks with a heavy hand – especially during the military-government years up through the end of the 1990s. On top of environmental pollution, Shell has also been charged with human rights abuses because of its alleged complicity in the rape, murder, and torture perpetrated by the local security forces hired by the Nigerian government to protect the joint venture's pipeline system. As such, Shell has also been labeled a violator of the UNGC's guiding principles around human rights and the environment. Tired of endlessly engaging on this ESG nonissue, Shell is currently in the process of selling off its onshore assets in Nigeria to rid itself of the problem, although it remains to be seen whether a simple divestiture will allow the company to expunge the ESG controversy from its record.

If there aren't real incidents to exploit, then ESG headlines are simply manufactured, often with theatrical protests and dramatic demonstrations at company headquarter buildings and annual shareholder meetings. Acting out and acting up in public corporate settings is another way to embarrass and send a message to ESG laggards about their lack of action on climate and other progressive policy fronts. All the corporate world is now a stage for ESG activists who, like Hamlet, believe that "the play's the thing" to "catch the conscience" of corporate suites and boards. In the name of "civil disobedience," these protest groups now regularly engage in corporate trespassing and vandalism in order to manufacture ESG controversies and pressure companies into compliance. Such theatrical displays basically serve as a random controversy generator for the ESG movement.[20] To ensure continued compliance across the board, the totalitarian rules of sustainability are not just applied to companies but also to investors and asset owners, which are similarly vulnerable to public intimidation. Increasingly, it is not just fossil fuel companies but also investment banks, asset management firms, and pension funds that must worry about controversies, board proxy fights, and protestors showing up at their headquarters with cans of red paint to stage a public die-in.

The 2022 annual general meeting season witnessed many breakout ESG performances. Shell's 2022 annual meeting was delayed for hours by Money Rebellion, the financial offshoot of Extinction Rebellion, both of which are unhappy with the pace of Shell's climate action plan. Members of Money Rebellion sang "We will, we will stop you" over and over again to the tune of the chorus from Queen's 1977 rock anthem "We Will Rock You," before the cops finally showed up. The previous month, the same group also disrupted the HSBC annual meeting with a flash mob singing a revised and well-harmonized rendition of ABBA's "Money,

Money, Money" to protest the bank's continued lending to the fossil fuels industry.

Climate protestors led by Greenpeace France blocked the entrance to the annual general assembly for the French oil company TotalEnergies SE to demonstrate against its environmental policies. Protestors were handcuffed together and sat toboggan-style in rows outside the company's Paris headquarters, thereby preventing company shareholders from attending. In May 2022, the Coal Action Network constructed a fake oil pipeline outside the headquarters of Lloyd's of London the day of its annual meeting to protest the company's insuring of real oil pipelines in Canada and Africa, prompting many syndicate members to dial in virtually for the event. This followed the shutdown of the same Lloyd's building the previous month by Extinction Rebellion in a well-televised event that included the dramatic unfurling of a 40-foot banner from an external staircase reading "End Fossil Fuels Now." Scores of environmental activists interrupted the 2022 annual shareholder meetings for Barclays, BNP Paribas, and ING Bank NV by setting off rape alarms and blowing whistles, ostensibly to draw attention to the sizable oil and gas loan portfolios of both institutions.[21]

Like a long-haul natural gas pipeline with compression stations every 200 miles, the entire ESG system is built on maintaining pressure on everyone involved. Asset managers strong-arm the companies that they invest in, while asset owners such as public pension funds and insurance companies hold the feet of their investment managers to the fire. Similarly, buy-side accounts lean on every counterparty for ESG compliance, particularly investment banks and investment consultants. No market participant can opt out because then they become the target. Companies must report and set targets, while investors and capital providers must demonstrate ESG leadership by documenting all of their corporate engagements – including follow-up actions and escalation plans – to prove their value-added and show how they are actually driving positive ESG outcomes and having a social impact. Conspicuous conformity is key because ESG is basically a massive surveillance state where Big Brother organizations like the PRI, the UNEP FI, the UNGC, and the WEF are always watching. Like Winston Smith in Orwell's *Nineteen Eighty-Four*, no one on Wall Street can turn off the two-way ESG telescreen.

Backstopping the negative publicity and reputational attacks associated with ESG noncompliance is the threat – both implicit and explicit – of legal and regulatory action for those businesses that fail to live up to their public statements around sustainability. If the ESG movement can't get you on the facts or the law, then it will get you on the cover-up. There is no shortage of friendly climate, environmental, and social activist groups willing to sue corporations and financial firms for consumer or investor fraud, misleading marketing communications, or deceptive advertising around ESG policies and public statements. The ESG data science firm RepRisk recently reported that approximately one in five corporate climate-related ESG incidents analyzed over the two-year 2020–2021 period were related to misleading communication or so-called incidents of greenwashing where companies overpromised and underdelivered on the ESG front or said one thing in public while lobbying politicians the other way behind the scenes.[22] Greenwashing legal cases, which are another ESG disciplinary tool, have already been brought against industrial companies and Wall Street firms. In the latter case, the Frankfurt offices of Deutsche Bank's DWS asset management arm, one of Europe's largest investment management firms, were raided by the German police in June 2022 looking for evidence of criminal prospectus fraud based on a tip provided by the firm's former sustainability chief Desiree Fixler. Since every aspect of ESG investing is morally and financially subjective, it is a simple matter for ESG whistleblowers to denounce any company to the authorities.

In January 2010, the US Supreme Court ruled in Citizens United v. Federal Election Commission that corporations also enjoy the First Amendment right of free speech, even when it comes to politics. For all the Democratic Party's repeated complaints about the *Citizens United* decision – including President Obama's State of the Union tirade shortly after the ruling was handed down – ESG integration and engagement over the past few years has rendered this legal ruling moot. Corporate CEOs are now afraid to speak their mind if doing so would contradict the liberal orthodoxy and, moreover, feel duty-bound to speak out in support of every progressive environmental and social cause. Like people, companies can also be canceled. Company displays of woke ideology are the public manifestation of sustainability and stakeholder capitalism and a leading indicator that the ESG system is working.

As clinical proof, business leaders now regularly take public stands on all the cultural and political issues of the day – including climate change, critical race theory, LGBTQ+ rights, gun control laws, COVID-19 vaccine mandates, voter identification requirements, and the Russia–Ukraine war – almost always staking out a position on the left side of the debate. CEOs now feel compelled to weigh in on every social headline and donate corporate money to every liberal cause. In 2020, after the death of George Floyd, US corporations sent millions of dollars to Black Lives Matter (BLM), a Marxist group intent on destroying the nuclear family, as well as the NAACP, the Equal Justice Initiative, and other self-described antiracism organizations. None of these overtly racial corporate donations helped stop the BLM protests that led to months of civil unrest, riots, and violence in major US cities, along with growing calls to defund and downsize police departments across the country. Most business leaders, even food retailers and retail banking institutions with large workforces and expansive networks, have remained silent about the recent spike in violent crime caused by criminal justice reform and no-bail policies, apart from regularly chiming in on demand about the need for tougher gun control laws.

In 2020, when most small, privately owned businesses were shut down to "slow the spread" of the COVID-19 pandemic, large publicly listed US companies were allowed to stay open and continue operating. Many, such as Amazon.com Inc., FedEx Corporation, United Parcel Service Inc., and Walmart Inc., minted money during the work-and-shop-from-home economic lockdown phase that partially persists to this day. The following year, many of these same large US employers returned the government favor by quickly instituting COVID-19 vaccine mandates for their employee workforces, even though none of the available emergency-use vaccines had yet received final approval from the Food and Drug Administration, significant adverse side effects from the shots were already being reported, and there was still no legally enforceable requirement by the federal Occupational Safety and Health Administration that they do so.

Despite all of the controversy and irregularities surrounding the results of the 2020 national elections – including universal vote-by-mail applications, privately funded ballot drop boxes, a synchronized suspension of vote-counting in key battleground states, and limited electoral observers – any subsequent state effort to protect the integrity of the ballot box by requiring voter identification has been dutifully opposed by the corporate sector. In 2021, more than 100 companies signed a statement decrying the passage of "discriminatory legislation or measures" aimed at "restricting access to the ballot box" in Georgia and other states. The list of signatories included American Airlines Group Inc., General Motors Company, Netflix Inc., PayPal Holdings Inc., and Starbucks Corporation.[23]

In 2022, when Roe v. Wade was overturned by the Supreme Court and the issue of abortion was returned to state legislatures, scores of American companies including Goldman Sachs, JPMorgan Chase, and Citigroup Inc. immediately rolled out a perverse new benefits perk by announcing plans to cover abortion-related travel expenses for their female employees. That same year, when the state of Florida passed a law protecting parental education rights by prohibiting all classroom discussions of sexual orientation and gender identity in public schools prior to the fourth grade, Disney, the beneficiary of several lucrative tax breaks from the Sunshine State, and several other major companies, including Apple, HP Inc., Microsoft Corporation, and Oracle Corporation, all with a presence in Florida, publicly condemned the legislation as hateful and anti-gay. As of May 2023, corporate leaders from 322 businesses had signed on with the Human Rights Campaign (HRC), an NGO focused on "the adoption of LGBTQ+-specific practices and language within existing business structures," to oppose a raft of state laws regarding transgender policy around public bathrooms, youth sports, and medical care for minors. In 2022, a total of 842 companies earned a perfect score of 100% on the Corporate Equality Index tracked by the HRC advocacy group.[24]

Also in 2022, after Russia invaded Ukraine, more than 1,000 international companies immediately announced plans to stop doing business with or in Russia, while the financial markets did their part to ensure that the country was "uninvestable" by removing Russian equities from all the major stock indexes, including S&P Dow Jones, MSCI, and FTSE Russell. At the same time, businesses draped themselves in the blue and gold of the Ukrainian flag and donated millions to refugee and relief organizations. Comparing the knee-jerk corporate response to the 2022 Russia–Ukraine war to the previous complacency around the Russian incursions into Crimea in 2014, Georgia in 2008, and Chechnya over

1999–2009 shows just how far the ESG movement has come in recent years. Or for that matter, contrast the harsh treatment of Russia with the fawning approach of international firms to China, where every aspect of the economy is state controlled and most businesses have direct ties to the Chinese Communist Party and the People's Liberation Army. From a geopolitical perspective, China dwarfs Russia as an economic and military threat to the United States and the rest of the developed world, yet most major companies are loath to call out the human rights record of China. Not coincidentally, ESG looks remarkably like the corporate equivalent of the social credit scores now used by the Chinese government for its citizens.

Judging by the past two years, the work of the ESG morality police is starting to pay off. CEOs now almost reflexively issue woke public statements to ensure that ESG controversies pass them over, the equivalent of smearing lamb's blood over their front doorposts. History is now starting to rhyme again as many of the recent state and national boycotts announced by public companies call to mind the chorus from Little Steven's *Sun City*. All these virtue-signaling corporate displays, though, are mainly a distraction from the larger threat posed by ESG as it works its way into the gears of the financial markets. Despite all the public attention paid to gender, abortion, and other social issues, climate action remains the overriding priority, with all other ESG goals secondary if not superfluous to the net-zero objective. And for all the focus on company resolutions, proxy fights, and board control during the annual shareholder meeting season, the main ESG battle is taking place not in the public equity markets but in the fixed income arena. Even though bondholders are only entitled to principal and interest payments and should not have a voting say on business strategy – another anomaly of the ESG movement – fixed income investors are being activated and taking the lead on ESG engagement, not only with public issuers but also with private companies, sovereigns, municipal bond issuers, and emerging market corporations.

The now-stated ESG goal is to choke off capital to certain industries and companies by either driving up their cost of capital to prohibitive levels or branding these issuers as basically unworthy of financing at any price, or both. Given that bank loans and institutional bonds are the main source of liquidity for most companies and the cheapest source of capital with which to fund ongoing operations and acquisition-related growth, the less transparent credit markets represent the kill switch for the ESG movement. Increasingly, ESG engagement activities and pressure tactics will be focused on financial institutions, particularly large money center banks.

The combination of bad press, investor coercion, and legal threats is typically enough for most companies to toe the ESG line, but for those that refuse or are unable to comply – such as the oil and gas industry, for which the climate-focused sustainable investment movement is an existential threat – these companies will be increasingly screened out from portfolios and eventually excluded from the politically acceptable investable universe, much like Russian securities. The UNGC, which many institutional investors now defer to, already excludes tobacco, weapons manufacturers, and thermal coal producers. It is only a matter of time before all fossil fuel companies are added to the UNGC exclusion list.

The end result of broad ESG acceptance and a sustainable global financial system predicated on stakeholder capitalism will be a submissive corporate sector. In the "more prosperous world for all" planned for 2030, capital flows will be controlled, analytical dissent will not be tolerated, and sustainable investment skeptics will be referred to as ESG deniers.

CHAPTER 6

IT TAKES A VILLAGE OF ESG ENABLERS

I listened for the echo and I heard only praise.
Friedrich Nietzsche

When everyone is looking for gold, it's a good time to be in the pick and shovel business.
Mark Twain

Almost overnight, a cottage industry of ESG research shops, rating agencies, consultants, accounting firms, and other service providers has sprung up in and around Wall Street to help facilitate the sustainable investment trade. Some are well-established players simply looking to leverage their expertise into a new market, but most are either pop-up firms looking to make a fast buck or ESG activists working in disguise to create an echo chamber around sustainability. Many are only one or two degrees of separation from a UN- or WEF-related entity, usually with an official Soviet-sounding name and often taking the form of a 501(c)(3) charitable nonprofit funded by a liberal green billionaire. While hawking their respective wares as a means of helping market participants to "think about sustainability," all are jockeying for position as the go-to incumbent in their particular niche of the nascent ESG market. And while some Wall Street firms are turning in-house to develop their own sustainability tools, most are looking to external ESG providers to help save time and provide political and regulatory cover through their third-party validation.

Like a Middle Eastern bazaar, there is something in the market for everyone, depending on what your ESG needs are. Do you need help ranking all the companies in your portfolio from an ESG perspective? There are several options to choose from. MSCI Inc., formerly known as Morgan Stanley Capital International, is an investment research firm that provides stock indexes, portfolio risk and performance analytics, and governance tools to institutional investors and hedge funds. Founded in 1968, the firm went public in 2007 before being completely divested by Morgan Stanley in 2009. The firm began diversifying into ESG research circa 2007 and fully embraced the concept in 2019, although its marketing materials retroactively put the start date in 1988 based on legacy corporate acquisitions along the way.

Currently, MSCI provides ESG ratings and scores for some 8,500 companies (including roughly 14,000 individual issuers and more than 680,000 equity and fixed income securities) globally, along with sustainability tools for evaluating funds and more than 1,500 benchmark ESG equity and fixed income indexes. MSCI's corporate ESG ratings are based on a seven-category AAA through CCC scale and are designed to measure a company's exposure to long-term, financially relevant ESG risks that are specific to a particular industry and its ability to manage those risks relative to peers. Industry leaders rank in the top two ratings categories (AAA and AA) while laggards fall in the bottom two (B and CCC), with average players coming in the middle of the pack (A, BBB, and BB) and every industry ratings distribution forming a normal bell curve. Using its custom rules-based methodology, the firm relies on a combination of analyst inputs, AI, machine learning, and natural language processing to research and rate all the companies in its global ESG universe. MSCI also assigns ESG ratings to 198 governments and regions plus 45 local authorities – essentially, every country in the world. These government ESG ratings are meant to identify a country's exposure to various ESG risk factors and how such factors might impact the long-term sustainability of its economy. MSCI's government ESG ratings also use the same AAA through CCC scale as its corporate ESG ratings, grouped by stage of economic development.[1]

The main drawback of MSCI is that its corporate ESG ratings are not comparable across different industries, while its government ratings are not relevant outside of preset developed, emerging, and frontier country buckets. While identifying top ESG performers within each industry or country cohort, there is no differentiation in terms of the type and magnitude of ESG risks faced by each group, thus leaving no room for standardization. Is the metals and mining industry with its disproportionate E factors more or less risky than consumer products with its exposure to S factors or financial institutions with their omnipresent G factors? In MSCI's subjective world, is an AA Leader in the food and beverage industry (like Darling Ingredients Inc., which recycles food waste) less risky than an Average A in the fast-food business (like Yum! Brands Inc.) or the gaming industry (like Caesars Entertainment Inc.), or a CCC Laggard in the energy sector (like Energy Transfer, forever stained by its DAPL project)? In this example, Energy Transfer would have the lowest MSCI ESG rating despite being an investment grade company and having the strongest credit in the bunch, showing how most ESG ratings are completely divorced from fundamentals, to say nothing of asset pricing and relative value. MSCI's best-in-class ratings system seems more designed to pressure ESG laggards – consistent with the PRI's preferred approach – as opposed to facilitating peer group comparisons by Wall Street analysts. This rating limitation hasn't stopped the firm, however, from using its individual issuer ESG ratings to construct ESG benchmark indexes and screen equity and fixed income funds and portfolios for aggregate ESG risk.[2]

The other ESG ratings leader is Sustainalytics, a boutique ESG shop that is now wholly owned by Morningstar, the publicly listed independent research firm. The sustainability-focused company was founded in 1992 as Jantzi Research before merging with its European counterpart in 2009 and rebranding itself as Sustainalytics. Between 2017 and 2020, the company was bought out by Morningstar in a two-step transaction that ultimately valued the company at approximately $185 million.

Sustainalytics currently assigns ESG ratings and scores to more than 16,000 companies worldwide using its own proprietary methodology, which is fed by analyst-compiled data and supplemented by AI-powered daily news monitoring from 60,000 media sources. Using both an open-ended numeric scoring scale starting at zero and a five-category qualitative risk rating system (Negligible 0–10, Low 10–20, Medium 20–30, High 30–40, and Severe 40+), the firm looks at 20 material ESG issues and sifts through more than 300 ESG indicators and 1,300 data points to come up with an ESG score for each company in its coverage universe. The company also assigns ESG ratings to 172 countries using the same five risk categories that factor in more than 30 indicators and assess both ESG exposure and the management of such risks in terms of a country's long-term prosperity and economic development. In addition to index and fund screening tools and controversies tracking services, Sustainalytics also offers second-party opinions and ratings on various specialty forms of ESG debt, including green, transition, social, sustainable, and sustainability-linked bonds.[3]

Like MSCI, Sustainalytics's ESG ratings are meant to gauge exposure to ESG risks – expressed through a calculated ESG beta value for each issuer – and assess how well a company or country manages such risks. Both sets of ratings look at the impact of ESG factors on a company's business, rather than how individual corporations are affecting the environment and society. Unlike MSCI with its relative, best-of-the-best approach, though, Sustainalytics's ESG ratings are meant to provide an absolute risk assessment that can be compared across sectors, industries, as well as countries. Nonetheless, the Sustainalytics system is also plagued by glaring relationship anomalies when its ESG ratings are applied to broader portfolio and market universes. Using the same peer group from above, in the Sustainalytics scheme of things, the high-yield trio of Darling Ingredients (20.8 score), Yum! Brands (20.3 score), and Caesars Entertainment (25.7 score) would all fall in the Medium Risk category, while Energy Transfer would face Severe Risk with a score of 52.1. As with MSCI, Sustainalytics's ESG ratings are totally disconnected from credit quality and financial strength.[4]

Because climate action is the top ESG priority, both MSCI and Sustainalytics also offer extensive suites of climate-related products to help benchmark, measure, and manage carbon risk in portfolios to facilitate the screening out of companies based on their greenhouse gas emissions profile and to help investors achieve their net-zero targets and navigate the energy transition. MSCI goes so far as to assign an implied temperature rise to each of the companies that it rates. Expressed in Celsius degrees, the reading is meant to indicate an issuer's contribution to global warming by the year 2100 and state of alignment with the goals of the Paris Agreement, including limiting global warming to well below 2.0°C through the end of the 21st century. To take the temperature of each company, MSCI starts with the remaining carbon budget of the planet through 2100, divides it by approximately 10,000 public companies in the world, and then compares each company budget to a projection of actual corporate emissions through 2050. Not surprisingly, large industrial conglomerates generate an off-the-chart temperature reading of over 4.0°C, landing them all in the red-lettered Strongly Misaligned category.[5]

Apart from the false precision implied by such a metric – MSCI cannot assign ESG ratings that are fungible across industries, yet it can somehow calculate down to one decimal point the contribution of individual companies to average global temperature changes decades down the road – these implied temperature readings highlight the fatuousness of most of the ESG-related scores and ratings currently on the market, the superficiality and artificiality of which is often obscured by visually emotive presentations relying on colorful displays and suggestive graphics such as heatmaps and thermometers.

Besides MSCI and Sustainalytics, there are a myriad of up-and-coming firms active in the ESG ratings space. By one recent count,[6] there are now more than 140 different rating firms providing proprietary ESG grades and scores to investors and companies. Refinitiv, which was formed in 2018 out of the financial and risk product portfolio of Thomson Reuters, provides ESG ratings for more than 12,500 public and private companies, roughly one-half of which are headquartered in North America, Europe, and Japan. Its ratings methodology is based on numeric scoring on a scale of zero through 100 across 10 ESG categories and 186 underlying ESG metrics, which are then combined with an ESG controversies overlay, forced into quartiles, and converted into letter grades ranging from D– at the Laggard bottom to A+ at the Leader top end of the spectrum.[7]

FTSE Russell, the global index provider and direct competitor to MSCI within that space, started diversifying into ESG ratings in 2019 with the purchase of the ESG boutique Beyond Ratings, although the company has been offering sustainability-related index products since the launch of its FTSE4Good Index series in 2001. FTSE Russell currently provides ESG ratings on 7,200 securities in 47 developed and emerging markets – essentially, all the corporate constituents of the FTSE All-World Index, the FTSE All-Share Index, and the Russell 1000 Index. Its ESG ratings are shown on a 1–5 number scale – with 5 being the best – and calculated based on more than 300 ESG indicators weighted across 14 themes within the three pillars of E, S, and G. Each company's

ESG score is meant as an objective measurement of both exposure to, and management of, material ESG issues, although the actual distribution of FTSE Russell's ESG ratings suspiciously resembles a normal bell curve. These corporate ESG ratings feed into the company's index business where it can now conduct portfolio screening and construct custom sustainable index benchmarks for clients.[8]

The problem with all the corporate ESG ratings now being assigned by the nouveau specialist firms in the sustainability space is that much like the title character played by Jodie Foster in the 1994 movie *Nell*, everyone is developing their own language when it comes to ESG ratings. Each rating firm uses its own in-house methodology in terms of which subjective environmental, social, and governance factors, themes, and indicators to feed into its proprietary model and then how to weight, scale, and score all these inputs to come up with an inherently misleading, objective-sounding quantitative numerical value or letter grade. This all-roads-lead-to-Rome approach to ESG ratings results in little consistency or comparability between firms. Michael Jantzi, the founder and former CEO of Sustainalytics, stated in a September 2021 interview with Morningstar that "the diversity of [ESG] ratings is a sign of a healthy market,"[9] which is like saying that schizophrenia or multiple personality disorder are signs of a healthy mind. Boiling down hundreds of metrics into one ESG number for a company is as meaningless as encapsulating the climate change argument into a single 1.5°C or 2.0°C average temperature reading for the entire planet. Moreover, since most ESG rating firms are making it up as they go along, methodologies are being perpetually revised, reclassifications are occurring almost annually, and companies are being regularly upgraded for doing absolutely nothing. The same goes for the ESG ratings being assigned to investment funds. In just the latest example of how the ESG ratings industry is not yet ready for prime time, MSCI announced in March 2023 that it would be revising its ESG ratings on approximately 31,000 funds due to a change in its scoring methodology.[10]

Compare the chaos and cacophony of the ESG ratings arena with the common language and similar approach used by the nationally recognized statistical rating organizations (NRSROs) to assign credit ratings to companies. For decades, the credit rating industry, led by Moody's, S&P Global Ratings, and Fitch Ratings, has maintained an orderly and standardized market whose rules and decisions, while often challenged and disagreed with, are nonetheless transparent to issuers and investors alike. All three regulated agencies use similar letter grade ratings scales that are translatable and largely interchangeable. Persistent ratings gaps of more than two notches between the three agencies for the same company are fairly uncommon. When new rating agency entrants have joined over the years, such as Kroll or Egan-Jones, they have not tried to build market share through a novel approach to credit analysis based on a new set of ratings criteria and presented with cartoonish colors and emoji-like icons. Such a competitive strategy would have quickly put them out of business in the real world of credit ratings – but not so in the surreal world of ESG, which is governed by the laws of relativity.

All three NRSROs have also supplemented their core credit ratings franchises with an array of ESG products in recent years, although mainly as a defensive move to protect their competitive turf and stake out their ratings territory in a changing market. Moody's is now assigning ESG credit impact scores (CIS) to companies – ranging from CIS-1 Positive down to CIS-5 Very Highly Negative – along with ESG issuer profile scores using a 1–5 scale for each pillar (e.g., E-3, S-4, and G-2).[11] S&P Global Ratings has developed a list of key sustainability factors by industry and started issuing ESG evaluations that score each company on a scale of zero through 100. Working with its S&P and Dow Jones index affiliates, the rating agency has also rolled out corporate sustainability assessments for all the companies in its benchmark ratings and market universes.[12] For its part, Fitch has launched a suite of ESG ratings, data, and analytical products within its Sustainable Fitch segment, including ESG relevance scores using the same 1–5 rating scale as Moody's.[13] All three rating agencies regularly monitor the airwaves for ESG controversies and incidents and also issue second-party opinions and ratings on sustainable and other specialty ESG bonds.

Notably, there has been no discernible movement or recalibration in credit ratings across the investment grade or high-yield corporate markets on the back of the Big 3 NRSROs upping their sustainability game and showily integrating ESG into their credit ratings process, which is either a reflection that financially material ESG issues were already factored into most company ratings or just another sign that ESG has absolutely nothing to do with fundamental value, credit quality, or solvency, the latter of which is the only meaningful measure of corporate sustainability. While further muddying the waters right now – Fitch also ranks companies for their impact on the environment and society at large – the NRSROs will play an important defensive role in the fight against the ESG takeover of the financial markets since ESG activists would like nothing better than for the major credit rating agencies to fallaciously redefine bankruptcy and default risk as sustainability risk.

Apart from ESG ratings, do you need to stay on top of potential ESG controversies so that you aren't blindsided by an adverse headline about potential human rights violations when you get into work? While most ESG firms track controversies and material incidents through their ratings process, some ESG technology companies focus exclusively on ESG controversy monitoring. For example, since 2006, the previously mentioned RepRisk has been using a combination of AI, machine learning, and human intelligence to translate big ESG data into actionable research, analytics, and risk metrics. The company's flagship product, its RepRisk ESG Risk Platform, is described as the world's largest database of its kind, covering more than 235,000 public and private companies and more than 65,000 infrastructure projects worldwide. RepRisk scans the world and systematically flags and monitors material ESG risks and violations of international standards that can have reputational, compliance, and financial impacts on a company – much as the Cerebro device in the *X-Men* comics allowed Professor Charles Xavier to locate mutants anywhere on planet Earth in real time. Every day, RepRisk screens over 100,000 public sources and stakeholders – including print, online, and social media, government bodies, regulators, and think tanks – and processes an average of 150,000 documents in 23 languages looking for hits on 102 ESG risk factors, including 28 core issues and 74 "hot topics." Notably, RepRisk does not verify or validate any reported allegations captured by its automated system when it goes spanning the world for ESG news daily. Moreover, the technology firm takes an outside-in approach to ESG risks and intentionally excludes company self-disclosures because, as the Swiss company says, "it is now well-accepted that self-reported information is not reliable data – especially when it comes to risks."[14] Such a nonsensical view that corporate management is inherently dishonest and untrustworthy is another indicator of the antibusiness mentality of ESG and stakeholder capitalism.

When it comes to sustainable investing, just collecting, organizing, and keeping track of all the requisite ESG data is more than half the battle, which has led to the rise of various ESG aggregators and information hubs. Arabesque, a technology-focused investment company, was established in 2013 to focus on "sustainable intelligence" using a combination of analyst research and AI. In 2018, the firm launched ESG Book, a sustainability data and technology provider offering a range of ESG-related data, scoring, and analytical tools. Its core research product analyzes 450 ESG data points for each of the more than 50,000 companies in its corporate universe.[15] Nasdaq, the electronic global marketplace for buying and selling securities, launched its own ESG Data Hub in 2021 to connect investors with sustainability datasets from leading providers across a wide range of ESG categories, including biodiversity, gender diversity, and carbon emissions. All the ESG data available on the Nasdaq's platform is connected back to the UN's 17 SDGs and is designed to help "both investors and corporates looking to support a more sustainable and inclusive capitalism."[16] FactSet, which was founded in 1978 and provides computer-based financial data and analytics for more than 185,000 financial and investment professionals, now offers more than 15 in-house ESG datasets plus 40 third-party databases (including RepRisk), including more than 200 information feeds, through its ESG Investing Solutions product.[17]

The clear industry leader in the ESG data and information category, though, is Bloomberg LP. With its ubiquitous hardware terminals – now software screens – sitting atop almost every desk on Wall Street, Bloomberg has a leg up on the competition given that it is already the default source for most company financial disclosure, regulatory filings, and market-related data and news, and is now positioning itself as the go-to central clearinghouse for all data and news related to ESG investing. Toward this end, Bloomberg now offers both proprietary and third-party ESG datasets – including both MSCI and Sustainalytics – that include metrics and disclosure scores for more than 15,000 companies in over 100 countries. Bloomberg's ESG company coverage universe equates to roughly 88% of global equity market capitalization. With historical data going back to 2006, its ESG database is organized into more than 5,100 fields and scores spanning several key sustainability topics including air quality; climate change; water and energy management;

materials and waste; health and safety; audit risk and oversight; compensation; diversity; board independence, structure, and tenure; and shareholders' rights.[18] Complementing its ESG data service, its Bloomberg New Energy Finance (BNEF) platform provides regular updates on the global commodity markets and the ongoing energy transition. Most of the "research" published by BNEF comprises self-serving long-dated forecasts for electric vehicle take-up and renewable power grid penetration consistent with an inevitable march toward a low-carbon global economy. Such BNEF projections, which are widely referenced by market practitioners, are, in turn, echoed by the green-tinted news coverage provided by Bloomberg's media arm. On any given day, Bloomberg's top news screen can be counted on for a handful of headlines related to climate, sustainability, and ESG. The media conglomerate also publishes *Bloomberg Green Magazine* to promote its commitment to climate solutions. Channeling the time-traveling future grifter Biff Tannen, Bloomberg's print advertising for its suite of sustainable finance products notes that ESG is "demanded by tomorrow." All these business moves are consistent with the progressive ideology of Bloomberg's billionaire founder and principal owner, Michael Bloomberg, whose personal wealth has been used to fund a litany of liberal activist causes including ESG and sustainability and especially climate change in recent years.

What if you need to check yourself before calling up the head of investor relations to complain about the poor quality of his company's sustainability disclosure? In that case, there is a veritable Alphabet City of companies to choose from. The CDP (formerly known as the Carbon Disclosure Project) runs a global environmental disclosure system with data covering more than 18,700 companies and 1,100 national and subnational government entities. Its goal is to study the implications of climate change for the world's principal publicly traded companies and help persuade them to measure, manage, disclose, and ultimately reduce their greenhouse gas emissions.[19] The GRI provides a sustainable reporting framework employed by more than 10,000 companies in over 100 countries worldwide. The group publishes universal, sector, and topic standards for sustainability disclosure to help businesses to be transparent and "take responsibility for their impacts" on people and the planet.[20]

The International Financial Reporting Standards (IFRS) Foundation created the International Sustainability Standards Board (ISSB) in November 2021 to serve as the consolidator within the sustainable reporting industry. The ISSB's remit is to launch global reporting standards for both general sustainability and climate-related disclosure. In recent years, the organization has swallowed up a number of smaller reporting framework groups including the Climate Disclosure Standards Board (CDSB), an initiative of the CDP, and the Value Reporting Foundation (VRF), which was itself the result of the merger between the Sustainable Accounting Standards Board (SASB) and the International Integrated Reporting Council (IIRC). The synthesized ISSB global standards, which were released in June 2023, covering sustainable finance and climate disclosures,[21] also factor in the recommendations of the TCFD, which are now publicly supported, albeit not necessarily implemented, by more than 4,000 organizations worldwide.[22] In its June 2017 final report to the FSB of the G20 intergovernmental forum, the TCFD laid out 11 recommended climate-related disclosures for both businesses and financial institutions touching on corporate governance, risk management, and strategic planning, along with a host of climate-related metrics and targets.[23]

Are you planning on launching a proxy fight because one of the companies that your fund owns does not have 30% women on its board of directors or refuses to disclose its Scope 3 greenhouse gas emissions or won't explicitly link its executive compensation to the achievement of ESG-related corporate goals? Both leading shareholder advisory firms, Institutional Shareholder Services (ISS) and Glass Lewis, which control approximately 97% of the proxy advisory market between them, have now been retrofitted for ESG, including new ESG product lines and a whole new sustainability-driven approach to corporate governance and shareholder proxy matters. ISS now provides ESG corporate ratings for 12,500 companies, ESG country ratings for 830 sovereign issuers, and ESG fund ratings for some 26,500 funds, while screening tens of thousands of issuers for ESG controversies and climate policy alignment.[24] Beginning with the 2022 shareholder meeting season, ISS's proxy voting recommendations have been increasingly driven by a list of ESG issues including climate, board diversity, board accountability, and compensation,[25] effectively crossing the line between shareholder advisor and ESG advocate. Glass Lewis also issues ESG profiles and scores for roughly 5,000 companies globally, ranking each on key sustainability issues such as climate risk mitigation, ESG transparency, ESG target setting, and board accountability (especially with regard to ESG policy).[26] As with ISS, Glass Lewis now uses a sustainable prism when issuing recommendations on shareholder proxy votes, and typically recommends voting straight down the ESG line.

Similarly, all the major consulting firms – both stand-alone and those with accounting parents – have now carved out separate practices to promote sustainability, the latest, and perhaps greatest, of all management fads. ESG and stakeholder capitalism can be viewed as the next logical step from, or iteration of, globalization, which the business consultants have been pushing for the past 20 years despite its negative effects on national economies. Even though globalization has led to a hollowing out of the US industrial base as manufacturing has been moved overseas, exposing economic supply chain vulnerabilities for everything from drugs and medical devices to semiconductor chips and critical minerals, the consultants are now doubling down on sustainability and touting the business need for a global focus on people and the planet. All repeat the boilerplate ESG arguments made by the tag team of the UN and the WEF. ESG is no longer a nice-to-have, it is now a necessity. Businesses must strive to build an economy that works for all. Companies must be mindful of their externalities to ensure that they do not lose their social license to operate. ESG is a form of risk mitigation that can also create or unlock business enterprise value over the long term.

All the leading business consultants now offer some client service variation on the sustainability theme: Client Change and Sustainability (Boston Consulting Group); ESG and Sustainability (FTI Consulting); Climate Change and Sustainability (EY); ESG Advisory (KPMG); Sustainability and ESG Services (Deloitte); and Sustainability and Climate Change (PwC). McKinsey, with its new Sustainability platform, has been one of the most aggressive ESG advocates within the industry, particularly regarding climate change and the energy transition. The company views net-zero policies as the "biggest capital reallocation of our lifetime," and its goal is to "help all industry sectors to transform to get to net zero by 2050 and cut carbon emissions by half by 2030."[27] Toward this end, McKinsey aspires to be the largest private sector catalyst on decarbonization, working with the WEF and its other strategic partners to pump out a significant volume of insights on the topic.

Or maybe you just need help justifying why your asset management firm is spending so much time and money on sustainability rather than, say, focusing on developments in the macroeconomy and global financial markets and trying to generate alpha for your clients? Spurred on by the PRI and other advocacy groups, many business schools have added sustainable business centers to produce supportive research and develop coursework on sustainability topics. Some universities even offer majors and concentrations in the emergent fields of business sustainability or sustainable finance. Most of these centers are run by environmental and social justice activists either hired from the professional protest industry or already working inside the walls of the academy. Based on numbers compiled by the Network for Business Sustainability, an organization focused on "advancing sustainable development to build a fairer and more environmentally sound future," there are currently some 200 sustainable business centers located at universities around the world.[28] In the US, the list includes Harvard, Yale, Stanford, MIT, Cornell, Dartmouth, Duke, Duquesne, the University of Pittsburgh, Pennsylvania State University, the University of Pennsylvania, and New York University (NYU).

Prototypical of these institutions would be the NYU Stern School of Business Center for Sustainable Business (CSB), which was founded in 2016 by Tensie Whelan, the former president of the environmental activist group Rainforest Alliance. From its vantage point in the ivory-hued Henry Kaufman Management Center tower overlooking Washington Square Park, the CSB pushes its sustainability agenda using a three-pronged approach built on research, education, and engagement. On the research front, the group issues a steady stream of advocacy white papers and promotional case studies, the majority of which are analytically challenged and more accurately described as propaganda for the cause. The list of recent CSB policy research includes such self-serving studies as "U.S. Corporate Boards Suffer from Inadequate Expertise in Financially Material ESG Matters," which, not surprisingly, concluded that increased board diversity – including younger directors with more open minds – is required to address the current ESG governance deficiency,[29] and "ESG and the Earnings Call: Communicating Sustainable Value Creation

Quarter by Quarter," which recommended – with a straight face – that companies plant ESG-specific questions with sell-side analysts so that earnings discussions are dominated by sustainability topics.[30]

A November 2021 CSB case study on ExxonMobil regurgitated all the same arguments made by Engine No. 1 in its proxy board fight with the company earlier that year – including ripping off its "Reenergizing ExxonMobil" title and reproducing many of the activist fund's exhibits – but failed even to mention how the global energy industry had been fundamentally changed by the US shale revolution during the 2010s even as it parroted the charge that ExxonMobil board mismanagement had led to "ten years of value destruction," which is an analytical sin of omission.[31]

Most of the CSB's research attempts to make the case that ESG leads to business or investment outperformance have similarly fallen short. Its Return on Sustainability Investment (ROSI) framework, introduced in 2019, is nothing more than a subjective projection model for future sustainability benefits, which are simply estimated and then discounted back to the present to create a theoretical net present value (NPV).[32] Its trademarked Sustainable Market Share Index highlights the obvious marketing point that, over the past few years, gullible consumers have tended to buy any product or service sporting a sustainable, green, or organic label.[33]

The CSB, whose motto is "a better world through better business," is also working actively to integrate sustainable business concepts throughout the existing curriculum at NYU Stern – effectively changing the meaning of a business education, particularly when it comes to finance. While the school offers a graduate-level specialization in Sustainable Business and Innovation and various sustainability-related elective courses, all Stern MBA students are now required to take a foundational course in sustainable business. The CSB also engages with corporate leaders and collaborates with other like-minded ESG advocates such as the PRI as a member in good standing of its PRI Academic Network and the WEF, occupying an important satellite position in the public communications network around sustainability.

At another level, the rise of sustainable business centers like the CSB highlights how the decomposition of the university system that Allan Bloom warned us about in his 1987 book *The Closing of the American Mind* has now made its way up from liberal arts colleges to graduate business schools and the harder sciences. Sustainability is just the latest blow for business schools, where educational standards have already been falling as rigorous quantitative topics have been replaced with faddish sociology and trendy technology courses, facilitated in large part by the decline in the power and prestige of most finance departments in the years since the 2008 global financial crisis. Outsized alumni donations – with the requisite naming rights – now drive shifts in business school curriculum. Adjunct professors and lecturers, many walking in right off the street with no instructor experience, do most of the teaching these days, both for core courses and esoteric electives. Class sizes now routinely average in the 40-to-50-student range, even for non-lecture courses. Group work now predominates to minimize the grading burden on professors and artificially inflate the GPA of weaker students and leave no adult behind. Students now wield enormous power through their course and instructor evaluations and effectively decide who teaches what to them. Professors whose courses are too difficult often find themselves out of a job.[34] Good luck trying to fail students – especially if underperformers fall in one of the many protected campus categories. Case studies no longer pose specific questions with right and wrong answers but instead ask students how they feel about different business situations and to diagram how many groups of stakeholders should have a say in the matter. Raising questions about climate change or focusing too much time on the fossil fuels industry during class discussion will trigger complaints to the dean. The result of all this student pandering has been a dumbing down of business school curriculum even as the cost has skyrocketed over the past decade. This has provided the opening needed for ESG and sustainability doctrine, with its lack of intellectual rigor, sloppy scholarship, and anticapitalist bent. With some of the country's top business schools now offering courses on "Reimagining Capitalism," the seeds of destruction are already being planted in young minds.

Lastly, are you still struggling to wrap your head around the whole concept of sustainability? Does your logical mind say one thing while your emotional heart tells you something completely different? Everything that you have read about the topic points to ESG as being a colossal scam, yet you still want to believe, just like Peter Pan, that companies can never grow old and hold within themselves the magic pixie dust to change the world. If this is what ails you, then there is no shortage of options to help train your brain. If paying roughly $250,000 (including room and board) for a two-year NYU Stern MBA degree with a specialization in Sustainable Business and Innovation does not make economic sense,[35] then there are cheaper educational alternatives. The PRI, through its PRI Academy, offers a menu of affordable online ESG courses at $1,000 a pop or less – even not-for-profits need to make money off ESG – including an introductory course on "Understanding RI," a comprehensive module on "Applied RI," and an advanced class on "Advanced RI Analysis."[36] Most of the sustainability-focused universities also offer online certificate programs in ESG, sustainability, and climate change or some combination thereof.

Even the vaunted CFA Institute, Wall Street's leading fraternal society of investment professionals with some 202,200 members as of year-end 2022, now offers a Certificate in ESG Investing as a complement to its grueling, three-year entrance examination to become a Chartered Financial Analyst, which has a less than 50% pass rate for its final Level III. Analytically, the three-part CFA test represents a cross between Marine boot camp, Navy SEAL BUD/S school, and Army Ranger training. Many Wall Street analysts and portfolio managers wear their CFA designations like a red badge of courage throughout their professional lives. So, it is more than a little surprising – and somewhat disheartening – that the CFA Institute would diminish itself and tarnish its image as the gold standard for Wall Street analysts by offering a certificate program in such a frivolous and fringe field as ESG investing. Even more troubling, the core CFA examination now includes questions on ESG, sustainability, and stakeholder capitalism. The organization has tried justifying such moves with vacuous statements like "sustainable investing is critical to the sustainability of investing,"[37] which reads like the script for a hostage video and shows how much public pressure everyone on Wall Street is now under to comply.

The market for ESG-related products and services for companies and investors has taken off since the signing of the Paris Agreement and the release of the UN's SDGs in 2015. Publicly disclosed ESG segment revenues by a handful of sustainability shops point to how rapid the recent growth has been. Since 2018, MSCI's revenues from its ESG and Climate segment have more than tripled to $228 million or 10% of its consolidated top line in 2022, with 98% of such segment revenues representing recurring subscriptions. Since Morningstar acquired 100% of Sustainalytics in 2020, segment revenues from the ESG subsidiary have increased at an annual organic rate of 40–45% over 2021–2022.

If ESG integration and engagement are taken to their logical, universal conclusion and sustainability is ultimately forced on every player in the global financial system, then the addressable revenue market would be huge – if not infinite, given the mutating nature of ESG with its ever-growing list of factors that never stops randomly generating new progressive controversies to leverage. To give you an idea of the size of the ESG market opportunity, imagine a world where every company, country, investor, fund, and individual security issue must be regularly inspected – just like food – and certified for sustainability purposes.

Given the pot of gold that lies at the end of the ESG rainbow, it is not surprising that ESG has become a kind of Wild West on Wall Street, with every service provider doing their own thing and jockeying for position. While all this rent-seeking does restore one's faith in capitalism – the Milton Friedman kind, not the Klaus Schwab stakeholder variety – the ESG investment movement feels like an exercise in modern-day cattle rustling. ESG rating and advisory firms say that they want to help their clients on their "ESG journey," but the reality is that all market participants are now being herded in the same direction and ultimately into holding pens. Anyone on Wall Street objecting or pointing out the inherent illogic of sustainable investing gets trampled.

It is also quite remarkable how the financial regulators have stood idly by as the market has been flooded for several years now with ESG specialists doling out investment advice, even though many of the firms now hanging out an ESG shingle have dubious qualifications and obvious conflicts of interest. Like a frontier town in 1880s Arizona, there are many grifters around the ESG trade, perpetually signaling each other, coordinating messaging, and talking their own book – effectively engaging in a form of market manipulation. There is often little transparency about the less-than-arm's-length relationships and behind-the-scenes money flows between companies looking to profit from ESG and the supposedly impartial sustainability thought leaders and technical experts from the private and public sectors and the halls of academia. Typically, the loudest public voices are the ones cashing in the most on ESG.

Many of the official-sounding organizations involved with ESG –

including the PRI, the WEF, and all the authoritative sustainable accounting and reporting bodies – are private not-for-profit organizations, most with close government ties and funding provided by progressive foundations. Donations from liberal benefactors also support many of the academic sustainable business centers now lecturing the public on the benefits of ESG. In the NYU Stern example, the CSB has received financial support since its inception from the Ford Foundation, one of the largest private foundations in the US with a current $16 billion endowment, which announced plans in 2017 to commit $1 billion over 10 years to mission-related investments. As part of this financial target, the Ford Foundation continues to make programmatic grants to advocacy groups that "enrich the evidence base and market standards for impact investing,"[38] with the former including academic outfits such as the CSB and the latter including ESG reporting frameworks such as the SASB, which is now being rolled into the ISSB. In related news, the Ford Foundation announced plans in 2021 to divest all its fossil fuel holdings.

The largest financial backer of the SASB, a 501(c)(3) organization whose misleading name evokes the officially sanctioned Financial Accounting Standards Board (FASB), is Bloomberg Philanthropies, the private foundation of the billionaire Michael Bloomberg, whose firm is going all in on ESG and sustainability. Bloomberg has been "a longtime champion in the fight against climate change."[39] As part of this personal green vendetta, he serves as chairman of the TCFD – which is pushing to require climate disclosure by all companies and financial institutions – and also as president of the board of the C40 Cities Climate Leadership Group and cochair of both the Global Covenant of Mayors for Climate & Energy and the "America Is All In" coalition. The funding that he has given to environmental groups has, by his own calculation, "helped retire more than 60% of all US coal plants since 2011 and more than half of all European plants since 2016." Working with the UN, he also formed the Climate Finance Leadership Initiative to accelerate private sector investments in climate solutions and was recently named the special envoy to the UN secretary-general on climate ambition and solutions. Now, the support that Bloomberg Philanthropies provides to the TCFD, the SASB, and other ESG advocacy groups drives more business onto his media and financial information platform.

In 2017, the final recommendations of the Bloomberg-chaired TCFD were presented to the FSB which, at the time, was chaired by Mark Carney, the former governor of both the Bank of England and the Bank of Canada. After leaving the FSB, Carney led the effort to sign up financial institutions for the GFANZ formed as part of COP26 in 2021, and he also now serves as the United Nations special envoy for climate action and finance. In his day job, Carney is the current head of transition investing at Brookfield Corporation, where he also chairs the company's asset management business.

Al Gore, who has been hectoring the world about climate change since the 1980s, has now parlayed the Academy Award and Nobel Peace Prize that he won for his 2007 documentary *An Inconvenient Truth* into a career in sustainable investing. He is currently the chairman of Generation Investment Management, a sustainability-focused fund manager with $32.1 billion of AUM as of March 31, 2023. He is also regularly held out as an expert on ESG despite the conflict of interest that all of his policy prescriptions and regulatory recommendations serve to benefit him both personally and professionally. In 2015, he partnered with the PRI to publish a policy white paper to "end the debate on whether fiduciary duty is a legitimate barrier to the integration of environmental, social and governance issues in investment practice and decision-making."[40] He also sits on the board of trustees of the WEF.

As Yogi Berra might say, all of this is "too coincidental to be a coincidence." Even as they criticize public companies for having interlocking boards, there is high-level synchronization between most players in the sustainability advocacy arena, where many are making a very good living off ESG. All this self-dealing behavior gives new ironic meaning to the "doing well by doing good" catchphrase of the sustainability movement. The oil and gas industry and other ESG-maligned sectors should keep this in mind the next time they are accused by climate and sustainability activists of arguing in bad faith for simply defending themselves and their livelihoods. Ditto for the investment community when the ESG crowd finally comes for the fiduciary rule. But probably the most important takeaway is that, while scores of ESG opportunists and grifters are now making money, many unwilling and unsuspecting investors are now paying for all of this extraneous administrative overhead without any incremental return to show for it. The price of virtue signaling is, indeed, very high.

CHAPTER 7

A PARALYSIS OF ANALYSIS

What we've got here is failure to communicate.
Strother Martin, *Cool Hand Luke*

Though this be madness, yet there is method in 't.
William Shakespeare, *Hamlet*, Act 2

Anyone who has worked on Wall Street will tell you that the environment is fast-paced and most people in the industry have very short attention spans, particularly during market hours. If you are pitching a new issue, trade idea, or other investment opportunity, you better keep it simple and get to the point. If you are putting something down on paper, bullet points are better than prose, a graph is worth a thousand words, and make sure that it all fits onto one page. Talking fast also helps.

Every workday – and most weekends and holidays, for that matter – research analysts, salespeople, traders, syndicate and capital markets personnel, investment bankers, and buy-side portfolio managers scan their Bloomberg screens, the *Wall Street Journal*, and myriad other media channels for any and all fundamental news – whether geopolitical, macroeconomic, industry-level, or company-specific – and then synthesize the information gleaned from the headlines with technical data to determine relative value, or the proper trading relationship between different sectors and companies, all in the context of the current market environment. Usually, company and industry fundamentals are the primary driver, but often macroeconomic trends and market technical factors can overwhelm idiosyncratic risk.

Relative value analysis provides the underpinnings for liquid two-sided secondary trading markets and a well-functioning primary market for new issues of debt and equity securities. It is a dynamic, real-time exercise that is global in nature and equal parts deduction and intuition, with market anomalies never persisting for long. It is the core function of Wall Street, and the main reason why the best and the brightest continue to be drawn to the industry. Every day, the facts on the ground can change and require a recalibration of valuations and risk relationships, which is both challenging but also very intellectually stimulating. Self-confident people with sharp analytical minds and good argumentation and marketing skills tend to do well in such a work environment.

The entire relative value process is built on having a differentiated view since financial markets only work when one side is willing to buy what the other side is selling at the agreed clearing price. While there is always room for subjective opinion, Wall Street does have its established rules when it comes to determining relative value. Broadly speaking, equity market valuations are driven by earnings momentum, dividend yields, and share price metrics due to the shareholder focus on dividends and capital appreciation. Bond market valuations mainly key off debt leverage, interest coverage, and cash flow measures due to the fixed income focus on coupon and principal payments. While customized by industry, a handful of financial ratios typically suffices for both equity and credit analysts in order to facilitate peer group comparisons. Supply and demand technicals and the potential for event risk (e.g., an M&A announcement or earnings surprise) are also factored into the valuation mix.

Lastly, the investment horizon is usually limited, never extending much past one year due to Wall Street's overriding focus on annual market (and personal bonus) performance and the fading accuracy of forecasts as one goes further out into the future. This, in a nutshell, is the basic approach to relative value analysis that Wall Street has used effectively for decades in its market-making and capital-raising activities, with technological advancements helping to streamline, simplify, and steadily improve the process. Notwithstanding periodic market blowups and corrections, the financial markets have become more efficient over time – particularly over the past 30 years – with many financial products now largely commoditized and Wall Street functioning as a manufacturing operation when it comes to raising capital.

It is onto this well-oiled financial machine that sustainable investment advocates are now trying to superimpose their convoluted and highly complex ESG framework and, in the process, fundamentally change the way that corporate debt and equity securities and other investments are valued by the financial markets. The effort thus far to create the "sustainable global financial system" envisioned by the PRI has been a logistical nightmare worthy of Freddy Krueger. Over the past few years, Wall Street research analysts have struggled to wrap their heads around the inchoate and incoherent system of ESG investing. Despite its pseudoanalytical framework and scores of metrics, ESG is a highly subjective security selection scheme built on qualitative factors and hidden behind a façade of quantitative analysis. Every market participant approaches the topic of ESG differently, including a sharp divergence between the US and European markets on a par with the "go metric" crusade of the 1970s.

Wall Street research analysts – whose fundamental sector and company analysis provides the underpinnings for security valuation and efficient primary and liquid secondary trading markets – stand in the way of the ESG mob now storming the financial markets, much like the lawyers marked for killing in Shakespeare's *Henry VI.* Since research underpins both market-making and investing activities, one of the first things that activists have focused on with their ESG integration efforts has been to co-opt research analysts on both the sell side and the buy side of the business. Toward this end, the PRI requires all its investment manager and asset owner members to incorporate ESG into their in-house research processes. All these buy-side accounts, in turn, are encouraged to withhold broker commissions and research poll votes from any brokerage firm whose analysts are not voicing support for sustainability. Since annual *Institutional Investor* research rankings are one of the main drivers of sell-side analyst compensation, this push is typically all that is needed to get sell-side analysts on board.

Investment banks and asset management firms are responding to PRI pressure by hiring an army of sustainability specialists to chaperone and look over the shoulders of seasoned fundamental analysts in their daily interactions with their coverage companies. Apparently, senior management imposing ESG top-down on Wall Street analysts is not a conflict of interest that currently needs to be disclosed in sell-side research reports or investment fund marketing materials. Research analysts are now being forced to suspend disbelief and forgo the traditional financial approach that they have used for decades to analyze and value company securities. This is unfortunate because fundamental research analysts are the best equipped to challenge the sophistry of sustainability. Using a Socratic method, it only takes a few basic analytical questions to expose the fatal flaws of the ESG argument.

When it comes to the morality-based system of ESG and the Schwab system of stakeholder capitalism, how does a Wall Street analyst come to grips with the exceedingly long and ever-growing list of ESG factors? Doing some simple math, the UN's 17 SDGs, 169 indicators, and 232 metrics translate into roughly 15,000 ESG data points for an analyst to track, assuming an average research coverage universe of approximately 50 to 75 companies. Moreover, how does one prioritize the universe of company stakeholders to reflect the new enlightened ESG focus on people and planet, apart from making sure that equity owners and bondholders are at the back of the line? Why would running a company for the benefit of every constituency in society except for capital providers such as shareholders and creditors necessarily lead to improved pricing for financial assets such as stocks, bonds, and bank loans?

Everyone on Wall Street would tend to agree – either tacitly or publicly – with the proposition that climate action should be the main ESG focus. This is both by default and design – the former because doing so avoids a political fight and simplifies life for financial market participants, the latter because climate change has always been the #1 ESG priority for sustainability activists. Just as Godzilla, the giant irradiated lizard with atomic breath, was the king of the Japanese movie monsters back in the 1960s, so too is climate change the greatest and most fearsome of the ESG factors.

But even when it comes to climate change, there is little analytical consensus. Do greenhouse gas emissions need to be reduced on an absolute basis or just in terms of intensity versus sales or some unit of production? Should the main focus be carbon dioxide or methane, which everyone now says is a more potent greenhouse gas? Is flaring associated natural gas to create carbon dioxide better than just releasing the unwanted methane into the atmosphere? Is a company responsible for the emissions of both its own operations as well as those of its suppliers and customers? Is there any price that a company should not be willing to pay for getting to net-zero emissions, even if such capital spending generates poor risk-adjusted returns or leads to a deterioration in corporate credit quality? Does the Paris goal of limiting the postindustrial increase in average global temperatures to less than 2.0°C and ideally 1.5°C justify any corporate means of achieving this end? Why is it that the ubiquitous hockey stick chart used to rally support for the cause (i.e., carbon emissions versus temperature anomalies since 1880) cannot be included in any Wall Street research report since it violates FINRA standards by being highly misleading due to its distorted scale and opaque data?

Why is the environmental pillar of ESG so myopically focused on the abstract concept of carbon pollution – and, by extension, fossil fuels – rather than the real and pressing pollution problems now facing the world? Take the case of plastics – single-use bags and otherwise – and the amount of plastic waste being dumped into the world's oceans, endangering sea life and the marine ecosystem. A 2018 report released by the WEF, an ally in the sustainability fight and hardly an unsympathetic source, noted that just ten rivers worldwide are responsible for roughly 90% of the plastic pollution being deposited in the Seven Seas.[1] Not surprisingly, all these rivers are located in the developing world, with eight in Asia – including five in China and two in India – and two on the African continent. Rather than confronting the environmental policy shortcomings of the Chinese and Indian governments, the ESG solution to the ocean plastic problem is to support bans on specific plastic products such as straws and polyethylene film bags and cut back on plastic production by companies in the industrialized world since such a response conveniently leads to more demand destruction for fossil fuels.

After climate change, things break down even further with the rest of the environmental agenda, with many more analytical questions raised than answered. For example, is water consumption a more important ESG indicator than energy usage? Exactly when did the memo go out stating that the world, particularly the developed industrialized portion of it, was running out of potable water and electric power? And if we are, isn't that more a failing of government rather than the responsibility of business? Is the problem that companies are not paying their water and electric bills? Are some of them opening up fire hydrants or illegally tapping into utility poles like a city block party in July? Why are Wall Street analysts in the 2020s being forced to track meaningless water and energy consumption statistics based on the discredited Chicken Little environmental warnings of the Club of Rome from over 50 years ago?

Maintaining biodiversity around the planet is a laudable objective, albeit one that importantly should be balanced against the economic needs of different human populations – especially those living in leafy poverty-stricken parts of the planet. It is also an issue that should be handled by national governments and multilateral development agencies, not by individual businesses and financial institutions. While refreshing on the major climate types and scanning the species list for each does provide a trip down memory lane for analysts who have forgotten what they learned in grade school science, tracking the natural resource endowments of different countries and regions around the world is a complete waste of time for Wall Street. Slapping the made-up label of "natural capital" on such environmental esoterica doesn't change that fact.

The category of social issues is arguably the messiest of the three ESG columns since it revolves around people and the emotional concepts of fairness and justice. Is operating safety and asset integrity more important for a company than the racial and gender composition of its workforce, contractors, suppliers, and clients? Is it more critical to keep the customer satisfied, as Simon & Garfunkel sang in their 1970 hit, or to ensure that your suppliers and service companies are happy? Do unionization rates trump diversity, equity, and inclusion statistics? Does a white card-carrying union worker earn a company more ESG points than a black or Hispanic nonunion worker? What is the social justice pecking order by race, gender, age, socioeconomic class, and sexual identity and preference? Why is it that social justice also doubles as an environmental issue to provide yet another line of attack for climate activists?

Most Wall Street analysts would be hard-pressed to quote the headcount number for each of the companies under their coverage off the top of their head. Yet under ESG, analysts will practically need to know each company worker by name, including whether they are content in their job and what they do in their spare time – which hopefully includes some form of giving back. Is high turnover and employee dissatisfaction necessarily a bad thing for certain companies and industries? Are companies with high operating cost structures still allowed to lay off employees? What insight can be gleaned from Glassdoor company reviews posted by former employees, which is basically the equivalent of asking an ex-spouse for a personal referral? Why are companies being evaluated based on how much time their employees spend volunteering? What is the appropriate amount of money that a company should donate to local charities if they operate worldwide? Why is donating to local communities acceptable, while perfectly legal political contributions are discouraged? Why just focus on the local geography when every company is purportedly a global corporate citizen beholden to the world?

In the governance pillar, why is the overriding ESG goal to make company boards less responsive to shareholders? Most S&P 500 companies already have majority independent boards, so why the continued push for change? Why is more board turnover a good thing, while employee turnover at the underlying company is a bad thing? Shouldn't it be more critical to have a diverse and inclusive workforce rather than focusing on the board of directors? Why is board underrepresentation of any group versus the general population always taken as a case of prima facie discrimination? When exactly did the quota system come back in vogue? Activist groups like the 30% Club and the Thirty Percent Coalition have been pushing for years for women to hold at least 30% of company board seats, even in the absence of data to back up the argument that more-female boards drive corporate outperformance. Why exactly does a company have to split the roles of chairman and CEO to avoid the dreaded duality? Is multitasking no longer allowed? What if the company's chairman and CEO is also its founder and majority shareholder? Do different governance rules apply if a company is privately held? Why are Wall Street analysts now being forced to calculate, in Dickensian fashion, the "fairness" of both corporate taxes and employee wages and the pay differential between a company's CEO and the lowest-level worker that reports to him (or hopefully her)?

Apart from such fundamental questions, what is the appropriate frame of reference to use when assigning an ESG grade to a company? Setting aside the question of relevance, if ESG were actual analysis, then it would be based on each company's metrics. Typically, getting one's hands on a clean set of numbers is all that Wall Street analysts need to do their job and develop a view. But with ESG, this is not the case. Sustainability disclosure is mainly a means to the end of forcing businesses to take action on climate and other sustainable development goals. Its main goal is not to facilitate analysis. In fact, the actual numbers reported by individual companies are fairly meaningless. For most industries, the data is already known, at least on an intuitive level, particularly for the ESG big-ticket item of climate change and emissions.

In what passes for due process in the ESG world, companies must first disclose their ESG metrics before they can be compelled to set sustainable targets for their business. This is why the initial focus of the ESG integration and engagement process has been on sustainable disclosure and reporting by companies. The entire ESG movement was never about simply factoring financially material ESG issues into corporate strategy and investment decisions. It is about investing for impact, aligning with the Paris Agreement, and achieving the SDGs set by the UN for 2030, even though none of this was part of the original ESG bargain when investors were first drawn into the trade by the siren's call of "responsible investing."

Should companies that do not disclose any ESG metrics be rated lower than issuers that set nonsensical targets based on reams of reported data? What if a company's ESG goals are simply aspirational or clearly unreachable or set so far in the future that they are effectively meaningless? Based on actuarial tables, most of the corporate executives now setting sustainable business targets will probably not be among the living when 2050 rolls around. Almost certainly, they will not be in their current management positions and still accountable. Do companies get ESG credit just for trying? Is ESG the financial market equivalent of a grade school participation trophy just for showing up?

Then there is the challenge of using ESG indicators to do peer group analysis, both within and across sectors. Given the step-change in the volume of metrics and the squaring of subjectivity when ESG moves from the company to the industry level, this routine quantitative exercise performed daily by Wall Street analysts now requires both Herculean effort and Solomonic judgment when applied to ESG. While energy and other carbon-emitting industries clearly reside at the low end of the ESG food chain, the cross-sector relationships become less clear-cut away from the core climate change thesis.

Are food and beverage producers such as Coca-Cola, PepsiCo Inc., General Mills Inc., and Kellogg Company that peddle sugary drinks and cereal products to children doing more harm than technology companies such as Alphabet Inc., Meta Platforms Inc., or Twitter Inc. whose social media applications are highly addictive and toxic for young minds? What about the negative societal impact of the online big-box merchandise juggernauts, Amazon and Walmart, which combined have laid waste to the brick-and-mortar retail sector in the US, shutting down local mom-and-pop shops, hollowing out small-town commercial districts, and turning shopping malls into ghostly structures mainly occupied by seasonal Halloween stores? Why did energy companies such as ExxonMobil and Shell and fast-food restaurants like MacDonald's Corporation all need to divest from Russia immediately after the country invaded Ukraine in February 2022, while media companies such as Disney, consumer electronics manufacturers like Apple, and sports apparel makers such as NIKE Inc. are given a pass to remain silent about the appalling human rights record and government policies of communist China, particularly the genocidal pogrom being conducted by Beijing against the Uyghur minority in Xinjiang province?

Looking to the third-party ESG experts for answers only adds to the confusion since each firm has its own unique ratings and scoring systems. Moreover, every company ESG report produced by MSCI and Sustainalytics approximates 100 pages and includes a staggering amount of minutiae, which is a clear violation of the Wall Street prime directive to "Keep it simple, stupid." Even if the analytical spirit were willing, it would take the average Wall Street analyst reading at a normal speed of 200 words per minute with no distractions a minimum of 2 to 3 hours to go through and thoroughly comprehend each ESG report, especially all the nonintuitive charts and graphs based on forced rankings rather than objective standing. This works out to a maximum of three ESG reports per day and approximately 15 to 25 workdays (3 to 4 workweeks) for the standard 50 to 75 companies within an analyst's coverage universe. And this math would be for just one ESG service provider.

ESG has now added a whole new pastime for financial analysts who must compare and contrast all of the ESG ratings by the leading third-party service providers, none of which match. Reconciling and justifying every ESG rating and score on individual companies is now a huge time sink for Wall Street. Take, for example, the case of Hess Corporation, the company formerly known as Amerada Hess, the global integrated oil and gas company and maker of the Hess toy truck. These days, Hess is a much smaller oil producer focused on two core operating areas: the Bakken

Shale in North Dakota and offshore Guyana. The company's carbon footprint, while currently modestly sized, is set to double over the next five years on the back of recent exploration success and increasing oil production out of Guyana, where it is partnered with ExxonMobil. Because of this, Sustainalytics places Hess in its High Risk ESG category with a 33.1 score. MSCI, on the other hand, gives the company its highest ESG rating of AAA based on its decarbonization goals and stated plans to decrease its emissions intensity even as its overall carbon emissions increase sharply. Good luck squaring that ESG circle.[2]

And then there is the fundamental disconnect between ESG ratings and the long-term credit ratings assigned by Moody's, S&P Global Ratings, Fitch, and the other NRSROs. For more than a century, these credit ratings have been used by the financial markets as the main predictor of bond default and bankruptcy risk. Corporate sustainability is another way of saying business solvency, which begs the question as to why ESG ratings are needed in the first place. While the NRSROs are not perfect and often get it wrong with their ratings, the current system works well and obviates the need for a new ESG-driven approach to divine true sustainability. This reality hasn't deterred ESG activists from their mission to ultimately supplant the NRSROs as the only ratings game in town.

Juxtaposing the two ratings systems highlights the inherent contradiction between ESG factors and corporate credit quality. Credit ratings are based on objective financial metrics and are designed to be comparable across industries as well as between corporates, financial institutions, and sovereign issuers so as to maximize the utility to investors and other market participants. ESG ratings, on the other hand, are highly subjective, nonfungible, and meant more to send a message to company management rather than protect investors from potential financial loss. The ESG movement primarily targets publicly traded industrial companies headquartered in developed countries in North America and Europe due to the size of their environmental and carbon footprints and their political vulnerability to media and other forms of public pressure – not because such issuers are particularly exposed to financially material ESG issues. To the contrary, US and European industrial companies have larger asset bases, more diversified business mixes, and greater financial flexibility, the combination of which results in solid investment grade credit ratings on average.

For example, the two US integrated oil and gas companies, Chevron and ExxonMobil, are strongly misaligned with the Paris Agreement as per Sustainalytics and carry fairly low ESG ratings from both MSCI and Sustainalytics. Chevron has an ESG rating of A at MSCI and a 36.6 High Risk ESG score from Sustainalytics; ExxonMobil has a BBB MSCI rating and a 41.6 Severe Risk score at Sustainalytics. At Moody's and S&P Global Ratings, the debt of both benchmark energy names is rated Aa2/AA–, at the upper end of the investment grade spectrum. The probability of companies rated in the Aa/AA category defaulting on their outstanding debt approaches zero. Yet, in the topsy-turvy world of ESG investing, both Chevron and ExxonMobil are classified as unsustainable, even though the two maligned integrated majors are the successors to the Standard Oil Company and Trust founded by John D. Rockefeller in the late 19th century. Chevron and ExxonMobil have each been around for more than 140 years, surviving two world wars, the Great Depression, and repeated oil price collapses over recent decades, yet the market is somehow supposed to worry about their financial health and life expectancy.[3]

The irony is that large, investment grade industrial companies – whether energy, chemicals, mining, or manufacturing – based in OECD countries have proven to be some of the most sustainable investments by providing exceptional asset coverage for bondholders. Moreover, investment grade companies have stronger track records when it comes to any objective measure of environmental (pollution spills), social (health and safety), and governance (transparency and disclosure) policies, along with better financial disclosure and reporting standards. Based on S&P Global Ratings data, over 1981–2021, the cumulative 15-year default rate for investment grade rated companies was 2.55%.[4] When the rare investment grade default does occur, it is usually due to idiosyncratic factors such as excessive leverage or occasionally fraud being flushed out by turns in the market, interest rate, or economic cycles.

In an interesting bit of ESG trivia dating back to the 2008 global financial crisis, in March of that fateful year when Lehman Brothers was struggling to survive and only six months from death, the company was forced to fend off a shareholder resolution related to sustainability during its final spring proxy season. As proposed by the Free Enterprise Action Fund, the proud owner of 452 Lehman shares at the time, the investment bank was asked to prepare an Environmental Sustainability Report by October 2008 detailing the company's plan to integrate environmental sustainability into all its operations. While the proposal was voted down, it is noteworthy that the report due date would have been roughly 30 days after the planet Lehman exploded – a stark reminder that the ESG agenda has nothing to do with company fundamentals, financial returns, or capital preservation. It completely ignores the one and only sustainability issue that should matter for Wall Street: bankruptcy.

There is no proven positive correlation between ESG factors and corporate fundamentals. If anything, the opposite is true. Often, when companies try to burnish their ESG image by setting virtuous sustainability targets, such efforts have a negative impact on credit quality and fundamental value due to their up-front costs and unquantifiable long-term monetary benefits – this on top of the distraction and time sink for executives and employees. For example, setting a net-zero target for one's business, while currently all the rage, is not a cost-free exercise. Depending on the company and the magnitude of the undertaking, it may involve some or all of the following: buying carbon offset credits; signing long-term wind and solar power purchase agreements; electrifying an entire vehicle fleet and building out the requisite in-house charging infrastructure; buying more expensive renewable transportation fuels to displace gasoline, diesel, and jet fuel volumes; and allocating scarce capital toward risky, unproven technologies such as carbon capture and sequestration (CCS). Carbon offsets, which are mainly used to plant trees in the developed world or pay developing countries not to cut down trees, currently cost about $3–4 per ton of CO_2 equivalent, although Bloomberg recently estimated that this cost could increase roughly 50-fold by 2050.[5] The cost of an electric Class 4–6 delivery van averages between $100,000 and $200,000, while an electric Class 8 freight truck goes for more than $300,000 – more than double what the internal combustion engine version would run. Biodiesel costs roughly twice as much as regular diesel, while sustainable aviation fuel – if you can get your hands on enough of the stuff – costs more than two to four times the average price of jet fuel. As for the chimera of CCS, The Southern Company, the Georgia-based regulated utility, wasted roughly $6.2 billion trying to make the technology work on its Kemper coal gasification and carbon capture power plant in Mississippi before finally pulling the plug on the project in 2017. The company's electricity rate payers and shareholders will bear most of the cost for this failure of technology and management.[6]

Apart from decarbonizing, increasing unionization rates to appease labor activists leads to a more expensive and rigid workforce while increasing the potential for work disruptions and stoppages around the contract renegotiation cycle. Hiring workers based on quotas rather than job skills and qualifications leads to higher training costs and, depending on the industry, may increase the risk of safety incidents. Cutting better deals for both customers and suppliers, baking in charitable contributions above the pretax line, and maximizing corporate tax payments – all in the interest of fairness – only serves to squeeze margins and shrink operating cash flow. The fact that ESG is antithetical to fundamental credit quality and financial strength should not come as a shock given that climate change and sustainable development have always been wealth redistribution programs at their heart.

Lastly, even after eight years of integration and engagement, ESG is still not affecting market pricing, much to the chagrin of activists. Apart from one-off negative headlines, ESG does not drive relative value and, thus far, has had no discernible impact on stock and bond prices or the availability or cost of capital for different sectors and issuing companies. Debt and equity markets don't move in lockstep and often react differently to the same news, whether company announcements or macro-developments, which does not jibe with the one-size-fits-all approach of ESG with its binary moral judgments. While the financial markets are efficient and capable of pricing all manner of risk – including actual, material business, financial, and legal risks related to environmental, social, and governance issues – and always factor in future expectations, they are not equipped to handle ESG futurism and corporate aspirations to be net-zero or SDG compliant some 10, 20, or 30 years down the road.

When the financial markets are faced with risks and uncertainties that cannot be priced – including known unknowns such as global terrorism and geopolitical risk – the typical response is to just ignore the issue and deal with it tomorrow, much like Scarlett O'Hara in *Gone with the Wind*. To date, the market response to the subjective system of ESG, which rests on the implicit threat of government action against noncompliant businesses and the potential loss of some theoretical social license that companies supposedly need to operate and fund themselves, has been to disregard it from a pricing perspective. Sustainable activists should probably count their blessings that this has been the case because if ESG factors were actually being taken seriously from a financial perspective as claimed, the market response to the recent flurry of distant open-ended management ESG promises would have been decidedly negative. If a publicly traded media company promised to respond in due course to a competitive threat from a new social platform by rolling out its own killer app by 2050, its share price would get pummeled. If an overleveraged high-yield industrial company with a looming maturity wall announced plans to pay down outstanding debt and strengthen its balance sheet over the course of the next decade, the response would be a sharp sell-off in its bonds.

The fact that ESG does not drive market pricing places Wall Street analysts in a difficult position when making research and portfolio calls since any recommendation based solely on ESG considerations, especially climate change, would leave a lot of money on the table at this point. Take the previously noted case of Energy Transfer, the maligned midstream company whose DAPL pipeline project has run afoul of Native American and environmental groups. Since 2017, the company has been branded as a violator of the UNGC. Because of this designation, many accounts – mostly European – have increasingly dropped the name from their portfolios, even though Energy Transfer accounts for roughly 10% of the Alerian MLP Infrastructure Index on the equity side and stands as the largest energy company issuer in most corporate bond indexes. Over the past seven years while the ESG press coverage of Energy Transfer and its management team was uniformly negative, the company also sharply decreased its capital spending, simplified its corporate structure, cut its distribution, and became free cash flow positive, which has facilitated the deleveraging of the firm's balance sheet. Most of the benefits from these management moves have accrued to Energy Transfer bondholders rather than shareholders. Between January 1, 2017, and December 31, 2021, Energy Transfer bonds outperformed both the energy subindex and the overall credit market. Any bond investor that screened out Energy Transfer on moral ESG grounds over the post-DAPL five-year period would have missed out on stellar returns. For any bond fund whose performance was measured against a benchmark index, the pain would have been amplified by the sizable market value of the company's outstanding bonds ($40.9 billion as of year-end 2021).

Just as avoiding certain names due to negative ESG perceptions can be detrimental to investment performance, so too can buying the securities of companies chiefly based on sustainability attributes and the mistaken belief that ESG is some kind of magic talisman capable of warding off all other negative drivers. All the leading US and European corporations that announced, to great fanfare, net-zero emissions targets during 2021 – including FedEx, General Motors, HP, and The Procter & Gamble Company – have seen their stock prices decline during the recent sharp market downturn driven by Federal Reserve monetary policy tightening and a slowing US economy. In 2022, the S&P 500 Index dropped by 19.44%,[7] with indiscriminate selling across the board and all sectors trading down except for energy, which was up 59.05% on the full year.[8] Just as there are no atheists in foxholes, no one ever pounds the table about ESG being a positive catalyst for long-term value creation in the middle of a market rout or when the broader indexes are moving into bear territory. ESG is a vanity project best suited for bull markets when volatility is low and analytical skills are dulled. Based on Morningstar data, net inflows into US sustainable funds turned negative during the second quarter of 2022 for the first time in five years and were barely positive for all of 2022.[9]

However, for a Wall Street analyst, pointing out the obvious contradictions of ESG can be toxic for one's livelihood. With ESG, as with every totalitarian system, there is no real room for analyst discretion or independent thought – plus you can't opt out of the program. Blowing off ESG or responding with a *no más* like Roberto Durán is not politically advisable given the pressure from all sides to conform, including from senior management, colleagues, and clients. Analysts who don't get on board with the ESG program – especially when it comes to climate action and the need to decarbonize – run the risk of not getting paid or being canceled. This is why Wall Street research analysts, who are paid to have an opinion and a differentiated view, are not speaking out about ESG and why no one currently working in the business has ever publicly questioned the sustainability orthodoxy. While the sounds of silence from the research rank and file are deafening – particularly from those analysts covering the oil and gas industry who will soon be out of a job if ESG investing is taken to its logical conclusion – the response is understandable given that Wall Street's motto has always been to keep your head down and focus on making money.

Some fundamental analysts – especially those covering the beleaguered energy and power sectors who are worried about their long-term job prospects in a transitioning world – have chosen to switch rather than fight, rebranding themselves as ESG specialists to increase their employment opportunities and take advantage of the recent explosion in hiring for sustainability-related roles across Wall Street. While a good short-term career move, such capitulation will only amplify the cognitive dissonance for those classically trained financial analysts opting for such Vichy-style ESG collaboration. ESG is a field best suited for sociology and gender- and race-studies majors, environmental activists, and professional social justice warriors. It is incompatible with the quantitative disciplines of economics, finance, and investments and antithetical to free-market capitalism. Analytical minds need not – or should not – apply.

What the ESG investment movement is attempting is truly breathtaking: a centrally planned global financial system designed to control the availability, allocation, and pricing of capital for different industries and individual companies based on their ESG or corporate social credit score. To achieve this goal, ESG uses the French Revolution as its model. During the 1790s, the revolutionaries running France tried to reorder all aspects of French and global society by developing new mathematical systems organized around neat groupings of 10 and used for the measurement of everything – units, weights, and even time. One common language – French – was also mandated for the entire country and, under the newly defined concept of French citizenship, all individual rights were subjugated to those of the "will of the community." Anyone caught criticizing the new enlightened way of doing things in France was imprisoned or executed, especially during the bloody Jacobin Reign of Terror when an estimated 17,000 people were guillotined.

In many ways, ESG is the financial market equivalent. The incredible ESG conceit that the financial performance of companies should be measured not by operating margins, cash flow generation, interest coverage, and leverage metrics but instead by such things as emissions levels, water consumption, electricity usage, and the skin color and chromosomal makeup (rather than the character) of their workforce is much like Revolutionary France decreeing that there be 100 minutes in an hour and 10 hours in a day and trying to replace the Gregorian calendar with a decimalized version. ESG aspires to be the one common financial language spoken on Wall Street. The ESG brand of stakeholder capitalism states that companies should be run for the benefit of society, which echoes the concept of the general will popularized by Rousseau and incorporated into the Declaration of the Rights of Man and of the Citizen by the French National Assembly in 1789. And just like back in the days of Robespierre, many on Wall Street – individuals as well as firms – are now terrified to speak out against ESG for fear of retribution or public charges of *J'accuse*.

The ESG goal of redefining the meaning of sustainable companies by replacing objective financial metrics with subjective moral criteria is yet another example of the progressive tactics of manipulating language and lowering standards that have been used very effectively to undermine other parts of society for decades, particularly the field of education. ESG is intended to debase and degrade the field of financial analysis and create controversy that deflects attention away from the sustainability movement and its takeover of the global financial system. A nominally voluntary approach to ESG adoption up until now has led to a modern-day Tower of Babel going up on Wall Street in recent years, with everyone talking past each other and no one comprehending the other. In the absence of standardization and any correlation with asset pricing, trying to select stocks and bonds on the basis of ESG factors is basically an exercise in picking colors. In the words of the late Pope Benedict XVI, ESG is a "dictatorship of relativism," with no absolute truths or objective standards. Arguably, ESG has always been a system designed to collapse under its own weight, with its resultant analysis paralysis providing the necessary pretext for regulatory intervention to impose government order on all the ESG chaos, consistent with the stated policy goals of the PRI and other sustainability activists.

CHAPTER 8

SUSTAINABLE RETURNS AND ESG PERFORMANCE ART

> *Nobody would confess that he couldn't see anything, for that would prove him either unfit for his position, or a fool.*
> Hans Christian Andersen, "The Emperor's New Clothes"

> *Go forth to find it, and it is gone: 'tis only a mirage as you look from the windows of diligence.*
> Ralph Waldo Emerson

ESG advocates have long argued that helping society and outperforming the market are not mutually exclusive activities. Sustainable investors really can have it all. Benjamin Franklin was on to something when he talked about "doing well by doing good." No need for after-tax charitable donations when your investments are already saving the world pretax.

According to the ESG party line, companies need to embrace sustainability to ensure "long-term value creation," while investors need to employ a responsible approach built on financially material ESG factors if they want to consistently outperform over the long term. In the words of the PRI, "Responsible investment can and should be pursued by the investor whose sole focus is financial performance."[1] Such performance guarantees, though, are heavily qualified and hedged with words like "could," "can," "may," and "should," which shows the lack of conviction on the part of ESG champions when it comes to financial return. Moreover, the long-term investment horizon is never actually defined. Like the actual horizon, it is something that is always just over the next hillside and forever out of reach.

After years of ESG integration and engagement, the financial promises of sustainable investing have not panned out. PRI membership currently totals nearly 5,400 signatories who, between them, manage more than $121 trillion in 2021 AUM. Adjusting for double counting, this implies that almost all invested AUM worldwide, which PwC estimated at $112.3 trillion in 2020,[2] is now subject to the ESG membership restrictions of the PRI. And yet, to date, empirical evidence has shown little correlation between ESG factors, corporate performance, and investment returns, mainly because ESG factors and moral considerations are still not driving the prices of debt and equity securities.

This point has been clearly illustrated by the market performance of the carbon-emitting energy sector over the past few years. Sustainable activists agree that climate change is the highest-priority ESG issue facing investors. In a sea of ESG metrics, decarbonizing and getting to net zero are the goals that always bubble to the surface. Energy is the most targeted sector on the PRI's Collaboration Platform, which is basically a public space where members can gang up on companies – much like teenage girls do on YouTube, Snapchat, and TikTok. Yet, such uniformity of climate opinion has not led to an exodus of investors from the energy sector or any discernible impact on capital market receptivity for energy issuers.

Following the 2014 shale-driven reset in global oil prices, the energy sector struggled for years to regain its financial footing and adapt to the new reality of an oversupplied world market. Spurred on by activist hedge funds and shareholders, management teams gradually came around to the need for capital spending discipline rather than reserve and production growth for growth's sake. Continued commodity price volatility, including the bottom dropping out again for oil prices during the fourth quarter of 2018, helped to reinforce this message while flushing out the last remaining overleveraged high-yield operators still hanging on from 2014. Nonetheless, US shale did not finally get that old-time religion about its business model until 2020, when the combination of an OPEC+ oil market share battle and COVID-19 pandemic lockdowns briefly turned crude oil prices negative, pushing more than 100 North American oil and gas companies into bankruptcy by year's end. The industry's near-death experience with negative oil prices in 2020 caused almost every surviving US energy company to embrace fully the concept of capital discipline and the need for free cash flow generation and shareholder returns. Toward this end, most US energy companies immediately laid down drilling rigs, turned off capital spending, and slashed operating costs and headcount. While the industry restructuring had taken nearly six years – with macrobroadsides along the way – the energy sector was in much better shape exiting 2020.

Given this fundamental improvement, it is not surprising that investors piled back into the sector beginning in 2021 as crude oil prices rebounded sharply, making energy the best-performing sector in both the equity and debt markets for the year. On the equity side, the S&P 500 Index increased by 26.89% in 2021,[3] while the Energy subindex jumped by 47.74%.[4] In fact, the best-performing company equity in the entire S&P 500 Index during 2021 was Devon Energy Corporation, a shale-focused US independent oil and gas producer, with a total return of 178.62%.[5] On the debt side, energy bonds also outperformed sharply in 2021, with the sector besting both the investment grade and high-yield credit markets. This energy sector momentum carried over into 2022 as the Russian invasion of Ukraine in February and the energy sanctions that it triggered led to a further increase in world oil prices, pushing WTI crude up from an average of $39.16 per barrel in 2020 and $68.13 in 2021 to over $120 by March 2022 and an average of $94.90 for the full year. In 2022, the S&P 500 Energy subindex jumped by 59.05%,[6] even as the broader equity market declined by 19.44%, while investment grade and high-yield energy bonds again outperformed on a relative basis.

Moreover, borrowing costs have not been rising for oil and gas companies. Apart from the recent increase in interest rates affecting all issuers, energy credit spreads have not been widening. Also, there has been a record amount of new energy bond issuance over the past few years, notably beginning in the tough trough year of 2020. Also, credit curves are not steepening for energy issuers, which would seem to indicate a lack of concern about potential stranded asset risk around the much-ballyhooed global energy transition. Notably, there has been no change in the appetite of institutional investors for 30-year energy bonds, which would seem to imply skepticism about the ability of the corporate sector to get to net zero by 2050. So even though the oil and gas industry will never be able to reconcile itself with SDG #13 (Climate Action) or achieve the PRI's #1 priority ESG goal, there appears to be no shortage of energy sector buyers at the right price.

The market persistence of the energy sector in the face of growing ESG criticism highlights the old Wall Street axiom, "There are no bad stocks or bonds, only bad securities prices." Dynamic pricing that reflects all currently available information is what allows the financial markets to clear and function properly – no different than the broader economy with its invisible hand of countless commercial transactions each day. On Wall Street, as in all free-market capitalist systems, pricing is an automatic and amoral mechanism that doesn't take sides between buyers and sellers and doesn't care what is being sold. The fact that energy debt and equity prices have not been affected by years of climate change and ESG hectoring should give pause to the sustainability movement, along with previous failed attempts targeting sin stocks such as tobacco, alcohol, private prisons, and defense manufacturers. If financial asset prices never respond to ESG integration and engagement, then this undercuts the argument that ESG will create long-term value for investors and lead to a sustainable global financial system.

This has not stopped a steady stream of Rorschachesque research being pumped out by Wall Street, business schools, and ESG activists in recent years to bolster the case for sustainable investing by establishing an ESG correlation with return performance – however weak and statistically insignificant. Notably, none of these papers points to specific company examples of ESG being a positive value catalyst. Rather, observation is replaced by interpolation. The typical ESG research approach is to take a 10,000-foot view of aggregated market data over time to paint an impressionistic picture. Like a Monet painting, it looks good from far away but, viewed up close, it is just a mess of random color streaks. Many ESG studies are second-order studies of other ESG research published over varying time periods. The fact that ESG activists must journey to the metadata universe to find the answers that they are looking for should call to mind the similarly spurious research approach used to fabricate the original 97% and now 99% scientific consensus about climate change.

Often, self-serving and exceedingly short time periods – sometimes a year or less – are used to extrapolate out ESG investing trends, which does nothing to bolster the case for long-term value creation. In March 2020, when government officials opted to shut down the global economy to deal with the COVID-19 pandemic, oil and gas names took it on the chin while technology companies were the main beneficiaries of the new stay-at-home protocol. Even as the world was locking down, ESG partisans were quick to highlight how sustainable funds outperformed during the first quarter of 2020, with 51 out of 57 Morningstar sustainable indexes and 15 of 17 MSCI sustainable indexes beating their broad market counterparts during the three-month period.[7]

Much of the ESG academic and investment research is flawed by definitional problems around what constitutes a sustainable company and the inherent difficulties with isolating the impact of specific ESG factors on corporate performance – especially if different sets of ESG ratings and scores are used. Then there are the challenges of separating alpha from beta factors when disaggregating returns, adjusting for sectoral tilt and quality bias, and controlling for different economic and market environments, particularly before and after the 2008 global financial crisis.

One of the most comprehensive empirical studies on the relationship between ESG and corporate financial performance was published in the *Journal of Sustainable Finance & Investment* in 2015 by the German academic team of Gunnar Friede, Timo Busch, and Alexander Bassen. Their research paper aggregated evidence from nearly all the ESG review studies conducted between 1970 and 2014, the majority of which focused on equities (87%). Looking at both simple vote-count studies (positive, negative, or neutral, winner-take-all) and econometric reviews or meta-analyses (studies of studies), the authors culled 60 review studies from this period encompassing approximately 2,200 unique individual academic studies for their second- and third-level review project. The study captures a broad view of corporate financial performance, which it defines dizzyingly as accounting-based performance, market-based performance, operational performance, perceptional performance, growth metrics, risk measures, and the performance of ESG funds and portfolios.

Given the different methodologies used in the thousands of primary studies underlying their review project and the multiple degrees of separation from the raw data, it is difficult to generalize from their findings that roughly 90% of the 60 review studies analyzed found a nonnegative correlation between ESG and corporate financial performance. For one thing, spinning the headline takeaway in this manner obscures the fact that the nonnegative category includes not just positive but also neutral and mixed findings, the latter two of which comprised in the aggregate

41% of vote-count studies. Only 47.9% of 35 vote-count studies and 62.6% of 25 meta-analyses actually found a positive correlation with ESG factors, and even then with a fairly weak average correlation level of 0.15. Even though their analysis only found that "empiric studies suggest a positive ESG relation," the Friede study was nonetheless categorical in its conclusions that "the business case for ESG investing is empirically very well founded" and "investing in ESG pays financially." Perhaps the strength of their conviction had something to do with the support that their ESG research project received from the PRI, a potential conflict of interest that was not reported by the authors.[8]

In 2020, the NYU Stern CSB rolled forward the work of the Friede group with its own "ESG and Financial Performance" study, which was published with financial support from Rockefeller Asset Management, a leading proponent of ESG integration and sustainable investing. The CSB study, which was designed to assess "whether it pays to be sustainable," conducted a quantitative analysis on an estimated 80% of the peer-reviewed academic research papers on sustainability published between 2015 and 2020. The study was subsequently updated in 2022 to capture the distorted COVID-19 period through May 2021. The total research universe started at 2,714 papers – which works out to more than one study per day during the six-year period, on a par with the climate research propaganda machine – before being boiled down to a representative 238 primary studies and 15 metareviews. This sample was then divided into two categories: those studies focused on corporate financial performance (e.g., operating metrics such as return on equity and return on assets or share price performance) and those studies focused on investment performance (e.g., idiosyncratic alpha measurement or Sharpe ratio calculations for a portfolio). The CSB's meta-analysis of 238 primary studies found a positive relationship between ESG and corporate financial performance in 60% of corporate studies focused on operating metrics – slightly better than even but still basically a coin toss, with a fairly low correlation coefficient between 0.05 and 0.13. For investment studies, though, only 38% of ESG funds surveyed showed similar or better performance relative to traditional investment approaches. As the paper noted, while there is "robust evidence for corporate managers that justify investments in sustainability for better corporate financial performance," the "returns from ESG investing – averaged across many portfolio management strategies – are indistinguishable from conventional investing." These "stylized facts" were confirmed by the CSB's meta-meta-analysis of its sampled 15 quantitative metareviews.

This schizophrenic finding is devastating to the case for ESG investing. How can it pay for companies to keep investing in sustainability if the financial markets don't recognize and reward the value? Who exactly is going to voluntarily fund all of this sustainable growth by the corporate sector if Wall Street doesn't view all this operating and capital spending as a fundamental positive? Scrambling, the CSB study qualified its analysis by despairing of the noise created by the variability of ESG data and the lack of distinction between different investment strategies, while decrying the same underlying methodological challenges that plagued the previous work of the Friede group. Then the CSB authors quickly changed the subject by confidently concluding the following: improved financial performance due to ESG becomes more marked over longer time horizons; ESG integration as an investment strategy seems to perform better than screening or divestment; ESG investing provides asymmetric benefits and downside protection, especially during a social or economic crisis; sustainability initiatives at corporations appear to drive better financial performance due to mediating factors such as improved risk management and more innovation; studies indicate that managing for a low-carbon future improves financial performance; and ESG disclosure on its own does not drive financial performance. Given the conflicting results of its research, these main takeaways are more a projected ESG wish list than anything else.[9]

Professor George Serafeim of Harvard Business School is another vocal public advocate for sustainability and stakeholder capitalism who has written extensively about ESG in recent years. Like much of the academic research on the subject, his work represents a quixotic search for quantitative justification for his personal ESG beliefs, including his novel theory that institutional and retail investors are "stewards of the commons" and have an important role to play in the process of social change,[10] which is another way of saying that investors need to become social activists. To date, the analytical proof that he has offered for the proposition that ESG leads to market outperformance remains unconvincing. His 2016 study "Corporate Sustainability: First Evidence on Materiality," which he cowrote with Mozaffar Khan and Aaron Yoon, found that investments in sustainability issues are shareholder-value enhancing and "firms with strong ratings on material sustainability issues [will] significantly outperform firms with poor ratings" in the future, based on an analysis of the stock market performance of 2,307 companies over 1991–2012. During this period, top-quintile performers on material ESG factors, as determined by the combination of MSCI ESG ratings and the SASB's materiality map by industry, generated an estimated 269 basis points more of annual alpha versus bottom quintile performers in an equal-weighted portfolio. While a headline-grabbing number, there is no way to drill down into the raw data to isolate the source of such incremental alpha by company, given the 30-factor SASB materiality map with differential weightings used for each industry. Also, a large part of the superior sustainable performance observed over the two-decade survey period was likely owing to ESG ratings upgrades driven by methodology changes rather than specific company initiatives, given that this was early days in the sustainability movement and the ESG rating agencies were still making up the rules as they went along.[11]

In his solo follow-up 2018 study, "Public Sentiment and the Price of Corporate Sustainability," which looked at a universe of 8,000 companies over the post–financial crisis years of 2009–2018, Serafeim qualified the findings from his previous joint 2016 study. Using a combination of MSCI ESG scores, basic market valuation metrics, and a big-data search of the more than 250,000 ESG articles published (in English only) over the 10-year period, Serafeim found that "the valuation premium paid for companies with strong sustainability performance has increased over time," but only because of the exogenous factor of "positive public sentiment momentum." Based on this revised thinking, it is public sentiment that influences investor views about the value of corporate sustainability activities and both the price paid for corporate sustainability and the investment returns of portfolios that consider ESG data. If sustainable investors want to outperform, then combining ESG performance scores with big ESG data would be helpful in identifying stocks with superior and undervalued ESG characteristics. Notably, such an approach would consign analysts and portfolio managers to forever monitoring the airwaves to somehow gauge public sentiment toward individual companies, while also diminishing their agency role in the investment function. It would effectively delegate investment decision-making to the global assembly of sustainability-focused NGOs, think tanks, and media outlets, all with ties to the UN and the WEF.[12]

Also, the 2018 Serafeim paper was distorted by the same underlying ESG ratings issues as the 2016 study. As *Bloomberg Businessweek* noted in its 2021 article on MSCI's ESG franchise, methodology tweaks continue to drive a significant portion of ESG ratings changes through the current day. During one 18-month stretch from the start of 2020 through the middle of 2021, roughly one-half of the 155 ESG rating upgrades MSCI awarded to S&P 500 companies were owing to changes in the way that MSCI calculated scores, rather than any change in the companies' behavior. In the same article, *Bloomberg Businessweek* also lamented how MSCI's ESG ratings didn't "even try to measure the impact of a corporation on the world" but instead were focused on "the potential impact of the world on the company and its shareholders." In the authors' opinion, such an ESG ratings approach "flips the very notion of sustainable investing on its head for many investors."[13]

Wall Street firms have also tried to make the analytical case for sustainable investing. The Morgan Stanley Institute for Sustainable Investing published a white paper in 2019 with the findings from its study of the relative performance of sustainable funds across multiple asset classes from 2004 to 2018. Using Morningstar data on 10,723 exchange-traded and open-end mutual equity and debt funds, the study compared the total returns (net of performance fees) and downside deviation of ESG-focused funds versus their traditional fund counterparts. The study found that the total returns of sustainable equity and debt funds were in line with those of traditional funds, with no meaningful difference in return performance between the two. Morgan Stanley also found that sustainable funds reduced volatility and downside deviation during the 2004–2018 survey period. Based on these results, the paper concluded that one can invest sustainably without sacrificing financial returns. The only problem with this analysis, though, is the fact that most sustainable funds are closet benchmark funds and index cheaters – tweaking a sector allocation here and a particular name there – so their performance will almost always mirror that of traditional funds since they deliberately minimize their active position so as to shadow the broader market. Moreover, the downside protection highlighted by the report was insignificant throughout the survey period except for instances of market turbulence such as 2008, 2014–2015, and 2018 – all of which were periods when crude oil prices dropped precipitously, causing the energy sector to underperform and benefiting sustainable funds sporting underweight positions – however slight – versus the industry.[14]

Zeroing in on the debt markets, Barclays Capital published a research report in 2018 that analyzed how ESG ratings affected credit spreads and excess return performance in both the US and European bond markets over the 2009–2018 period. The discrete, rated company universes for both MSCI and Sustainalytics were each segmented into high and low ESG scoring cohorts to compare their relative bond market performance over time. The results, however, were confusing. Barclays found that, since the 2008 global financial crisis, the spread premium between high and low ESG scoring companies (i.e., higher-rated issuers trade at tighter credit spreads) in the investment grade bond market had averaged between 31 and 36 basis points in the US and between 15 and 22 basis points in Europe, while compressing over time. Despite trading at a spread concession, Barclays also found that high ESG scoring companies generated significant excess returns (i.e., incremental return over a riskless Treasury security with the same maturity) versus their low-scoring counterparts using either MSCI or Sustainalytics as the ratings frame of reference. For US investment grade bonds, the excess return advantage averaged 27–43 basis points more per year, while for European investment grade bonds the annual pickup averaged 43–51 basis points. In addition, Barclays found that high-scoring ESG companies in both the US and European markets generated a cumulative 3.50–4.50% more of total return based on MSCI scores and a cumulative 2.50–3.50% more using Sustainalytics ratings. It is difficult to reconcile these analytical results. Typically, higher-quality bonds marked by compressed spreads don't tend to outperform outside of flight to quality market moves, which was not the case for most of the low-interest-rate and low-volatility 2009–2018 survey period. Moreover, most of the higher ESG–rated companies in the study were scored one or two notches higher in terms of credit ratings than their lower ESG counterparts, which would seem to indicate that the study was simply capturing stronger corporate credit quality and better-run companies, consistent with Barclays Capital's conclusion that governance was the most important of the ESG factors.[15]

Recently, some publications have started to point out the obvious problems and inherent contradictions associated with the theory of ESG investing. A 2020 joint research study by the Korea Advanced Institute of Science and Technology and Northwestern University found that becoming a PRI signatory and implementing an ESG framework often results in decreased portfolio returns and alpha generation,[16] which should not come as a shock. Integrating 17 UN SDGs and hundreds of related corporate targets into a firm-wide investment process tends to have a stupefying and stultifying effect. Haranguing company management teams about ESG esoterica eats up a lot of time, and only distracts from real fundamentals and market monitoring. Excluding certain sectors (particularly commodity cyclicals like energy) will eventually catch up with you.

In 2021, Scientific Beta, a joint venture between the Singapore Exchange Limited and the EDHEC Business School Risk Institute, released a scathing report stating that there was no solid evidence supporting the claims that ESG strategies generate outperformance. In their study, the researchers at Scientific Beta reconstructed 12 ESG strategies that had been shown to outperform in popular papers and then assessed the performance benefits to investors when accounting for sector biases, factor exposures, downside risk, and attention shifts. The study found that, when accounting for exposure to standard factors, none of the 12 different strategies that tilted toward ESG leaders added significant outperformance, whether in the US or other developed markets outside of the US. To the contrary, roughly 75% of any positive alpha identified was attributable to quality factors that were mechanically constructed from balance sheet information. The Scientific Beta team also found that ESG strategies do not offer significant downside risk protection either. When accounting for the exposure of each ESG strategy to a downside risk factor, it did not alter its conclusion that there was no value added beyond implicit exposure to standard factors such as quality. Lastly, the paper noted that claims of positive alpha in popular industry publications were not valid because the analysis underlying these claims was flawed and skewed by the increase in investor attention around ESG seen since 2013. As the authors concluded, "Omitting necessary risk adjustments and selecting a recent period with upward attention shifts enables the documenting of outperformance where in reality there is none."[17]

Still other academic research studies have started to call out the suspect nature of all the ESG ratings and scores now swamping the financial markets. In a 2020 paper titled "Sense and Nonsense in ESG Ratings," Ingo Walter, Professor Emeritus of Finance at NYU Stern, noted that "ESG ratings seem conceptually and practically challenged," and "composite ESG-scoring and its use as a guide to capital allocation, business strategy, and public policy seems a stretch." Even though "alphanumeric displays and rankings tend to command disproportionate attention in most people's minds," Walter highlighted a list of key weaknesses with ESG ratings including "identification and causality problems, self-reporting and greenwashing, quality of the primary data collection process, indicator mismatch in the use of secondary data, factor aggregation and weighting, setting scoring breaks, and reporting formats."[18] Other than that, the current system works fine. Similarly, in a 2022 research report titled "ESG Ratings: A Compass without Direction" published by the joint academic team of David F. Larcker, Lukasz Pomorski, Brian Tayan, and Edward M. Watts from the Stanford Graduate School of Business and the Yale School of Management, the authors concluded that "while ESG ratings providers may convey important insights into the nonfinancial impact of companies, significant shortcomings exist in their objectives, methodologies, and incentives which detract from the informativeness of their assessments."[19]

Even Professor Serafeim of Harvard seems to be coming around to the failings of ESG as an investment approach. In his 2021 working paper "ESG: Hyperboles and Reality," which presented a synopsis of his ESG work to date, Serafeim made several observations that seemingly undercut many of his previous research conclusions. For example, he noted that the capital markets do not react significantly to the "vast majority of ESG news," which indicates that such news is largely irrelevant for assessing the value of companies and implies that investors do not place much reliance on ESG information. Also, he noted that "one cannot have much confidence in the performance outcomes of most ESG investment products." Since most ESG products are quasi-index funds designed to minimize tracking error and only change portfolio weights on holdings to optimize certain ESG metrics or ratings, these sustainable funds will always deliver very close performance to their respective market benchmarks.[20]

The accumulated body of ESG research can best be described as a dog's breakfast of analysis – more promotional and aspirational than confirmatory and conclusive. Through no lack of trying on the part of sustainable proponents, no compelling quantitative data has yet been produced to demonstrate that investors can consistently outperform over the long term by relying on nonfinancial ESG factors. At best, the research published to date suggests some correlation, while critically failing to distinguish between coincidence and causality. However, with each less-than-satisfying report hinting at the appearance of some relationship between ESG and investment returns, there are calls for still more research and a redoubling of efforts to confirm the foregone conclusion of ESG outperformance. As with climate change, there has been an ESG publishing frenzy in recent years to overwhelm the opposition and smother ESG critics with a mountain of research papers. At another level, it is amusing that academic studies are being used to prove to traders and portfolio managers that there is money to be made in ESG. Much as a bloodhound has no use for a picture, Wall Street has never needed a diagram to help it sniff out profitable new market opportunities before.

Most of the quantitative analysis used to prove the ESG argument is hindered by two major problems. First, it is almost impossible to isolate the financial impact and performance contribution of scores of subjective ESG factors that vary by industry, country, and market and also interact with and often offset each other. Separating out ESG factors from fundamental company drivers is also problematic. In this regard, including the G in the mix only serves to confuse the issue and obscure the analysis. Since governance or management quality is central to any corporate investment, the G becomes a catchall for everything. The tautology that well-run companies tend to perform better over the long term, both operationally and financially, is then used to prove that ESG is a positive catalyst. Conversely, any unexpected headline or event affecting stock and bond prices – even missing quarterly earnings guidance – is now taken to indicate a governance or ESG problem to further bolster the case for responsible investing.

Second, there is the price signaling problem. Despite years of pushing sustainability and integrating ESG into the global financial system, equity and debt prices are still not reacting to any of the myriad ESG ratings, scores, factors, and themes swirling around the market. This nonresponse is basically the market's way of saying either that the entire ESG agenda is financially immaterial or that sustainable investment horizons are too distant to be discounted back into current prices or both. Just as the genetically reconstructed Tyrannosaurus Rex in the movie *Jurassic Park* cannot see nonmoving creatures, the financial markets do not see ESG as an important pricing variable. If financial asset prices never respond to ESG factors, there is no way that sustainable investing can ever pay off for investors over any time horizon.

In the absence of hard data showing that a sustainable approach leads to better market outcomes, the ESG argument has started to change. Along with qualifying their return promises with more prominent legal disclaimers, many sustainable proponents have begun talking about return in risk-adjusted terms, consistent with the spin that ESG is also a risk management framework. Since high ESG scoring companies purportedly have lower volatility – which, again, may just be a function of higher fundamental quality – this magically converts lower absolute returns into higher risk-adjusted returns. If investors would just "think in a more comprehensive fashion," as the PRI puts it in its promotional research, they would be able to appreciate the ESG benefits of relative underperformance and perpetually leaving money on the table. This subtle tweak in the argument paves the way for replacing return with impact as the overriding objective, which has always been the plan with ESG investing. Environmental and social outcomes are increasingly what ESG investing will be measured on, with investment flows used as the chief barometer.

This is why ESG advocates are now changing the subject entirely from performance to the amount of capital being raised for funds with sustainable mandates as an alternative form of validation. Since 2016, the amount of net capital inflows to sustainable funds has increased sharply worldwide, from less than $100 billion in 2017 to more than $600 billion in 2021. Based on Morningstar data, as of December 31, 2022, the global AUM of sustainable open-end mutual and exchange-traded index funds – including equity, debt, and allocation strategies – totaled $2.5 trillion, up from $500 billion as of year-end 2017. Roughly 83% of this sustainable AUM was managed out of Europe, demonstrating how ESG remains a Europe-centered investing approach spearheaded by sovereign pensions and national financial institutions with close ties to the European governments pushing the climate change and sustainable development programs of the UN. Highlighting the European obsession with ESG, in recent years, more capital has been raised in Europe for sustainable funds than for conventional strategies.

Outside of Europe, only 11% or $286 billion of sustainable AUM is currently located in the US. While growing more than fivefold over the past six years, this is still a rounding error compared to the size of the overall US investment arena. For further perspective, based on the above-noted PwC-estimated 2020 figure for global AUM of roughly $112.3 trillion, dedicated sustainable funds currently represent less than 3% of the worldwide market. Moreover, when $2.5 trillion of AUM is spread across 7,012 different individual funds, the average size of the typical sustainable fund is only about $356 million, which is comparatively small, further reinforcing the image of ESG as a niche investment strategy despite all the hype.[21]

To date, the lion's share of capital raised for sustainable mandates has been for equity strategies and actively managed funds, the latter of which are able to charge more for their investment management services than passive funds. For example, the Vanguard Global ESG Select Stock Fund, a mutual fund focused on global equities, charges a 0.57% management fee, which compares to a 0.41% expense ratio for a conventional mutual fund such as the Vanguard Global Equity Fund. More surprisingly, additional management fees are also charged for passive ESG strategies. The Vanguard ESG US Stock ETF has an expense ratio of 0.09%, which is three times the 0.03% expense ratio for the Vanguard S&P 500 ETF.[22]

But despite earning more in fees, most sustainable funds bear a striking resemblance to their conventional counterparts, as noted ruefully in much of the ESG research. The extent of such greenwashing became abundantly clear over 2021–2022 when the energy sector snapped back after the annus horribilis of 2020 but most sustainable equity and debt funds still performed broadly in line with the overall market. The S&P 500 ESG Index, a more sustainable version of the benchmark S&P 500 equity benchmark, bested the price return of the S&P 500 in both 2021 (29.90% versus 26.89%) and 2022 (–19.03% versus –19.44%).[23] The main driver for this counterintuitive performance was the fact that the ESG equity index had a higher energy sector weighting than the S&P 500 benchmark in both years (5–6% versus 4–5%) which, despite slightly lower carbon intensity metrics overall, would still seem to be a violation of the spirit of ESG.

Similarly on the debt side, the significant outperformance of energy bonds in 2021 helped flush out much of the greenwashing associated with sustainable credit funds. One would think that ESG bond funds primarily focused on the issue of climate change (as per the PRI's mission statement) would have trouble making up for such industry outperformance, especially given how large the energy sector is relative to the investment grade corporate bond (7–8% at year-end 2021) and high-yield credit (13–14%) universes. Yet, the Bloomberg SASB US Corporate ESG Ex-Controversies Select Index and the Bloomberg SASB US Corporate High Yield ESG Ex-Controversies Select Index both performed broadly in line with their respective bond market benchmarks in both 2021 and 2022, mainly due to a roughly market weight position on energy over the period. All this index fudging and sustainable fund mislabeling is just further admission that ESG investing doesn't lead to outperformance.

The amount of capital that has been raised through the issuance of ESG-labeled bonds sporting either green, social, sustainability, or sustainability-linked labels is also held out as another proof of concept – even though ESG bonds only add to the greenwashing image of the industry and provide more fodder for the sustainable investment critics. Since the beginning of 2015, a total of $1.3 trillion of such bonds had been issued through year-end 2022, based on data tracked by Barclays Capital. To date, more than one-half of the aggregate supply of ESG bonds has been issued out of Europe, denominated in the Euro and British pound, and largely comprised of green bonds, all to take advantage of strong demand from climate-focused European bondholders. Most ESG bonds carry second opinions by MSCI, Sustainalytics, or another ESG rating service, which are separate assessments from the credit ratings of the NRSROs that vouch for the sustainability framework of the issuing company. Thus far, the largest group of issuers has been higher-quality financial institutions rated A/A or above by the NRSROs, as opposed to carbon-emitting industrial companies looking to fund their green energy transition, which is the first red flag about ESG bonds.[24]

None of these virtuous-sounding debt issues are asset-specific or project-level bonds or have any real teeth in their documentation. Structurally, there is no difference between an ESG-labeled bond and an issuer's other outstanding senior unsecured bonds. Despite what management may promise in its bond prospectus, money is fungible and there is no legal restriction on how a company may ultimately choose to allocate the use of proceeds. Sustainability-linked bonds, an increasingly popular ESG flavor over the past two years, do contain springing penalties (such as a coupon step-up) if certain stated sustainable goals (such as net zero by 2040) are not achieved. However, most of these self-determined corporate targets are pretty much in the bag when the bonds are issued or set so far into the future that current management has little to no personal liability. Moreover, it would be fairly easy just to refinance out any outstanding sustainability-linked bonds that become problematic down the road.

Despite this, most ESG bonds tend to price at tighter credit spreads than a company's other outstanding senior unsecured bonds, often by 15 to 20 basis points. This pricing anomaly, which cannot be justified on a fundamental basis, is mainly due to technical factors. Given the significant amount of debt capital from green-eyed bondholders chasing sustainable investments, new-issue ESG bonds tend to be oversubscribed and print at very tight levels – often through an issuer's secondary market curve. For issuers, ESG bonds offer better pricing, few corporate restrictions, and good sustainability press. For sustainability-driven investors gullible enough to participate in these expensive ESG debt deals, there is definitionally no way to outperform by consistently buying bonds priced through the market, which further complicates the ESG return argument.

Increasingly, the amount of capital deployed toward specific causes is being tracked as the measure of success for the ESG movement, which is consistent with the stated wealth redistribution goals of the UN's climate change and sustainable development programs. Recall the initial UN estimate that $5–7 trillion per year would be needed from the private sector to achieve the 17 SDGs by 2030. Since climate change puts the E in ESG and impact is the name of the endgame, the amount of investment flowing into green, clean, and renewable energy projects is a key indicator. In its "World Energy Investment 2023" publication, the International Energy Agency (IEA), another captured supranational agency, estimates that a total of $10 trillion was invested in clean energy projects – including EVs, biofuels, CCS, energy efficiency, and renewable power – over the 2015–2022 period, with the annual amount steadily increasing from $1.1 trillion in 2015 to $1.6 trillion in 2022.[25] If the world wants to stay on track for net zero by 2050, current investment levels need to ramp up sharply. The IEA is calling for a near tripling of clean energy investment to $4.6 trillion annually by 2030, along with an end to new investment into fossil fuels production.[26] Reading from the same hymnal, Bloomberg estimates that current energy transition investment levels need to immediately triple to $3–4 trillion annually and then jump to the $4.6 trillion range through 2030.[27] By 2050, Bloomberg and other ESG advocates are calling for annual clean energy spending in the range of $6–8 trillion.

The vast pool of capital that has been raised thus far for clean energy initiatives includes scores of targeted green energy or similarly labeled funds – both equity and debt, active and passive, public and private – that have been raised over the past few years, many of which have significantly outperformed versus the overall market. On the active equity side, BlackRock's BGF Sustainable Energy Fund generated an annualized return of 12.45% over 2020–2022, which is nearly triple the 4.68% three-year return of the BGF Global Dynamic Equity Fund. On the passive equity side, BlackRock's iShares Global Clean Energy ETF posted a total annual return of 20.32% over the past three years, which is nearly triple the 7.72% annual return posted over the same period by the iShares Global 100 ETF.[28] Many of these sector-specific funds include high-flying single clean energy names that have had stellar equity performance in recent years. A partial list would include the following publicly traded companies: Plug Power Inc., a hydrogen fuel cell developer (up 463.3% cumulative price return over the last five years); First Solar Inc., a solar panel manufacturer (up 144.8%); NextEra Energy Inc., a Florida utility with significant solar power generation in its mix (up 100.9%); and Clearway Energy Inc., a solar and wind power project developer (up 69.9%).[29] These returns compare with a cumulative return of 43.61% for the S&P 500 Index over the same 2018–2022 five-year period.[30]

Doesn't such outperformance prove that ESG investing does pay, especially when you can point to specific company names as examples? The financial markets seem capable of seeing and pricing the sustainability benefits to clean energy companies, so doesn't this refute the ESG performance criticism? The short answer is no. Clean energy companies are the direct beneficiaries of both supportive government policies – including subsidized loans, investment and production tax credits, and forced demand – and favorable ESG-driven market technicals – mainly billions of dollars of sustainable capital chasing a small number of deals and company investments. With the green energy sector being the most favored by governments across the developed world and the likelihood of an abrupt reversal in environmental and climate policy between now and 2030 diminishing with each passing year, the risk–reward balance is heavily skewed to the positive for investors. No, the main takeaway from the recent outperformance of clean energy investments is that ESG is all about climate change and crony capitalism.

At best, the ESG system is a broad catchall for all negative corporate event risk. While ESG is not a proven driver of long-term value in either direction, it can be a source of surprise news that leads to a sudden drop in equity and bond prices. Just as climate change is purportedly demonstrated by every severe weather event, so too is ESG with every unexpected adverse headline related to environmental, social, or governance issues. The only repeatable, actionable way to make money and generate excess return from ESG is to buy the stock or bonds of companies hit by negative environmental headlines immediately after such news hits. As opposed to social factors, which rarely move the needle, or governance factors such as fraud, which may prove terminal, one-off environmental spills caused by industrial accidents tend to push down securities prices but typically are manageable for most large-cap companies once the dust settles, creating an opportunity for investors.

Ironically, negative ESG events often represent a strong signal to buy. Any investor with a strong conviction about BP's financial staying power that bought the integrated energy company's shares shortly after the April 2010 blowout of its deepwater Macondo well would have realized a gain of nearly 50% over the second half of that year as its stock price recovered. As previously mentioned, BP paid out more than $65 billion for legal penalties, environmental remediation, and economic restitution around the Gulf of Mexico oil spill but was never in danger of insolvency due to its Aa/AA credit ratings and ample asset coverage at the time. In 2011, a magnitude 6.6 Mw earthquake struck off the coast of Japan and triggered a tsunami that damaged the Daiichi nuclear power plant in Fukushima, causing the release of radioactive contamination into the Pacific Ocean and surrounding atmosphere and forcing the evacuation of approximately 154,000 local residents. Any nimble trader who picked up shares in Tokyo Electric Power Company Holdings Incorporated, the owner and operator of the Fukushima plant, after they tumbled by 90% in the three months following the disaster, could have tripled his money in just a few weeks when the shares finally bounced. In 2019, the Brazilian mining company Vale SA was hit by the collapse of its Brumadinho tailings dam in the state of Minas Gerais, which released 12 million cubic meters of toxic mine waste and killed 270 people. Despite being rated borderline investment grade at the time, the company was able to financially absorb the roughly $7.8 billion settlement reached with the Brazilian government to cover local community reparations and environmental remediation. Investors who bought the company's shares immediately after the Brumadinho news would have realized a roughly 25% return over the first half of 2019 and would have doubled their money if they stuck with their position through mid-2021.

One of the unintended consequences of ESG is that bad environmental news is often good news for investors, which would seem to run counter to the raison d'être of sustainable investing, which is to benefit both people and the planet. While it seems clear that ESG-minded investors should avoid companies with bad environmental track records and would be well within their rights (albeit ill-advised) to short such issuers, are they also allowed to buy the same companies on the ESG dip? Is making money off bad environmental news acceptable in the new ESG market paradigm? Is it morally upright to root for a negative environmental headline, much like bottom-feeding distressed debt players do when they are looking for a better entry point?

No one on Wall Street is getting particularly rich off ESG. While investment managers are charging higher fees for both active and passive sustainable funds, the capital flowing into these outwardly virtuous portfolios is mainly being reallocated from existing conventional accounts. Moreover, investment firms are bearing the incremental overhead cost of integrating ESG into all of their existing funds, which is more of a loss leader for the industry. Ditto for the growing volume of ESG bonds, which are largely cannibalizing other plain-vanilla corporate bond issues while also paying the same level of underwriting fees to the investment banks involved. At the same time, the last few years of ESG integration have exposed the extensive greenwashing now taking place across Wall Street, including the false advertising associated with many sustainable funds and ESG bonds, which increases the liability exposure of buy-side and sell-side firms.

ESG investing is still a work in progress for Wall Street. Like climate change, it is a theory in perpetual motion, its tactics and messaging constantly changing. Like a clever predatory pack of Velociraptors on Isla Nublar, the aggressive ESG movement is learning from its mistakes, adapting to setbacks, and remembering along the way. The lack of quantitative proof for its core argument of ESG outperformance is simply shrugged off and replaced with new impact-oriented goals. That sustainable funds have not lived up to their public promises is merely a distraction from the capital being siphoned out of the significantly larger body of ESG-integrated funds. ESG bond ratings have proven ineffective at measuring impact, but they are conditioning the debt markets to seek an ESG seal of approval as a prerequisite for raising capital, perhaps as a dry run for all bond issuance down the road. The European debt markets are already headed in this direction as 29% of Euro-denominated investment grade bonds issued in 2022 came with some form of sustainable label, based on data sourced by Barclays Capital. As previously mentioned, for all the focus on shareholders, stock funds, and the equity markets, the credit markets are the main target of ESG activists since bonds and bank loans are the chief source of liquidity for the corporate sector. If financial asset prices are still not responding to the voluntary integration of ESG into the research and fundamental investment processes of market participants, then an involuntary approach that controls pricing from the technical side through the supply and demand of capital may be in order.

Sustainable investing sets up as a highly unique type of asset bubble for the financial markets. While many investors are piling onto the sustainability trade, ESG factors are not having an impact on securities prices in the debt and equity markets, so there is no price bubble to pop. While ESG facilitators are making money, most investors are being pushed into the sustainability trade by moral arm-twisting rather than being motivated by the opportunity for attractive returns. By the time accounts realize that they have been duped, the regulators will have made sure that all of the exits are blocked and no one will be allowed to leave.

CHAPTER 9

THE CHILDREN'S HOUR

Now the little crazy children are jangling the keys of the kingdom, and common vengeance writes the law.
Arthur Miller, *The Crucible*

It was almost normal for people over thirty to be frightened of their own children.
George Orwell, *Nineteen Eighty-Four*

The moral imperative behind climate change and its longer-form version of sustainable development rests on the premise that current generations should "Do no harm" to the world that we are leaving behind for posterity. Assorted UN agencies regularly warn us that unchecked climate change will affect "the lives of today's children tomorrow and those of their children much more than ours," and that economic growth and development cannot compromise "the ability of future generations to meet their own needs." As with every progressive initiative, the argument assumes the psychic ability of precognition – often expressed as "being on the right side of history," even though no one knows what the future will hold – and reflects a deep pessimism about the future of humanity, while also seeking to divide the population into warring tribes – in this case, the old versus the young. The climate change and sustainable development movements have both been very effective at exploiting young people and children – both as victims and as their vanguard – and this cynical tactic is now being copied by ESG activists. As the PRI chair, Martin Skancke, has noted, investors need to "create long-term value for their beneficiaries, the societies they inhabit and that future generations inherit."[1]

Ever since the signing of the Paris Agreement in 2015, the UN has led on climate from behind angry teenage protestors and staged youth climate conferences to justify the need for extreme government and corporate action to curtail greenhouse gas emissions and fossil fuels production. In true *Hunger Games* fashion, the adults working at the UN are letting children do the heavy fighting for them on climate. In the past few years, youth-oriented climate change advocacy groups have proliferated, helped in large part by logistical and networking support from the UN. Sadly, getting to net-zero emissions is now the defining issue for younger generations. With earnest names such as iMatter Youth Movement, Zero Hour, TREEage, and Youth vs. Apocalypse, many of these organizations regularly meet and march for the cause.[2]

Youth climate activism had its breakout moment in 2019 when the Swedish teenager Greta Thunberg, the founder of the school-skipping Fridays for Future, attended the climate festivities at the annual General Assembly of the UN in New York, sailing over from Europe rather than flying so as to minimize her carbon footprint. In her distraught "How dare you" speech delivered to the UN Climate Action Summit, Thunberg – who has been diagnosed with Asperger's syndrome – excoriated the crowd of UN dignitaries for stealing her dreams and her childhood by not doing enough to stop man-made climate change. Because of this inaction, she claimed, people are already suffering and dying, entire ecosystems are collapsing, and the world is looking at a "mass extinction" event. She warned every adult within earshot that "the eyes of all future generations are upon you" and "if you choose to fail us ... we will never forgive you." Any parent watching the speech doubtless found the entire scene highly disturbing, although probably not in the way that Thunberg's adult handlers expected. For their part, the UN crowd celebrated the performance of the young climate activist and basked in her criticism, much like a self-flagellating medieval religious sect. UN Secretary-General António Guterres admonished the gathering to "heed the calls" of Thunberg and other "young people who are taking to the streets to demand that we change our relationship with nature now."[3] Three years later, Guterres was still firing up the UN's underage base, solemnly tweeting to "the youth of today" before jetting off to Sharm el-Sheikh, Egypt, for the COP27 climate confab: "I urge you to be the generation that succeeds in addressing the planetary emergency of climate change."[4] COP27 was the first annual climate gathering that included a youth pavilion, a kind of insult tent where UN delegates could stop by and be belittled by children for not doing enough on climate.

A number of these youth climate advocacy groups are highly litigious. For the past few years, the US legal system has been clogged with climate change–related federal and state lawsuits brought on behalf of sympathetic young plaintiffs and based on the novel legal concept of intergenerational equity, which states that man-made global warming will mainly harm future generations (i.e., today's children) and, therefore, is a violation of their constitutional due process rights to life, liberty, and property. Many of these cases continue to work their way through the courts, including the Juliana v. United States lawsuit filed in 2015 by Our Children's Trust, an Oregon-based nonprofit created to file such climate change lawsuits. In the *Juliana* case, 21 young people ranging in age from 11 to 22 sued the federal government for failing to limit the country's carbon emissions and contributing to climate change – a violation of both their constitutional rights and the public trust doctrine that government has a responsibility to preserve the ecosystem. The young *Juliana* group was represented in the proceedings by climatologist James Hansen, the grandfather of one of the plaintiffs and the NASA scientist who first warned the American public about global warming in a staged congressional hearing choreographed by then-Senator Al Gore back in 1988. The *Juliana* case never went to trial before being blocked by the Ninth Circuit Court of Appeals for lack of standing and judicial remedy, with the US District Court directing the plaintiffs to engage in settlement discussions with the DOJ, which is a common backdoor tactic used by environmental activists to implement policy by consent decree. These settlement talks ended in 2021. In June 2023, US District Court Judge Ann Aiken, a Clinton appointee, ruled that the *Juliana* plaintiffs could amend their complaint and have their evidence heard in open court. Currently, there is no end in sight for the yearslong litigation.

Our Children's Trust has also launched similar legal actions across all 50 states. In Held v. State of Montana, 16 young people are claiming that state lawmakers have consistently prioritized fossil fuel infrastructure and profits to the detriment of their future and in violation of their right to a healthy and safe environment under the state's constitution. The *Held* lawsuit was filed in 2020 and, unlike *Juliana*, went to trial in June 2023, with Helena District Judge Kathy Seeley ruling in favor of the precocious plaintiffs, marking the first time that such a climate case has had its day in court. This was followed by the group's filing of its Natalie R. v. State of Utah lawsuit in 2022, wherein seven youths – or more appropriately, yutes, as in the 1992 courtroom comedy *My Cousin Vinny* – claimed that the state of Utah, through its policies promoting the development of fossil fuels, had contributed to hazardous air quality and dangerous climate crisis impacts, thereby harming the young plaintiffs and violating their state constitutional rights to life, health, and safety. The *Natalie R.* lawsuit was initially dismissed by a state district court but has since been appealed to the Utah Supreme Court. The state governments of Florida, Hawaii, and Virginia have also been served with similar complaints.[5]

Youth climate lawfare has now become a global trend. In 2021, Germany's Constitutional Court ruled in favor of nine young climate activists by finding that parts of the country's climate legislation were insufficient and a violation of the freedoms of the young complainants and ordering the government to set post-2030 greenhouse gas reduction targets. Also in 2021, the Australian Federal Court ruled in a class-action case brought on behalf of all Australian children and teenagers that the national government owed a duty of care to children to protect them from the harm caused by climate change, which immediately set up government ministers for negligence claims on the back of any new coal project approvals. The case was subsequently reversed on appeal the following year, and the plaintiffs did not seek special leave to appeal it to the highest court in the country. Six Portuguese youth recently sued 32 European governments to force them to transition away from fossil fuels through a legally binding decision from the European Court of Human Rights, with the case now pending before a 17-judge Grand Chamber.

All of these frivolous lawsuits are basically an attempt to set climate policy by working through the courts and hiding behind sympathetic young plaintiffs. Complementing this effort, childish green legislation has also been introduced in several countries around the world, often by younger, up-and-coming political leaders. In 2019, when the Zero Carbon Bill, which would set a target of zero carbon emissions for the country by 2050, was being debated in New Zealand's parliament, the 25-year-old lawmaker Chlöe Swarbrick responded to heckling by her older legislative colleagues with a flippant "OK boomer." Also in 2019, the 34-year-old Sanna Marin was selected as the youngest Finnish prime minister in history. Shortly after taking office, Marin's Social Democratic Party–led government set a national goal for Finland to become "Europe's first climate neutral welfare society by 2035," with negative net emissions thereafter.

In the US, a Green New Deal was first proposed in 2019 – introduced, appropriately enough, by one of the youngest members of the US Congress, 29-year-old Representative Alexandria Ocasio-Cortez, working in concert with the youth climate activist group Sunrise Movement. Not surprisingly, the Green New Deal with its stated goals of "decarbonization, jobs and justice" reads more like a Christmas wish list for Santa Claus – with some socialist stocking stuffers thrown in – than a serious piece of legislation.

Nonetheless, US politicians – many septuagenarian and octogenarian grandparents who should know better – have infantilized themselves by agreeing with the dreamy goals of the Green New Deal rather than challenging its nonsensical technological and economic underpinnings. Pandering to young voters is a terrible political misreading of the axiom "Youth will be served." Many of the core elements of the Green New Deal, which the American Action Forum think tank estimated would cost between $51 and $93 trillion,[6] have been broken down and incorporated into other legislative bills such as the mislabeled Infrastructure Investment and Jobs Act of 2021 (IIJA) and the highly misleading Inflation Reduction Act of 2022 (IRA) and signed into law by President Biden.

Some of these youth climate groups are now employing adolescent Alinksy tactics to target directly and increase the pressure on government officials for climate action – often with great success. Groups of children and young adults now regularly show up to publicly shame and confront recalcitrant legislators and politicians. In 2019, the late Dianne Feinstein, then the oldest sitting US senator, was ambushed in her San Francisco office by middle and high school students from the Sunrise Movement demanding that she sign up for the Green New Deal. Still feisty at 85, she told the young group that there was no way to pay for the resolution with its excessive price tag, cutting short the surprise meeting with a curt "I know what I'm doing." Four years later, though, she voted with fellow Democrats along party lines for both the IIJA and the IRA, which, combined, included more than $500 billion of unfunded green pork spending.

In early 2022, Rishi Sunak, then the UK chancellor of the exchequer, was accosted at a Tory conference for his support of North Sea oil and gas development by puerile protestors from Green New Deal Rising, a youth climate group – no one over age 35 need apply – focused on imposing a version of the Green New Deal on the UK (including climate reparations). Showing the cowardice of his policy convictions, he quickly retreated once he realized the conversation was being videotaped and recorded. Barely nine months later after being selected prime minister, Sunak came out in support of a continued UK ban on fracking even as the country and the rest of Europe were staring down an energy crisis brought on by natural gas shortages and ill-conceived renewable power policies.

Mostly, these young climate protestors act out in public – as children are wont to do – through demonstrations and theatrical performances which, under the guise of civil disobedience, have grown more disruptive and criminal over time. One of the more radical groups, Extinction Rebellion, has staged several protests worldwide in recent years. In the US, this has included a die-in at the NYSE building, a human blockade of the Brooklyn Bridge, a rush-hour roadblock of the FDR Drive, and the obstruction of the printing presses used by Dow Jones publications such as the *Wall Street Journal* and the *New York Post*. Over in Europe, Extinction Rebellion has also blocked major bridges, roads, and public transit, blockaded UK oil refineries and terminals, sprayed fake blood across the City of London, and dropped a miniature "sinking house" in the River Thames to call attention to the sea level rise caused by climate change. Like-minded UK protest groups such as Just Stop Oil and Insulate Britain have also added to the public disorder, with the latest publicity gimmick being the defacement of art masterpieces by Monet, Picasso, and Van Gogh. Young climate protestors are now throwing tomato soup and other viscous liquids on priceless Western paintings, gluing themselves to museum walls, and then spouting off like members of Chairman Mao's Red Guards for the benefit of the cameras and the cell phones in the room.

Exploiting young people to further the climate change cause makes perfect demographic sense. As the UN has noted in its self-serving praise for youth climate activists, "The world is home to 1.8 billion young people between the ages of 10 to 24 – the largest generation of youth in history," and it will be up to these young people to hold "the older generation" accountable for preserving the planet and saving mankind.[7] More ominously, with millennial and Generation Z cohort members now outnumbering baby boomers, nearly two-thirds of the world's population of approximately 8.0 billion as of 2022 was below the age of 40 – meaning that, during their lifetimes, all they have seen and heard are repeated warnings about global warming and the impending climate emergency. Climate alarmism is deliberately targeted at young people to increase their anxiety levels and scare them witless about their uncertain futures. These younger generations will soon be moving into positions of decision-making authority across society – including the government sector, the business world, and the financial markets – and will bring with them their preconceived notions about climate change and sustainability when they do. Parading children around as climate victims is merely a distraction; grooming them and shaping their worldview is the main goal.

Since the ratification of the Paris Agreement, the scaremongering around climate change has ratcheted up significantly, fueled in large part by the UN marketing machine. When it comes to climate change, every day feels like Halloween. On a regular basis, new and frightening factoids are rolled out to scare the public – especially kids – into coordinated, collective action against the global climate threat – like *Reefer Madness* for climate change, with the messaging just as subtle. All of this would be humorous were it not for the fact that today's young people are being taught in the classroom and lectured by the media that such cli-fi futurism should be accepted as scientific fact. Impressionable youth are now believing everything that the climate computers are telling them. A 2021 study by the University of Bath that was published in *The Lancet* found that eco-anxiety affects the daily life of nearly half of the world's young people. In a survey of 10,000 young people aged 16 to 25 across 10 countries, over half of respondents thought that "humanity is doomed" and roughly 75% said they believed that "the future is frightening." More than 45% of survey participants reported that distress over climate change affected their daily life and ability to function, adding a whole new dimension to the typical teenager angst.[8]

The pessimism about humanity's prospects that marked the 1960s and 1970s was overstated back then and is clearly out of place in the current technology-blessed century. And yet, baby boomers continue to engage in an intergenerational transfer of environmental fear by projecting such anachronistic anxieties onto today's youth – spooking kids into believing that the world is going to end or pass a climatic point of no return in the year 2030. This exploitation of young people is a transparent attempt to move public opinion on climate change and control the minds of adults.

To start the indoctrination at an early age, climate activists and government officials have moved to embed climate education into the K–12 public school curriculum and the course offerings at colleges and universities, thereby controlling what students are taught during their formative learning years. Both the UN and the WEF have called for compulsory climate studies to be integrated into the primary and secondary education policies and curricula of all the world's countries. As the UN has stated, "Education is a critical agent in addressing the issue of climate change."[9] Toward this end, the United Nations Educational, Scientific and Cultural Organization (UNESCO) has rolled out its climate-focused Education for Sustainable Development framework and lobbied to include it as a core component of all education systems at all levels by 2025. As of 2020, roughly one-half of surveyed UNESCO member states had integrated climate and environmental topics into their national education documents.[10]

The US is doing its part to teach its children well on climate change by rolling out a green Common Core for K–12 schools over the past decade, even as average math and reading scores for fourth and eighth graders have failed to improve over the past 20 years. Forty-three states and the District of Columbia have adopted the Next Generation of Science Standards, which were designed to provide students with an internationally benchmarked science education, including climate science. Introduced in 2013, the new science standards rely on a framework developed by the Washington, DC–based National Research Council (NRC). This is the research arm of the National Academy of Sciences that works closely with the federal government on most scientific matters.

All of the NRC's work around global warming proceeds from the initial premise of its 2011 report "America's Climate Choices," which states that "climate change is already occurring, is based largely on human activities, and is supported by multiple lines of scientific evidence." From the council's perspective, the science of climate change has already been settled. Not surprisingly, global climate change is one of the disciplinary core ideas embedded in the Next Generation of Science Standards, making it required learning for students in grade, middle, and high school. The NRC framework for K–12 science education recommends that by the end of Grade 5, students should appreciate that rising average global temperatures will affect the lives of all humans and other organisms on the planet. By Grade 8, students should understand that the release of greenhouse gases from burning fossil fuels is a major factor in global warming. And by Grade 12, students should know that global climate models are very effective in modeling, predicting, and managing the current and future impact of climate change.

Many of the background materials and classroom resources used by instructors in teaching the new climate curriculum are sourced from the UN and various government agencies. The UN provides an online video game called Mission 1.5°, a Sims-like life simulation game called Stop Disasters!, and a 2030 SDG board game called Go Goals that resembles Hasbro's classic Chutes and Ladders. The EPA has an array of ready-to-download climate change primers for classroom use by teachers, including handouts on the link between carbon dioxide and average global temperatures and tear sheets on the causal relationship between greenhouse gas emissions and rising sea levels. Similarly, NASA has published "A Guide to Climate Change for Kids," which can be found on its ClimateKids website, while NOAA and the DOE have their own Climate Literacy & Energy Awareness Network, which serves as an online portal for the distribution of digital resources to help educators teach about climate change. One such learning module requires students to measure the size of their family's carbon footprint and come up with ways to shrink it.

Relying on a climate change curriculum and teaching materials largely sourced from ideologically biased multilateral and national agencies is obviously problematic. Along with the undue authoritative weight that such government-produced documents carry in the classroom, most of the work is one-sided and presented in categorical terms, with no discussion of the limitations and gaps with the underlying data and the remaining uncertainties about the scientific theory. Moreover, too much blind trust is placed in the predictive power of long-range computer simulations, despite the weak forecasting track record of most climate models to date.[11]

Anyone requiring further proof that climate curriculum is classroom thought control and just another red brick in the progressive wall that has gone up around schools over the past four decades need only note that the Zinn Education Project, which was founded to continue the work of the late Howard Zinn, has also developed its own climate teaching materials including a 400-page textbook titled *A People's Curriculum for the Earth: Teaching Climate Change and the Environmental Crisis.* Zinn's history textbook *A People's History of the United States*, which was first published in 1980 and has since sold more than two million copies, offers a distorted Marxist take on American history designed to undermine national pride and patriotism by highlighting the country's racist past and calling into question the moral authority and exceptionalism of the US. The leftists carrying on Zinn's legacy are now looking to replicate this subversive success on the climate front, again from a racial and social justice angle.

Post-secondary, there is no shortage of climate courses to choose from at the college and graduate school level, both as science electives and for degree requirements. Even the Core Curriculum at Columbia College, which for more than 100 years has set the standard for an undergraduate education in the classical humanities, now requires a Frontiers of Science course that includes a learning module on global climate change. At graduate professional schools, whether for the study of medicine, law, or business, climate change and climate justice have also permeated the pedagogy. By the time most students complete their formal education, they have filed away climate change alongside gravity and thermodynamics as a scientific given, never to be revisited again intellectually.

Many of the progressive tenets of corporate sustainability – chief among them, climate change – have been incubated on college campuses and indoctrinated into young minds by university professors and academic administrators over the past two generations. The fossil fuel divestment campaign targeted at college endowments that started on college campuses roughly a decade ago has now made its way to Wall Street, with the handwritten protest signs for the quad now being replaced by sleek financial dashboards that calculate the size of a company or portfolio's carbon footprint at the press of a button. Climate change and environmental activist groups ideologically opposed to the production of fossil fuels are now the driving force behind the ESG movement. Each year, Wall Street's sustainability ranks grow as another undergraduate class of climate and social justice warriors moves out into the business world. In 2022, 47% of the workforce in the US securities industry was younger than 45 years old, highlighting how demographics are the friend of the ESG trend.[12] By 2030, a supermajority of the people working on Wall Street – which has never been a country for old men or women – will have been raised on the belief that climate change is an emergency and sustainable development and finance is the only answer.

As with climate change, sustainability proponents also make the generational argument that millennials feel more strongly about environmental and social issues than baby boomers, so businesses need to be more sensitive to the needs of their evolving employee ranks and customer bases. This warning also applies to the financial markets. Millennials represent the largest workforce in history and are very eco-conscious when it comes to consumption and the products that they buy. These same young people also gravitate toward social and responsible investing because they need to find a purpose both for their investments as well as in their day-to-day jobs. A 2017 survey of 1,000 individual investors by the Morgan Stanley Institute for Sustainable Investing found that millennials were twice as likely to purchase from a sustainable brand, were three times more likely to seek employment with a sustainably minded company, and were twice as likely to invest in companies targeting ESG goals as compared to the total population of individual investors. The same study found that 86% of millennial respondents were interested in sustainable investing, the majority of which acknowledged the trade-off between financial returns and societal impact.[13]

Similarly, a 2022 joint survey of 2,470 investors by the Hoover Institution and Stanford University found that older and younger investors have diametrically opposed views of ESG. Older investors who rely on retirement savings to pay for living expenses are largely opposed to sustainability initiatives and unwilling to sacrifice financial returns to advance environmental and social goals. ESG is overwhelmingly supported by young investors who want investment managers to take an active stance on climate change, diversity, and other stakeholder initiatives. Moreover, the study found that young investors – those aged 41 and below – were willing to lose between 6% and 10% of their retirement savings to support ESG causes, compared to zero for older investors closer to retirement age. The relative sanguinity of the younger investors polled was partially owing to their self-confidence about their investment skills and their higher expectations for future market returns – an interesting combination of financial market optimism and environmental and social pessimism.[14]

With ESG, the implicit threat is that eventually the lion's share of assets under management across Wall Street will comprise millennial (followed by Generation Z) money driven by moral goals, so market participants, especially money managers, should get on board the sustainability train now to position themselves for this coming shift. Based on Federal Reserve data as of the fourth quarter of 2022, millennials currently hold only 5.7% of the wealth in America, versus 53.0% for the baby boomer generation.[15] Household wealth for baby boomers approximated $73.0 trillion at year-end 2022, more than nine times the $7.8 trillion accumulated by millennials. When only market investments are included, the financial gap is even wider: $19.0 trillion in corporate equities and mutual fund shares held by baby boomers versus just $0.8 trillion for millennials. It would seem the only way to close such a wide generational gap in wealth would be if millennials were able to inherit a significant amount from their baby boomer forebears over the coming decades – assuming they remain on good terms with their parents and familial elders. The current market reality about millennials hasn't stopped ESG advocates from trying to exploit this generation to give the appearance of greater numbers on their side. Much as the invading Mongols tied tree branches and leaves behind their horses to create dust storms and the appearance of a much larger attacking army – thereby forcing the enemy to surrender without a fight – everything about climate change, sustainability, and ESG is meant to project overwhelming numbers to shut down the opposition and force capitulation.

Sustainability activists have adopted the same "A child shall lead them" strategy as they work to spread the gospel of ESG across the global financial system. As with climate change, the process of ESG integration espoused by the PRI and other sustainable advocates relies on juvenile and sophomoric tactics to achieve its stated goal of conformity, including peer pressure, nagging, whining, and public shaming. Even though your parents always warned you about giving in to peer pressure when you were growing up and strenuously avoided comparing you to your siblings, these basic rules apparently do not apply to corporate behavior. While comparative analysis is a staple of Wall Street research, sustainability takes this approach to a whole new level. Companies and investors are regularly compared to the best-in-ESG-class in their industry category (as subjectively defined) and force-ranked to achieve the highest degree of compliance. As a defensive maneuver, many businesses have tried to argue their ESG bona fides by virtue of their strong management and good governance, which only serves to trip them up and get them into trouble, much like bragging middle schoolers hanging out in the playground. Corporate leaders and investment managers touting their ESG credentials are now regularly called out for greenwashing and not living up to the spirit of sustainability.

Recalcitrant market players are targeted for engagement by sustainability-minded analysts, which usually means intervention meetings structured around a wish list of "I want" ESG demands plus a timetable for completion, as any child's chore list would require. And when such measures fail and companies are still misbehaving from a sustainability perspective, matters are escalated, with mostly Generation Z youth protestors used to publicly shame and confront companies and investors for their ESG failings – especially with regard to climate action. In the current social media age, it is fairly easy to gin up a flash mob of young people on short notice and have them show up at the corporate headquarters or annual shareholder meeting of an ESG laggard. By doing so, an ESG controversy can be created out of thin air to sully a company's reputation and stain its sustainability record – often permanently. Such public spectacles give new meaning to the New Testament phrase, "Suffer the little children."

The irony of exploiting young people to push climate change and the broader sustainability agenda is that, by demonstrating the lack of a reasoned argument, these juvenile tactics may ultimately backfire on ESG activists. Children are innocents, but innocence also connotes inexperience, naïveté, and lack of wisdom, which can be problematic traits for standard-bearers of a movement. Relying on youngsters as your spokespeople can also be tricky when it comes to managing and controlling the message. As W.C. Fields warned, "Never work with children or animals," because they invariably upstage you or screw up their lines or both. This old show business adage also applies to the climate-driven ESG business, as seen of late with Greta Thunberg, the now-emancipated poster child for the youth climate movement. At the COP26 warm-up youth jamboree event held in Milan in September 2021, Thunberg noted that all the net-zero promises of governments and corporations basically amounted to nothing more than "blah, blah, blah."[16] A year later in 2022 when she was out promoting her new book on – what else – climate change, she went a step further by declaring that the only way to avoid a global climate catastrophe was by forcing Western countries to forgo economic growth and development and abandoning the "whole capitalist system," which she views as being responsible for "imperialism, oppression, genocide, and racist, oppressive extractionism."[17] Sometimes the truth spills out of the unscripted mouths of babes, exposing young climate activists for the socialist jabberwockies that they are.

The cofounder of Extinction Rebellion, Stuart Basden, disclosed in a lengthy 2019 *Medium* article that his environmental protest group really had nothing to do with climate. Rather, the goal was to tear down the entire system of Western capitalism because European civilization and colonialism are to blame for spreading cruelty and violence throughout the globe for centuries and bringing "torture, genocide, carnage and suffering to the ends of the earth."[18] For good measure, he also highlighted white supremacy, patriarchy, class hierarchy, and heterosexism as the other negative consequences of capitalism. Similarly, after the Green New Deal resolution was introduced in the US Congress back in 2019, Saikat Chakrabarti, the chief of staff for Representative Ocasio-Cortez, admitted that the true motivation behind introducing the Green New Deal was to overhaul the entire US economy. As he noted at the time, it was less of a "climate thing" and more of a "how-do-you-change-the-entire-economy thing."[19]

Children and young people are being used as human and moral shields to shut down discussion and cut off debate around climate change and sustainability. While it is true that you can't reason with kids – particularly millennials and Generation Z members, many of whom have been showered with participation trophies and micromanaged by helicopter parents for most of their early lives – corporate leaders and investment managers should not be afraid to have an awkward tough-love conversation about ESG with these young activists. Doing so would rip off the socialist mask of the stakeholder capitalism being used to disguise ESG and quickly expose the infantile nature of the demands being made by youthful protestors and the adults hiding behind them. Whitney Houston was correct when she sang about children being our future, but letting them lead the way on climate change, sustainability, and ESG would be a recipe for disaster. As anyone who has read *Lord of the Flies* can attest, there is a reason why we don't let kids run society, manage the economy, or set national energy policy.

CHAPTER 10

THE FIDUCIARY RULE: BROKEN, NOT BENT

> *Law is the highest reason implanted in Nature, which commands what ought to be done and forbids the opposite.*
> Cicero

> *To have a right to do a thing is not at all the same as to be right in doing it.*
> G. K. Chesterton

Notwithstanding all the rules and regulations governing the industry, the main reason why the global financial markets operate in an ethical manner is because of the people who work on Wall Street. From investment banking to investment management, the concepts of fiduciary duty, account stewardship, fair dealing, and avoiding undue advantage inform almost every aspect of day-to-day market-making activities – this despite the inherent adversarial nature of the securities business and the zero-sum game of generating return and profit. Most compliance rules are superfluous and unnecessary for anyone in the industry with a basic understanding of fairness dating back to the playground days of childhood and an appreciation of the fundamental ethical principle of the Golden Rule to "Do unto others as you would have them do unto you." Ironically, a key obstacle facing the morally driven market utopia that ESG activists would like to create is the personal ethics guiding most of the people who work on Wall Street.

It is next to impossible to monitor all the countless interactions and conversations that take place every day as part of the information flow that drives the markets. As of December 2021, there were approximately 1.0 million people – including more than 600,000 FINRA-registered representatives – working at roughly 135,000 different establishments across the US securities industry, based on BLS data.[1] In 2021, the average daily trading volume of the major US equity markets – NYSE, Nasdaq, and regional – was $565 billion based on SIFMA numbers. That same year, SIFMA estimated that the average trading volume of all US fixed income securities – including corporate bonds, Treasury and agency securities, municipal bonds, and mortgage- and asset-backed securities – totaled $955 billion.[2] Moreover, such secondary trading figures only reflect public securities and do not capture activity in the private equity, debt, real estate, and infrastructure markets. In contrast, the SEC reported only 697 enforcement actions with an aggregate $3.9 billion in assessed penalties and disgorgement proceeds during fiscal 2021.[3] When compared to overall market throughput or financial industry headcount, the level of SEC police activity has been minimal and relatively constant over the years despite changes in market conditions and financial technology, highlighting how criminality has always been the exception rather than the rule on Wall Street.

However, one would never know this fact based on how the financial industry is portrayed by the press and in popular culture. Since the barbarian LBO and M&A days of the 1980s, Wall Street has been consistently cast in a negative light, with every bad actor spotlighted and every scandal sensationalized. Corporate raiders like Ivan Boesky, boiler room operators like Jordan Belfort, rogue traders like Joseph Jett, and Ponzi schemers like Bernie Madoff and Sam Bankman-Fried – all their crimes have been exploited by the media to feed the perception of Wall Street as a casino where the odds are stacked in favor of the house and all rules were made to be broken. To reinforce the message – lest the public forget due to the dearth of actual Wall Street crimes – the CNBC business cable channel runs a regular series called *American Greed* to highlight cases of white-collar financial crime every week. Even though corporate fraudsters such as Enron's Jeff Skilling and Andrew Fastow, WorldCom's Bernie Ebbers and Scott Sullivan, Adelphia Communications' John and Timothy Rigas, and Tyco International's Dennis Kozlowski and Mark Swartz are in a separate class and mainly victimized the financial industry, the two categories are conflated and lumped together to feed the narrative.

Over time, the perception of Wall Street as lawless has gradually stuck. Almost every industry misstep or extreme volatility event is now automatically labeled as fraud, even when there is no criminality involved. In 1998, when the sudden collapse of LTCM sent shock waves through the global financial system, there were no calls to lock up the managers of the quantitative hedge fund and only minimal criticism of the bailout that was organized to limit the contagion. Few challenged the perfectly logical explanation that the fund collapsed due to a combination of poor risk management and excessive leverage. Nobody cried fraud. Ten years later during the 2008 financial crisis, when Lehman Brothers went bankrupt and several other financial firms collapsed due to the same combination of poor risk management and excessive leverage, everyone on Wall Street was accused of criminal behavior. No criminal charges were brought and nobody on Wall Street ever went to jail for the events of 2008, although billions of dollars in legal payments were made to settle civil lawsuits, which many took as an admission of guilt. The industry has struck a meek public posture ever since, which is why it has been so easy for ESG to make inroads on Wall Street. Instead of trumpeting the many positive contributions of the finance industry to society – including funding global economic growth, technological innovation, energy infrastructure, and emerging markets development – Wall Street has forgotten how to defend itself, at least in the court of public opinion, because it is perpetually on the defensive around the well-publicized sins of a few within its ranks.

Since the insider trading scandals of the 1980s, there has been a regulatory backlash, even though there have been statutes on the books since the 1930s outlawing the practice. Section 10(b) of the Securities Act of 1934 is the general anti-fraud provision of the law that has been most frequently applied in cases of insider trading over the years. Under Section 10(b), it is unlawful for any person, either directly or indirectly, to use or employ any "manipulative or deceptive device or contrivance" to conduct transactions in stock and other securities in contravention of the rules and regulations set by the SEC to further the public interest and to protect investors. To provide further clarity, the SEC passed Rule 10b-5 alongside the 1934 Act. Formally known as the Employment of Manipulative and Deceptive Practices rule, Rule 10b-5 spells out what constitutes securities fraud – including making false or misleading statements, omitting relevant information, or otherwise conducting business operations in a deceptive manner – to make matters clear. Since the New Deal era, insider trading or using confidential information to manipulate the stock market has been a fraudulent act and a violation of the fiduciary responsibility owed to a company by its executives and surrogates. Moreover, this prohibition has always applied not just to corporate insiders and constructive insiders but also to any person in receipt of nonpublic inside information.

This hasn't stopped the US Congress and the SEC from passing additional laws and rules in recent decades aimed at expanding the universe of market players with a fiduciary responsibility, while increasing the penalties for insider trading. President Reagan signed into law the Insider Trading Sanctions Act of 1984, which was enacted in response to the perception of rampant insider trading on Wall Street, which threatened to undermine "the public's expectations of honest and fair securities markets." Under the 1984 Act, the SEC may bring legal action against any person who has bought or sold a security while in possession of material nonpublic information (MNPI) and seek a civil penalty of up to three times the profit gained or loss avoided in any such transaction. Four years later, the Insider Trading and Securities Fraud Enforcement Act of 1988 was also signed by President Reagan to expand the scope of civil penalties related to insider trading by targeting corporate executives or control persons who fail to take adequate steps to prevent the leakage of MNPI and the fraudulent securities market activity therefrom.

Two additional rules – Rule 10b5-1 and Rule 10b5-2 – were issued by the SEC in 2000 effectively to prohibit any person from trading while in receipt of MNPI. Under Rule 10b5-1, anyone knowingly trading securities on the basis of material nonpublic information would be violating a "breach of a duty of trust or confidence" that is owed to the issuer of the security or the company's shareholders or the insider who passed along the confidential information. Rule 10b5-2 took this chain a step further by explicitly stating that these "duties of trust or confidence" also include a fiduciary duty to the source of the MNPI provided in confidence, whether a business associate or family member. As opposed to the classical theory of insider trading mainly focused on corporate insiders, Rule 10b5-2 adopted a new misappropriation theory of insider trading to cast a very wide liability net and essentially target every MNPI transmission point. To cut down on the selective leaking of MNPI at the source, the SEC then created a positive duty to disclose in the wake of the 1990s dot-com stock market bubble by passing Regulation FD under the 1934 Act in 2000. Regulation FD generally prohibits public companies from disclosing previously nonpublic, material information unless the information is also distributed to the public first or simultaneously, typically through the filing of a Form 8-K. While the regulation has had no perceptible impact on the volume of insider trading violations, it has meaningfully reduced the information edge of market experts such as research analysts and traders while also casting a pall over all nonpublic information.[4]

For years, the only other Wall Street constituency with hard-coded fiduciary responsibilities apart from corporate insiders has been investment advisers. Under the Investment Advisers Act of 1940, investment advisers are required to act in the best financial interest of their clients, owing both a fiduciary duty of loyalty and care to act prudently and in good faith while avoiding conflicts of interest and putting their clients' interests above their own. Under the prudent-man rule, fiduciaries are required to invest trust assets as a "prudent man" would invest his own assets. During the modern age, the conventional definition of prudent investing has taken into account modern portfolio theory and a diversified approach, eliminating category restrictions on different types of investments and placing a primacy on total return generation. Fiduciary duty requires a high standard of financial professional conduct and a demanding level of client care consistent with an ongoing investment relationship, discretionary power, and an asset-based compensation structure. Up until recently, such a blanket fiduciary responsibility toward investors has not applied to the sell side of Wall Street where customer relationships are more transaction oriented.

Broker-dealers – which execute securities trades and provide discrete investment recommendations and are compensated via commissions for individual transactions – are licensed and regulated by state securities regulators, the SEC, and FINRA, the SEC-regulated entity that was formed in 2007 as the successor to the regulatory arms of the National Association of Securities Dealers (NASD) and the NYSE. All US broker-dealers must register with FINRA and every individual working in the securities business must be licensed as a registered representative, subject to regular disclosure and educational requirements. Despite the industry's transactional focus, for decades, investment banks, broker-dealers, and boutique financial advisers have been subject to rules – first NASD and NYSE and now FINRA – requiring them to perform due diligence to know their customer and ensure that any recommendations made are both reasonable and suitable for each particular investor.

The Dodd–Frank Act passed in the wake of the 2008 global financial crisis directed the SEC to evaluate gaps in existing regulations for investment advisers and broker-dealers given the widespread confusion over the respective client obligations of the two groups of market players. Dodd–Frank specifically authorized the SEC to impose a fiduciary standard of care on broker-dealers akin to that already applied to advisers. In 2011, the SEC staff issued a report recommending that the SEC do just that and adopt a uniform fiduciary standard. After back-burnering the issue for several years, in 2019 the SEC passed Regulation Best Interest (BI) under the 1934 Act, which establishes a "best interest" standard of conduct for broker-dealers and associated persons when they make a recommendation to a retail customer of any securities transaction or investment strategy involving securities, including recommendations of types of accounts. Under Regulation BI, the required standard of conduct is to act in the best interest of the retail customer at the time a recommendation is made without placing the financial or other interests of the broker-dealer ahead of the interest of the retail customer. The new regulation only applies to retail accounts, and the obligation to act in the best interest of the investing client is only temporal and measured at a point in time.

Other federal agencies besides the SEC have tried to get into the act and use their regulatory powers to impose a uniform fiduciary standard on both sides of Wall Street. In April 2016, the Department of Labor (DOL) under the Obama administration issued a final regulation that redefined the term "investment advice" within pension and retirement plans and subjected all financial professionals – including broker-dealers – who work with private sector retirement plans governed by the Employee Retirement Income Security Act of 1974 (ERISA) to an elevated fiduciary level of customer duty. The ERISA Act was promulgated to protect retirement savings from mismanagement and abuse and safeguard pension benefit plan participants and their beneficiaries, mainly by holding plan administrators to a high standard of conduct. Under the 1974 statute, a person who provides investment advice to a retirement plan has a fiduciary obligation, which means that the person must provide the advice in the sole interest of plan participants. As originally conceived, securities brokers and dealers who provided services to retirement plans did not qualify as fiduciaries and were not required to act in the sole interests of plan participants; rather, their recommendations simply had to be reasonable and suitable. By broadening the definition of investment advice, the 2016 DOL rule effectively reclassified broker-dealers as fiduciaries whenever these financial firms provided recommendations to participants in retirement and pension plans. After taking effect in 2017, the 2016 DOL rule was immediately challenged by various business groups who successfully argued in court that it constituted statutory overreach. In 2018, the US Court of Appeals for the Fifth Circuit vacated the rule.[5]

Over time, the concept of fiduciary duty on Wall Street has evolved from an issuer- or client-specific contractual obligation to a broader duty owed to all investors and the markets in general, with the goal being to ensure public confidence in the integrity of the financial system while increasing control over all market players through the threat of legal action. The fiduciary rule that has historically governed the behavior of investment advisers has gradually seeped over to the sell side of the business over the past two decades. Based on the current legislative and regulatory momentum, the standard of putting the interests of investing clients first will eventually be applied to investment banks and broker-dealers, with negative implications for market liquidity. The same trend can be seen in the corporate sector as stakeholder capitalism theory has slowly gained ground, with corporate purpose becoming a malleable concept and the fiduciary focus of business executives and board directors expanding beyond shareholders and profitability.

Even as fiduciary obligations have been ratcheted up across the business world and Wall Street, ESG activists, led by the PRI, have gone to work to change the meaning of fiduciary duty to allow for ESG considerations. Because there is little compelling market data to make the economic case that sustainable business practices create value or sustainable investing leads to better returns for investors, the fiduciary rule represents a kind of ESG Maginot Line for the global financial markets, which is why proponents have been actively targeting this last line of defense for years.

There is nothing currently standing in the way of fund managers seeking to raise capital for ESG mandates where investors are fully aware of the risks associated with the defined strategy and are willing and able to bear the return consequences of the chosen strategy. A significant amount of new money has flowed into dedicated sustainable funds in recent years. The fiduciary problem arises, though, with the ESG integration process being pushed by the PRI and other sustainable activists where existing broad-based market funds are being rebranded as sustainable. The majority of present-day investors – especially in the US – did not sign up for an environmental and social justice agenda when they allocated capital to an asset manager, making the ex post application of such criteria – even if mandated by an activist regulator – a fiduciary breach. While segregated accounts would be the more appropriate means of satisfying the vocal minority of ESG-driven investors, such a customized response would not move the needle toward the stated goal of creating a "sustainable global financial system" by the year 2030. This is why the concept of fiduciary duty must be relaxed and redefined to clear the way for a systemwide application of ESG.

For years as part of their advocacy agenda, the PRI and its UN affiliate, the UNEP FI, have been pushing the argument that the "modern interpretation" of fiduciary duty not only allows but actually requires investors to incorporate ESG factors into their investment decision-making. In 2005, the UNEP FI commissioned the international law firm Freshfields Bruckhaus Deringer to issue a report analyzing the legal framework for the integration of environmental, social, and governance issues into institutional investment. The report was prompted by the fact that fiduciary duty represents the key source of legal and regulatory limits on the discretion of investment decision-makers to focus on other criteria such as ESG rather than just financial return. Freshfields looked at whether the integration of ESG factors into investment policy – including asset allocation, portfolio construction, and stock or bond picking – was voluntarily permitted, legally required, or hampered by law and regulation in nine jurisdictions: Australia, Canada, France, Germany, Italy, Japan, Spain, the UK, and the US. The Freshfields analysis was mainly focused on pension funds and insurance companies, given that these two groups of asset owners comprise the lion's share of investable AUM in the global market. Using somewhat circular legal reasoning, the

2005 report concluded that, regardless of the legal framework of the jurisdiction – whether common or civil law – integrating ESG considerations is clearly permissible given that "the links between ESG factors and financial performance are increasingly being recognized," even though recognized is not the same thing as proven. Moreover, Freshfields found that ESG integration is arguably required in all the jurisdictions surveyed as part of the duty of loyalty owed to the best interests of the investing client so as "to give effect to the views of the beneficiaries in relation to matters beyond financial return." Simply pointing to an ESG market consensus or "clear breaches of widely recognized norms" would suffice to justify investment decisions to exclude individual companies or entire sectors from portfolios. The main objective of the 2005 report was to provide the legal cover needed to start shifting the fiduciary focus away from objective goals such as return maximization and portfolio diversification and more toward subjective nonfinancial factors such as ESG.[6]

In 2009, the UNEP FI published its follow-up study to the Freshfields report, which looked at the legal and practical aspects of integrating ESG issues into institutional investment from a fiduciary perspective. Dubbed "Fiduciary II," the report conducted a review of the law and the literature and surveyed investment management consulting firms to come up with best practices for legally embedding ESG into the investment process, particularly with regard to investment mandates and management contracts. Whereas the Freshfields report provided the legal justification for ESG, the 2009 sequel provided "the legal roadmap for fiduciaries looking for concrete steps to operationalize their commitments to responsible investment." Moreover, coming three years after the formation of the PRI and in the immediate wake of the 2008 global financial crisis, "Fiduciary II" was highly prescriptive – almost urgent – in its ESG conclusions and recommendations. The report's top-level takeaway was that "the global economy has now reached the point where ESG issues are a critical consideration for all institutional investors and their agents." Only by integrating ESG issues into investment policymaking and decision-making will institutional investors – and the companies that they invest in – be able to "sustain their wealth creation role and play their fundamental role in the creation of a more sustainable global economy." More specifically, the paper concluded the following: investment advisers have a duty to proactively raise ESG issues within the advice that they provide to institutional investors; a responsible investment option should be the default position; ESG should be a routine part of all investment arrangements, and not just an optional add-on; and global capital market policymakers should ensure regulatory frameworks that legally impose such ESG requirements on investment fiduciaries.[7]

The ESG fiduciary mantle was next picked up by the PRI. Working with the UNEP FI and the Generation Foundation, the charitable organization funded by Al Gore's sustainable investment management firm, the PRI produced a white paper aimed at "ending the debate" on whether fiduciary duty is a legitimate barrier to ESG integration. The report, "Fiduciary Duty in the 21st Century," was released in September 2015 and found – not surprisingly, given its foregone conclusion – that "far from being a barrier, there are positive duties to integrate environmental, social and governance factors in investment processes." Much like the climate science being purportedly settled, the PRI also decreed that "the conceptual debate around whether ESG issues are a requirement of investor duties and obligations is now over." Like the Freshfields study, the findings of the PRI 2015 fiduciary report have been dutifully parroted by the group's membership and like-minded ESG institutions, including those embedded in the halls of academia.

Based on the PRI's take, modern-day fiduciaries are required to incorporate ESG factors into their investment decision-making and obligated to be active owners by regularly policing the ESG performance of all the companies in which they are invested. Supporting the "integrity and stability of the financial system" would also be a fiduciary responsibility in the new ESG world order. Notably, the PRI report also adopts a lower threshold of care for fiduciaries to facilitate broad ESG integration. Rather than the traditional prudent-man rule – which requires trade and portfolio decisions that an investor of reasonable intelligence, discretion, and prudence could be expected to make – the PRI argues that fiduciaries nowadays only need to invest as an "ordinary prudent person" would, which represents a dumbing down of the process and a lowering of stewardship standards. Moreover, using the time machine construct of the sustainability argument, investment fiduciaries should now consider the long-term interests of their beneficiaries, both financial and non-financial, whether known to them or not.[8]

In 2021, the PRI, along with the UNEP FI and the Generation Foundation, took it a step further by commissioning another report by Freshfields to explore the current legal framework for impact investing. Specifically, the project was focused on determining whether investing for sustainable impact and social outcomes to benefit "people and the planet" is legally required or permitted under the fiduciary rule and other legal duties owed by asset owners and investment firms. The study looked at 11 jurisdictions – including Australia, Brazil, Canada, China, the EU, France, Japan, the Netherlands, South Africa, the UK, and the US – and concluded that, while current laws and regulations varied across different markets, most jurisdictions permitted such impact-oriented investment moves as overweighting, underweighting, or exiting particular sectors and companies based on how their activities aligned with the SDGs of the UN. Freshfields noted that more legal clarity is needed to facilitate sustainable impact investing and justify those situations where there is no financial return argument to be made. Toward this end, the report also included a list of reform suggestions for global policymakers to consider.[9]

The PRI's crusade to deconstruct fiduciary duty has thus far found the most policy traction over in Europe, both in the UK and the EU. With regard to the former, the Financial Reporting Council (FRC) is an independent regulator with delegated powers from the UK government that serves the public interest by overseeing auditors, accountants, and actuaries and setting corporate governance and stewardship codes for the country. In recent years, at the PRI's prodding, the FRC has revised its UK Stewardship Code for investment managers and asset owners (and their service providers) to incorporate ESG and mandate sustainability as a positive fiduciary duty. The code, which was first promulgated in 2010 and subsequently revised in 2012, made no mention of ESG in its earliest iterations, instead focusing on generic principles of good investment stewardship such as avoiding conflicts of interest, monitoring and maximizing corporate value, and maintaining adequate disclosure and reporting standards.

All of this changed, however, with the updated version of the code released by the FRC in 2020. In it, the FRC explicitly cites ESG and lays out 12 principles for investment managers and asset owners to follow – all of which require a sustainable approach to investing. Under Principle 1, investment stewardship is defined as creating "long-term value" for clients and beneficiaries, which in turn will lead to "sustainable benefits for the economy, the environment and society." Under Principle 4, investors must identify and respond to marketwide and systemic risks – including, specifically, climate change – to promote a well-functioning financial system. Under Principle 7, asset managers and owners need to integrate "material environmental, social and governance issues, and climate change" into their investment processes to fulfill their stewardship responsibilities. Under Principle 9, investors must engage with issuers to enhance the value of their assets by holding them to account on material issues including ESG.

The latest iteration of the UK's stewardship code has the fingerprints of the PRI all over it. Besides leaving open to interpretation such concepts as the appropriate length of investment horizon and client and beneficiary needs (especially around nonfinancial issues), the new code includes many PRI buzzwords and catchphrases such as active ownership, company engagement, investor collaboration, and stewardship escalation, as well as the concept of holding service providers accountable. With regard to the latter, there are also six principles enumerated for service providers, including a requirement to address systemic risks such as climate change and the need to support their clients' stewardship efforts including the integration of environmental, social, and governance issues into their respective investment approaches.[10]

The stewardship codes of the FRC are technically voluntary. Asset managers and asset owners sign up and pledge to follow the FRC's 12 principles, much like PRI members sign up and pledge to follow its six guiding principles. As of February 2023, 254 financial firms were signatories, even though the FRC's soft law sets a higher standard than the current minimum UK regulatory requirements. However, when certain large accounts – such as Scottish Widows Group Limited, the UK-based life insurance and pensions company with £152 billion in AUM as of December 31, 2022 – mandate that all their counterparties must be signatories to the stewardship code as a prerequisite for doing business, this helps to get the membership ball rolling. Once again, an official-sounding, nongovernmental group is effectively setting regulatory policy, in the model of the PRI and the rest of the ESG nonprofit network.[11]

On the continent, the EU, as part of a series of recent sustainable finance regulations aimed at implementing the Paris Agreement, fighting global climate change, and achieving the 2030 Agenda for Sustainable Development, has also issued several regulatory amendments spelling out how financial market participants and financial advisers must now integrate ESG risks and opportunities in their investment processes, as part of their fiduciary duty to act in the best interest of clients. Released in April 2021, the amendments to the EU's Markets in Financial Instruments Directive (MiFID) and its Insurance Distribution Directive require investment advisers to obtain information about a client's sustainability preferences as part of their suitability assessment and to ensure that such sustainability considerations are taken into account on a systematic basis when making investment decisions and recommendations to clients. The EU amendments, which came into force in August 2021 and apply to the asset management, insurance, reinsurance, and investment sectors, make clear that, from a European legal and regulatory perspective, fiduciary duty encompasses sustainability risks such as climate change and environmental degradation and requires a proactive ESG stance by investment stewards.[12]

Since the US holds the largest share of pension assets globally – approximately $34.0 trillion as of 2022,[13] roughly 71% of the OECD total – the PRI has also taken aim at this market by pushing for a rewrite of ERISA regulations to allow for the incorporation of ESG factors. Here the US government has been playing catch-up over the past three years as the Biden White House has worked to reverse the anti-ESG DOL rulings of the previous Trump administration. Since ERISA was first enacted nearly 50 years ago, the DOL has had a long-standing position that ERISA fiduciaries may not sacrifice investment returns or assume greater investment risks as a means of promoting collateral social policy goals. For years, however, the DOL's nonregulatory guidance has recognized that, under the appropriate circumstances, ERISA does not preclude fiduciaries from making investment decisions that reflect ESG considerations, which has led to growing confusion in the financial markets.

In late 2020, the Trump DOL reinstated the first principles of ERISA with two new rules that redirected plan fiduciaries to put the economic interests of retirement account participants and beneficiaries ahead of any other investment goals – including those related to ESG and sustainability – and reiterated that only pecuniary factors that had a material effect on financial performance and risk–return trade-offs were relevant for pension fund managers. In November 2022, the Biden DOL issued a new final rule that superseded the two Trump ERISA rulings. Dubbed the "Prudence and Loyalty in Selecting Plan Investments and Exercising Shareholder Rights" rule and taking effect in January 2023, the Biden DOL rule makes clear that "a fiduciary's determination with respect to an investment or investment course of action must be based on factors that the fiduciary reasonably determines are relevant to a risk and return analysis," but that such factors may include the economic effects of climate change and other ESG factors on the particular investment or investment course of action. Moreover, the new rule also recognizes that the fiduciary act of managing employee benefit plan assets includes the management of proxy voting rights and other shareholder rights connected to the ownership of stock, and that management of those rights, as well as shareholder engagement activities, are subject to ERISA's prudence and loyalty requirements. Said another way, ERISA fiduciaries are expected to be active asset owners and aggressive stewards in the model of the PRI.[14]

The PRI has been warning for years that "investors that fail to incorporate ESG issues are failing their fiduciary duties and are increasingly likely to be subject to legal challenge."[15] While perfectly in character, such a threatening statement betrays a lack of confidence in the ESG argument being made and foreshadows calls for regulatory reinforcement down the road. A major goal of the PRI-led ESG agenda is to change the legal and regulatory frameworks within which investors operate and make the ESG program compulsory. Toward this end, the PRI has been closely coordinating for years with government regulators worldwide to convert its ESG recommendations into legal requirements for all financial market participants. In fact, after publishing its 2015 report on modern fiduciary duty, the group spent the next four years lobbying government officials worldwide for financial market regulations that would enforce its conclusions.

From the outset, changing the fiduciary rule has been the first and most important step in the regulatory strategy of the ESG movement. By emasculating the fiduciary responsibilities of investors and corporate managers – mainly by diluting down financial performance and return as primary goals and injecting subjective nonfinancial factors and client preferences into the mix – it will remove the last remaining legal stumbling block for ESG. Much like lowering your deflector shields in an episode of *Star Trek*, it will leave Wall Street defenseless and open the regulatory floodgates for sustainable finance mandates, which have always been part of the plan to achieve a "sustainable global financial system" by the year 2030. As the PRI laments in its 2015 report, the "capital markets remain unsustainable" because ESG factors are not yet driving valuations or investment allocations, so "changing this will be our next phase of work."[16] Moral suasion, collective guilt, and implicit threats were the main tools used to spread ESG integration over the past few years, but these drivers can only get you so far. The only way to impose order on the current ESG chaos and standardize the application of sustainability is through regulatory force. The only way to influence the cost of capital and direct investment away from politically incorrect industries such as fossil fuels and toward government-favored sectors such as green energy is through legal mandates. The only way to suppress animal spirits and rein in the price mechanism of the financial markets is by controlling market access and the supply of capital. The central planning aspect of the ESG movement will become abundantly clear over the coming years as sustainable finance enters its final authoritarian phase between now and 2030. And, as with everything related to ESG, it will be Europe leading the charge on the regulatory front.

CHAPTER 11

EUROPE ATTACKS!

It is Europe, it is the whole of Europe, that will decide the fate of the world.
Charles de Gaulle

During my lifetime most of the problems the world has faced have come, in one fashion or other, from mainland Europe, and the solutions from outside it.
Margaret Thatcher

Every progressive cause eventually requires the use of government force. We have now reached that point with the quixotic sustainable investment movement. Despite a lot of public lip service, ESG considerations are still not driving investment decisions by most asset managers, particularly in the US. In its 2020 Annual ESG Manager Survey, Russell Investments found that 71% of 400 respondents did not use any portfolio performance measures directly tied to ESG or climate risk criteria.[1] Similarly, in its 2022 ESG Survey of 109 institutional investors, the Callan Institute disclosed that only 35% were incorporating ESG into their investment decision-making process.[2] Such findings are not surprising given the preposterous premise of sustainable investing. Pressuring companies to toe the progressive line with their public statements is one thing; reengineering the financial markets based on a chaotic and ever-changing list of morally subjective ESG factors is quite another. Clearly, a voluntary approach to ESG integration over the past few years has not worked. Nothing is yet standardized, asset prices are not responding, and global investor capital is still not being redirected away from those politically incorrect sectors and companies deemed "unsustainable," especially when it comes to the "highest-priority ESG issue" of climate change. Moral suasion can only get you so far.

Calling in government reinforcements by weaponizing regulatory agencies was always part of the plan for the PRI and other ESG advocates, most of which are self-aware enough to realize that no amount of public shaming, implicit threats, and herd mentality was ever going to convince everyone on Wall Street to get on board. Aligning the global capital markets with sustainability goals was always going to require compulsion on a grand and global scale. This is why the PRI has been pushing its ESG agenda with government officials and financial regulators worldwide for years. The PRI has compiled a regulation database that tracks policy tools and guidance that support, encourage, or require ESG considerations by market participants. The PRI database includes sustainable finance policies and regulations that target a range of ESG-related issues and outcomes: supporting national policy goals on climate change and the SDGs; enhancing the resilience and stability of the financial system and the economy; improving market efficiency by clarifying and aligning investor and company expectations; and increasing the attractiveness of countries as investment destinations to help drive investments toward "sustainable, inclusive and zero-carbon economies."

For the PRI, the database is a barometer of the group's success since its members are required to promote acceptance and implementation of its ESG agenda through support for regulatory and policy developments that facilitate the organization's six guiding principles. The group published a white paper titled "Policy Frameworks for Long-Term Responsible Investment: The Case for Investor Engagement in Public Policy" in 2014, which spells out the duties of its members.[3] Working directly through its membership and indirectly through like-minded ESG affinity groups, the PRI has actively lobbied government policymakers and regulators for years through its public consultations and policy recommendations, with the volume of both increasing of late. Per the PRI's self-serving vision, all ESG regulatory frameworks need to be aligned globally and government officials must articulate the role that capital markets should play in creating a sustainable financial system and world economy. Specifically, financial regulations need to be strengthened to improve monitoring, measure impacts, and preclude "easy opt-outs" by market participants, starting with mandatory reporting on climate and other ESG issues by companies and investment firms alike.

As of April 30, 2022, based on the PRI's numbers, the worldwide count of ESG policies and regulations stood at 868, almost all of which (96%) have been put on the books since the year 2000. Since 2015, the number of ESG policy instruments has more than doubled as the pace of regulatory intervention has accelerated, with 225 new additions in 2021 alone. The aggregate number tracked by the PRI includes approximately 300 policy revisions in recent years as ESG rules have been steadily tightened across the board, with the lion's share of responsible investing regulations now mandatory as opposed to voluntary. To maintain the public ESG pressure on market participants – particularly those still sitting on the fence around sustainability – the PRI has published its regulatory database since 2016 to highlight the increasing ESG policy count and remind Wall Street of the growing regulatory threat.[4]

With the all-important 2030 inflection point for the planet and society now less than a decade away, the sustainability movement needs to pick up the pace. Cue the European regulators. Since European national governments were the driving force behind the Paris Agreement and the follow-on UN Sustainable Development Goals, and since sovereign-related European financial institutions and pension funds have been the loudest champions of sustainability to date, Europe is now leading the charge on ESG disclosure mandates and fund regulatory requirements. Roughly 75% of the currently outstanding 868 ESG regulations tracked by the PRI have been passed by European nations, including the EU and the prodigal UK.

Since the 2015 signing of the Paris Agreement and the companion SDGs for 2030, the EU has plunged headlong into the legal and policy work required to implement the UN's climate and sustainable development agenda across its member states and collective territory. In December 2019, the European Commission introduced the European Green Deal, an aggressive, whole-economy approach designed to make Europe the first carbon-neutral continent on the globe by 2050. On top of no net emissions of greenhouse gases by the mid-century mark, the EU has also committed to at least a 55% reduction in net emissions by 2030 versus a 1990 baseline, which compares to an actual cumulative decline of 33%

through 2020 as measured by Eurostat.[5] Besides making Europe environmentally sustainable and enhancing its natural capital and biodiversity, the comprehensive green plan to decarbonize and decouple the European economy from fossil fuels has also been billed as a growth driver that will increase employment and transform the EU into "a modern, resource-efficient and competitive economy." Also, a "just transition" away from fossil fuels will create "an economy that works for people," improves the well-being and health of all citizens, and leaves no person or place behind.[6]

The EU has been one of the leading government proponents of climate change since the early days of the 1980s. In November 2022, it was the EU that threatened to walk out of the COP27 meeting in Egypt to shut down any collective backtracking from the 1.5°C global temperature target set by the UN group. European nations have a lot of political capital vested in the progressive climate project at this point. Neither current world events nor economic reality or realpolitik considerations will keep the EU from its appointment with climate destiny in 2030. Many of the EU's climate targets and green goals have been ratcheted up further over the past two years – the headline emissions reduction target for 2030 was inched up from 55% to 57% at COP27 – despite the onset of an energy crisis triggered by the Russian invasion of Ukraine in 2022, which finally exposed the geopolitical and security risk of Europe's long-standing dependence on Russian energy imports. In 2021, Europe relied on Russia for 40% of its natural gas, 25% of its crude oil, and 45% of its coal needs. Even though the main energy takeaway from the Russia–Ukraine war should be that Europe needs to develop its own in-house natural hydrocarbon resources – starting with the regulatory approval of hydraulic fracturing – and fortify its sovereign oil and gas supply lines, many EU officials have used the conflict to double down on renewable power by dusting off the old 20th-century canard about fossil fuels being a leading cause of war. While such an argument is nonsensical on its face – national economies based on intermittent power sources such as wind and solar cannot project economic or political power to discourage adventurism and aggression, and military forces cannot run on sustainable fuels and solar panels – many European countries have nonetheless rallied behind an acceleration of the continent's green transition as the means to achieving energy independence from Russian fossil fuels.

Pushing down the EU's 2030 green goals to the national level shows how the European climate movement is now entering its "White Rabbit" phase – the one, as described by Jefferson Airplane, "when logic and proportion have fallen sloppy dead."[7] Norway, while not an official EU member, has signed up for the same 55% emissions reduction by 2030 as the EU even though the oil and gas sector accounts for 40% of the Scandinavian country's exports and 14% of its GDP and supports its generous welfare state and rainy-day sovereign fund. Norway is one of the world's largest oil and gas producers and supplies 25% of the EU's natural gas imports, second only to Russia in 2021. Rather than aggressively positioning itself to replace Russian natural gas, Norway is actively suppressing its normal competitive response. Officials in Oslo have announced plans to steadily raise carbon taxes on its domestic energy industry through 2030, while the country's already punitive 78% marginal tax rate on the petroleum sector was modified in 2022 to increase the cash receipts flowing to the Norwegian government.[8] Even though Norway's upstream development pipeline shows its oil and gas production and hydrocarbon reserve base both peaking by 2025, the current Labor government has still voiced its support for the proposed EU ban on exploiting oil and gas in the Arctic Ocean. In the view of Norway's climate and energy minister Espen Barth Eide, the economic future of the High North Arctic region lies not in oil and gas but hydrogen and battery factories, green shipping, and modern sea farming.[9]

Similarly, to live up to its pro rata climate goals as part of the European Green Deal, the Netherlands is now moving quickly to expropriate and shut down 3,000 farms to reduce the country's nitrous oxide emissions, even though the nation is the world's second largest agricultural exporter and Dutch farmers feed the rest of Europe. Shockingly, any Dutch farmers taking a government buy-out must also sign noncompete agreements promising that they will not return to farming (mainly livestock breeding) activities anywhere within the EU.[10] Based on World Bank data, the Netherlands was responsible for just 8.3 million metric tons of CO_2e of N_2O emissions in 2020, or barely 0.3% of the worldwide total.[11] Moreover, nitrous oxide comprises a relatively small piece of the atmospheric GHG pie, roughly one-quarter the volume of methane and one-twelfth that of carbon dioxide (all measured on a global CO_2 equivalent basis). And finally, the Dutch government's extreme steps to further shrink its N_2O footprint come despite the country's nitrous oxide emissions having been cut in half over the past 30 years, mainly due to the increased efficiency of its farming sector.

The race to zero is rapidly devolving into a race to the economic bottom for Europe. If energy producers like Norway and food producers like the Netherlands are allowed to carry through with their self-destructive climate-driven economic policies, Europe will be faced with both energy insecurity and food scarcity as the continent reconfigures itself for the sustainable new world order by 2030. European history seems destined to repeat itself. Food shortages, famines, and people dying from the elements, which have not been a problem for Europe since the 19th century, have led to revolutions in the past. European civilization destroyed itself twice over within a span of 30 years during the first half of the 20th century, and there is no reason why it could not happen again, even if the method of suicide will be different this time around.

The lunatic fringes of the climate movement are now starting to show. To fight climate change, the WEF has proposed a variety of draconian measures including eating insects,[12] replacing meat with synthetic food,[13] banning private car ownership,[14] using a digital ID to track personal carbon usage,[15] and enforcing climate-related lockdowns that build on the 2020 COVID-19 pandemic model.[16] The French government recently banned short-haul commercial flights within the country so now only the elite will be able to fly by private jet directly to their destination.[17] In the UK, more than 300 local councils have drawn up plans to become net zero by 2030.[18] Toward this end, Oxfordshire county officials have designed a new travel plan for the Central Oxfordshire Area that seeks to "rapidly reduce carbon emissions from all transport related activities" and create 20-minute walking neighborhoods – the building blocks of smart cities – notably by restricting private automobile usage to only 100 trips per year and by permit only.[19] In January 2023, the Scottish city of Edinburgh voted to ban all meat and dairy products in schools, hospitals, and government buildings.[20] The WEF vision of society is already playing out in Europe, with technology making it all possible.

Given that the EU has led the climate change charge for decades, it is not surprising that the EU is also taking the lead on the ESG regulatory front. To realize its self-imposed climate goals for 2030 and beyond, the EU estimates that the European Green Deal will require total investment of €1 trillion over the next 10 years, of which roughly 25–30% would need to be funded with private sector investment. The actual financing cost is likely to come in much higher – perhaps three times higher based on the calculations of the Brussels-based think tank Bruegel.[21] Given the weak state of public sector finances across Europe, this means that private sector capital will need to fill this funding gap. To redirect private sector financing toward the European Green Deal, the EU has taken several regulatory steps to make the European financial system more sustainable – just the latest proof that sustainability and ESG are synonymous with climate change.

To steer investment toward clean energy businesses and projects across Europe, the EU has put in place a sustainable finance regulatory framework built around three core components. First, the Taxonomy Regulation, which went into force in July 2020, establishes a classification system for a range of economic activities across various industries to show which are environmentally sustainable and conducive to the goals of the European Green Deal, and which are not. This green taxonomy, which purports to be science-driven and based on technical screening criteria but is compiled and maintained by politicians, is meant as a foundational sustainability tool for companies and investors to use – first to standardize reporting and disclosure and then to change behavior and reorient the flow of capital spending and investment. The EU Taxonomy was initially applied to 13 sectors which, in the aggregate, accounted for roughly 80% of European greenhouse gas emissions: forestry; environmental protection and restoration activities; manufacturing; energy (including electricity); water supply, sewerage, waste management, and remediation; transport; construction and real estate; information and communication; professional, scientific, and technical activities; finance and insurance; education; human health and social work activities; and arts, entertainment, and recreation. More economic activities and industries – notably farming and agriculture – will be added to the running list over time.

Economic activities deemed environmentally sustainable would be those that contribute substantially to one or more of the EU's six environmental objectives and, in Hippocratic fashion, do no significant harm to any. The list of environmental objectives is skewed toward climate action and includes the following priorities: climate change mitigation;

climate change adaptation; sustainable use and protection of water and marine resources; transition to a circular economy; pollution prevention and control; and protection of healthy ecosystems. To achieve green taxonomy alignment, an economic activity must also comply with certain minimum social safeguards which eventually will be spun out into a separate, stand-alone social taxonomy. The list of sustainable economic activities is fairly intuitive. For example, activities that make a substantial contribution to the environmental objectives of climate change mitigation and adaptation would include such things as hydrogen manufacturing, biofuels production, solar, wind, and geothermal power generation, and permanent carbon sequestration.

Even though the EU Taxonomy does not define or explicitly label any activity as environmentally unsustainable, this is the clear signal sent by not making the sustainability list. For the bureaucrats in Brussels, the system is binary: either an economic activity makes a substantial contribution and lands in the green category, or it is doing substantial harm, implicitly placing it in the brown category of unsustainable activities not worthy of financing. Crude oil production, refining, and coal mining are nowhere to be found on the energy sector activity list, which is heavily weighted toward non–fossil fuel electricity. Essentially, the EU Taxonomy is the environmental equivalent of Santa's naughty and nice lists, with politicians populating both columns and companies and investors doing what they can to avoid landing up on the latter. As Eldridge Cleaver, the leader of the Black Panthers, used to say back in the 1960s, "If you're not part of the solution, you're part of the problem."

The EU Taxonomy regulation applies to approximately 12,000 large publicly listed companies and all financial market participants. On an annual basis, companies must report what percentage of their total revenues and capital expenditures are comprised of taxonomy-aligned and sustainable economic activities – basically, the green and brown split for how they make money and where they are investing their cash. Using this company-level detail, investment firms must aggregate the percentage of taxonomy alignment at the investment and product level. The corporate reporting requirements for the first two climate-focused environmental objectives started in January 2022, while those for the remaining four began a year later in January 2023.

The EU Taxonomy represents the cornerstone of the EU's ESG

regulatory agenda. The classification system underpins the ESG mandates set for European corporations and investment firms, while also feeding into the EU's labeling standards for green bonds and climate benchmark indexes. The green taxonomy is meant as a transparency tool, although transparency weapon would be a more accurate description. It has two main goals: standardizing the approach to ESG investing, starting with climate change, by laying out which economic activities and business operations are irrefutably green; and using reporting as the means to the end of driving capital toward companies and projects that support the goals of the European Green Deal. Once European companies and investors start disclosing how much or how little they are doing to help the transition to a low-carbon economy, then individual firms can be isolated and pressured to act and do more for the cause. While designed to cut through the ESG noise in the market by replacing all the competing ESG methodologies with one set of objective sustainability criteria, the EU Taxonomy is equally subjective and mired in the same level of minutiae. For example, the list of sustainable activities that contribute to the environmental objective of climate change mitigation includes 72 different operations, while the approved activities for climate change adaptation number 70. The main difference, though, is that the official EU Taxonomy approach to sustainability is mandatory. Gone are the days when ESG was optional and voluntary, customized approaches were encouraged, and just focusing on financially material factors was allowed. Now, companies and financial institutions must demonstrate concrete action on the EU's environmental goals, and nobody gets a free pass just by having good ESG reporting and disclosure.[22]

Under the Corporate Sustainability Reporting Directive (CSRD), the second major piece of EU ESG regulation passed in November 2022, designated European companies are required to disclose a broad array of information under the E, S, and G pillars, building off the structure of the environment-focused EU Taxonomy. The CSRD applies to any companies doing business in Europe that are either publicly listed or have more than 250 employees, €40 million in annual sales, or €20 million in total assets. Any EU company meeting the criteria must produce an annual ESG report meant to satisfy the requirements of EU regulators and supersede all the ESG reporting formats currently outstanding in the market. Under the CSRD, companies must conduct a materiality assessment of their operations – and those of their suppliers and other operating counterparties – and report on the impact of their businesses on people and the environment, as well as the risks posed to them by climate change and other ESG issues. Sustainability must be embedded in the long-term strategy planning of every company and must also permeate its business and financial policies. Companies must set clear ESG targets and regularly monitor their progress in achieving these goals, while clearly identifying those managers with ESG oversight responsibilities. All ESG reporting, target setting, and performance tracking must comply with EU standards and be audited by an independent auditor for inclusion alongside financial information in a company's annual report. The EU estimates that more than 50,000 companies will be subject to the CSRD ESG mandate, which went into effect in 2023, a fourfold increase from the corporate universe subject to the EU Taxonomy. Affected European companies will need to start reporting against the CSRD beginning in early 2025 for the 2024 fiscal or calendar year.[23]

The third key ESG regulatory component is the Sustainable Finance Disclosure Regulation (SFDR), which imposes ESG disclosure requirements on all investment managers and investment products marketed in the EU. The SFDR, which is being phased in over an extended time frame, applies to all EU financial market participants, including portfolio managers, fund managers, pension providers, and financial advisers. It requires managers to disclose how sustainability risks are considered in the investment process and what metrics are used to assess ESG factors. All funds – both sustainable and nonsustainable – must disclose their level of ESG integration so that EU investors have the information they need to make investment choices that are in line with their sustainability goals. With such greater ESG transparency, investors will be able to make better-informed investment decisions that steer the flow of investment dollars toward sustainable investments and increase the growth of the so-called sustainable economy. If fund managers want to remain relevant and competitive in an increasingly ESG-focused market, they will need to offer more sustainable fund options to their investing clients, which is the ultimate desideratum of the regulation.

Under Phase 1 of the SFDR, which went into effect in March 2021, financial firms must comply with a series of high-level ESG disclosure requirements at both the firm and fund level. These include a rundown of the sustainability risks (mainly climate change) that could impact the value of an investment; a description of the principal adverse impacts or negative effects that an investment could have on the sustainability goals set by the EU, particularly for carbon emissions; and an attestation to the accuracy of any statements made regarding ESG characteristics or sustainable investments. The SFDR also mandates transparency around remuneration policies in relation to the integration of sustainability risks into the investment process. In addition, the first phase of the SFDR requires European asset managers to start disclosing sustainability data for their managed funds, both commingled and segregated, all of which needs to be classified into three groups to help investors understand the different kinds of sustainable investing. Under the SFDR fund taxonomy, Article 6 funds would largely ignore sustainability considerations and have no ESG-related portfolio exclusions or restrictions; Article 8 funds would integrate ESG considerations and promote environmental and social characteristics while observing good governance standards, even though sustainability would not be the stated investment goal; and Article 9 funds would have sustainable investment as their core objective and be designed to have a sustainable impact and show positive outcomes. Under Phase 2 of the SFDR, enhanced disclosure requirements kicked in for sustainability-focused light green Article 8 and dark green Article 9 funds beginning in 2023.[24]

Thus far, the SFDR appears to be succeeding in its goal of steering more capital toward the European Green Deal. As intended, the tripartite fund category system has been interpreted as a competitive scale and led to a positioning contest for asset managers focused on the sustainability-minded European market. Since an ESG-indifferent Article 6 label would be out of step with the sensitivities of most European investors and likely to trigger fund outflows, one would expect to see an increasing number of sustainability-focused Article 8 or Article 9 funds over time, and the market data bears this out.

Based on Morningstar data, the European market share of Article 8 and Article 9 funds has grown from roughly 30% in April 2021, shortly after Phase 1 of the SFDR was implemented, to 56% or €4.6 trillion as of December 2022. During the fourth quarter of 2022, Article 8 and 9 funds accounted for 57% of all new European fund launches. As the number and market share of Article 6 funds has decreased over time, there has also been an increasing downshift from Article 9 to Article 8 funds as the 2023 deadline for enhanced Phase 2 reporting requirements has approached. Since an Article 9 designation sets a high bar for actual achievement and sustainable outcomes (i.e., fund managers must capture and report all the negative effects of a particular investment on the world's environment and global society), many of these funds have been reclassified to the Article 8 category (with its looser ESG-integrated approach) going into year-end 2022. During the fourth quarter of 2022, 307 or 40% of all outstanding Article 9 funds were downgraded to Article 8 status.[25]

Notably, Article 8 funds can only invest in companies demonstrating good governance standards which, in the absence of any definitional clarity from EU regulators, means that fund managers will now be forced to justify every investment that they hold. Such a portfolio line-item "comply or explain" standard is likely to push most managers to outsource the name approval process to so-called ESG third-party experts – in particular, the UNGC with its 10 governance principles for businesses, which it describes as international norms – to simplify decision-making and limit manager liability. Outsourcing the governance call, which is arguably the most critical aspect of the investment function, is just one of the fiduciary breaches created by the SFDR. Other fiduciary issues include affixing a sustainability label to an existing pre-SFDR fund, effectively changing its investment strategy and overhead cost structure ex post, as well as actively discriminating against investors who don't care about sustainability by limiting their available fund choices. However, in the wake of the recent evisceration of the fiduciary rule across the European financial markets, such obvious violations of trust and care are now legal and have gotten lost in the ESG movement's one-two regulatory punch.

Given the never-ending wave of delegated acts, enabling rules, and follow-on technical criteria out of Brussels in recent years, the complexity of EU ESG regulations will only grow over time. Compounding the problem, many individual nations and country blocs in continental Europe have imposed their own customized rules on top of the SFDR. Moreover, this heavy administrative burden will extend not only to Europe-based firms but also to any company or investment manager operating in Europe, given the extraregional reach of the EU's ESG regulations. The ESG disclosure requirements of the CSRD will affect global and non-European companies with at least €150 million of annual revenues from the EU. The SFDR rules will apply to any investment managers or advisers based outside of the EU who market or plan to market their products to EU clients or seek to raise money in the EU. Based on PwC estimates, Europe accounted for 28.8% of the industry's $112.3 trillion in global assets under management as of year-end 2020, with European firms (many with US operations) comprising 17 of the world's top 50 investment managers.[26]

The EU's aggressive regulatory approach has spurred other national regulators – mainly those in developed, industrialized countries – to either call or raise the EU on ESG disclosure and reporting. The post-Brexit UK is now developing its own sustainable finance regulatory framework through its Financial Conduct Authority (FCA). The UK is the first country in the world to make TCFD disclosures mandatory. Since 2022, all UK-listed companies and large asset owners such as banks, insurers, and investment firms have been required to report climate-related data in line with the framework recommended by the G20-empaneled TCFD – including Scope 3 greenhouse gas emissions. In addition, the FCA is working on its own set of Sustainability Disclosure Requirements (SDR), building on the TCFD's climate platform. The outline of the SDR rules was first proposed in October 2022 and, following a brief public consultation period, is scheduled to be finalized by the fourth quarter of 2023. In-scope companies will need to start reporting SDR data for the 2024 financial year beginning in 2025. Like the EU's SFDR, the UK's SDR has its own three-category sustainable labeling convention. Funds with a sustainable focus need to invest mainly in assets that are sustainable for people or planet or both. At least 70% of the assets in such investment portfolios must meet a credible standard of environmental and social sustainability or align with a specified ESG theme. Funds targeting sustainable improvement would invest in assets with the potential to become more environmentally or socially sustainable over time. Such funds may be invested broadly across sectors, but the asset manager would be expected to play an important role in spurring improvements in the sustainability profile of a fund's portfolio assets, mainly through its investor stewardship activities. And funds designed to have a sustainable impact would invest in solutions to problems affecting people or the planet and be expected to achieve real-world impact. Such funds would aim to achieve predefined, positive, and measurable environmental or social goals based on a clearly articulated theory of change and asset selection process. While broadly in line with the SFDR's three-part classification system, the SDR approach is more a labeling regime laying out the requirements for each category, while the SFDR is more focused on the disclosure required for each subjectively applied fund category. Moreover, the UK system would come with its own set of ESG reporting and measurement criteria.[27]

The Biden administration is also following Europe's ESG lead and responding in kind with its own set of US ESG financial regulations to complement the scaled-down version of the Green New Deal recently passed by Congress and signed into law. During the first half of 2022, the SEC issued three proposed rulemakings about climate and ESG disclosures for publicly listed companies and financial firms. The three new SEC disclosure rules draw on the TCFD framework and its recommended climate disclosures regarding strategy, risk management, metrics, and targets. In March 2022, the agency proposed a new rule that would require all publicly listed corporations to disclose climate-related risks that are reasonably likely to have a material impact on the issuer's business operations or financial condition. All public companies would also be required to report audited data on their Scope 1 and Scope 2 (and potentially Scope 3) greenhouse gas emissions at the consolidated enterprise level.[28] This was followed in May 2022 by two new SEC rules aimed at standardizing ESG disclosures by investment advisers based on its own three-part ESG naming convention for funds. Based on fund type, specific ESG disclosures would be required in fund prospectuses, annual reports, and adviser brochures, including a standardized ESG table allowing for comparability across funds. The three fund categories would include integration funds that integrate ESG factors alongside non-ESG factors in the investment process; ESG-focused funds where ESG is the main consideration; and impact funds that have as their investment objective the achievement of a particular nonfinancial environmental or social impact. For all ESG-labeled funds, 80% of invested assets must be consistent with the stated ESG objective. Impact funds would also need to spell out their strategies for effecting change and measuring progress, including the extent to which proxy voting and issuer engagement are used to achieve ESG outcomes. Any ESG funds that consider environmental factors in their strategies would also be required to disclose greenhouse gas emissions data for their individual investments and funds. Previously, any ESG disclosure included in SEC filings has been subject to a financial materiality standard, which has now gone out the regulatory window.[29] If implemented largely as proposed, the SEC's three new rules would create a new ESG reporting requirement that replicates, both in terms of cost and scale, the regular financial reporting under the 1934 Act. The SEC is expected to finalize all three ESG rules by year-end 2023.

Complementing the SEC's ESG rulemaking, the Federal Reserve, the FDIC, and the OCC under the Treasury Department separately have also issued proposed disclosure rules that large financial institutions must follow around climate-related financial risk management. All three sets of principles are modeled on the framework of the TCFD and are substantially similar. If approved in roughly their current form, the principles will require financial firms with total consolidated assets of $100 billion or more to incorporate climate-related risks into their policies and procedures and strategic planning. Senior executives and bank boards will be responsible for overseeing climate risks as part of their governance duties. Financial firms must also embed climate into their risk management approaches by tracking key climate risk indicators, setting appropriate climate risk limits, and conducting scenario analyses to gauge enterprise vulnerability to climate change.[30]

The immediate effect of the competing sets of sustainable finance regulatory mandates coming out of Europe and the US – and eventually the Asia-Pacific region – will be onerous new reporting requirements, increased compliance costs, and heightened litigation risk for companies and investment managers alike. This ESG administrative burden is likely to increase going forward as financial regulators continue to tighten the screw and scale up the bureaucracy. To justify their new ESG mandates, the regulators have pointed to several explanatory factors, none of which is particularly convincing. First, the recent growth in investor interest in sustainability has been used to make the case for regulatory oversight. However, Google searches for the term "ESG" are highly misleading and do not an investment trend make. Over the past few years, it has been mainly ESG advocacy groups such as the PRI that have had the ear of financial regulators worldwide. The PRI has been lobbying government officials for years to normalize ESG as a part of investment policy and risk management on Wall Street by making sustainability a regulatory requirement, so it is not surprising that the current wave of global mandates codify most of the PRI's ESG wish list. While a vocal minority, these sustainability activists do not speak for most return-oriented investors active in the global financial markets, particularly in the US.

Second, the need for regulatory intervention has been spun as a necessary response to investor demand for more clarity and standardization of ESG market protocols. Here again, it has been mainly the PRI and its member surrogates talking their own book with the regulators and, in the process, overstating ESG as a demand-driven, populist grassroots movement. A hyperregulated Wall Street calling for more financial regulations – particularly highly restrictive ESG-related rules – to make its market-making life even more difficult is counterintuitive, since it would be the equivalent of a battalion commander calling in an air strike on his own position. Even in Europe, the epicenter of ESG, the support for sustainability mandates has been decidedly mixed across the investment community and especially weak among the industry's rank and file. A 2018 survey of roughly 24,000 CFA Institute members working in the EU found that most respondents – roughly 60% of which were comprised of portfolio managers, analysts, and traders, the people in the markets every day – agreed that mandating specific ESG factors was inappropriate (61%) and legislating ESG as an override of investor discretion was also inappropriate (72%).[31]

Third, regulators have justified their ESG rulemaking actions on risk management grounds, arguing that climate – the #1 ESG factor – represents a systemic risk for the financial markets. The PRI has been making this argument since its inception and has published regularly on the subject, including a handy investor resource guide on climate risk released in January 2022.[32] Many ESG players with skin in the sustainability game have also echoed this view. In his January 2020 Letter to CEOs, Larry Fink, the CEO of BlackRock, noted in bold letters that "climate risk is investment risk."[33] In a September 2022 opinion piece published on his own media site, Michael Bloomberg stated unequivocally, "The fact is: climate risk is financial risk."[34] Government officials have dutifully parroted the party line. The TCFD recommendations are premised on the preconceived consensus view among the G20 nations that climate poses a risk to the global financial system.

Scratching below the surface of the argument, though, the assertion – as with most other claims about climate change – does not stand up to scrutiny. Climate change represents two types of risks for the financial markets: physical asset risk and transition risk. The former category captures the risk posed to specific real estate assets by catastrophic storms, mainly along coastal areas due to damaging hurricanes. Setting aside the fact that there has been no discernible increase in storm frequency or intensity in recent decades as global atmospheric carbon dioxide levels have continued to climb, this is weather risk and not climate risk despite the self-serving conflation of the two terms. The risk of a storm-related casualty event to a specific corporate asset or location is company-specific and has been well handled and mitigated up until now by insurance coverage. Given the automatic premium pricing adjustment built into most property and casualty policies, outsized weather events or active storm seasons in the past have never spilled over into the broader markets.

The latter category of transition risk is better described as regulatory risk given that the term basically translates as the risk of a disorderly transition to a green economy caused by an abrupt change in government climate policies and regulations. The risk of such a scenario playing out is fairly remote given the lack of meaningful government action on the climate front over the past 30 years, most recently on display at the COP27 meeting in November 2022. Not surprisingly, the CDP noted in a February 2023 report that only 81 out of 18,600 reporting companies surveyed had credible climate transition plans currently in place.[35] Moreover, the concept of ESG was mainly conjured up to cajole the private sector into the fight against climate change and pin the blame for the economic fallout on businesses rather than elected officials. Using the noncredible threat of aggressive government climate policies to paint climate as a systemic financial risk to justify the case for ESG regulations shows the hellish concentric-circular arguments now being made around climate change. It also smacks of desperation since it is essentially a regulatory cry of "Stop me before I kill again."

Lastly, regulators have pointed to the need to protect unsophisticated institutional and retail investors from false and misleading ESG statements by cutting down on greenwashing activity. The greenwashing claim is even more dubious given that ESG is inherently a subjective approach to investing and will always mean different things to different people. The old joke about putting 10 economists in a room and coming up with 11 opinions also applies when it comes to putting the concept of ESG into practice. The original promise of sustainability – repeated by the activists as recently as 2015 – was that converted companies and financial institutions would be able to figure out for themselves what worked for their businesses and how to customize their approaches to ESG integration, engagement, ratings, and metric reporting. Financial materiality was still the main determinant of what – if anything – a corporation or investment firm needed to do around ESG. Most importantly, ESG was still optional despite the moral pressure involved. Now, a mandatory ESG regulatory regime is being rolled out to protect investors from the wholly expected disorderly ESG market that has developed over the past eight years.

The EU has stated that its SFDR rules are designed to protect investors from greenwashing or deceptive sustainability marketing. UK and US financial regulators have similarly echoed this greenwashing objective in their proposed ESG rulemakings. To justify sustainability fund mandates and ESG reporting requirements as a means of protecting investors, financial regulators in Europe and the US have been working in tandem in recent years to lay the predicate and fire a compliance warning shot over the bow of Wall Street. Toward this end, in March 2021, the SEC created a Climate and ESG Task Force within its Division of Enforcement to "proactively identify ESG-related misconduct."[36]

As previously mentioned, in May 2022, the German federal police and regulators from the Federal Financial Supervisory Authority raided the Frankfurt offices of DWS, the largest asset management firm in the country, majority owned by Deutsche Bank, looking for evidence of greenwashing based on whistleblower allegations of misleading investors about green investments.[37] Apparently, ESG factors were only taken into account for a minority of investments in certain DWS funds sporting a sustainable label. The CEO of DWS, Asoka Woehrmann, was forced out shortly after the raid. That same month, the investment arm of BNY Mellon paid a $1.5 million fine to resolve SEC charges that the firm had misstated ESG policies for some mutual funds that it managed.[38] In November 2022, after being under public investigation for six months,

Goldman Sachs Asset Management agreed to pay a $4.0 million penalty to settle SEC charges of ESG policy and procedure failures at the firm between 2017 and 2020.[39]

Much as the Sudetenland was used to justify Nazi Germany's invasion of Czechoslovakia back in the 1930s, greenwashing is now being used as the main pretext for regulators to push through standardized ESG rules and requirements for the global financial markets. The recent flurry of enforcement actions related to ESG is noteworthy given the glaring need for better regulatory oversight in other market areas such as cryptocurrency. Moreover, such a preemptive regulatory intervention in the investment process is rather unprecedented. When was the last time there was a police raid for investment fund strategy drift? How many mutual fund managers were charged with prospectus fraud in the wake of the 2008 financial crisis because they piled into illiquid assets despite having a liquid fund mandate or bought too many stocks in their bond fund? How many hedge fund managers have gone to jail for side-pocketing or gating their fund investors when the markets have turned on them? ESG started out as a voluntary individual process, but now investment firms can be brought up on criminal charges and have a SWAT team show up at their offices for not adhering to a certain sustainable standard. The ESG movement has come a long way in just a few short years. Ironically, with ESG regulations now sprouting up around the world, the risk of being accused of greenwashing will only go up.

As the first mover on the regulatory front, the EU's more prescriptive sustainable finance rules with their overriding climate focus and outcome orientation will raise the bar for the global industry. The Euro vision of ESG regulations will set the global default standard. Given the world's interlocking financial markets and the global nature of the asset management industry, bureaucrats in Brussels may soon be dictating what US investors can buy in their 401(k) accounts. While most of the ESG regulations now being put in place globally are similar in their focus on environmental and social objectives as opposed to governance-related issues – even though the G was the original foot in the door for the ESG movement – there is still no global standard for ESG metrics and outcomes. Faced with a myriad of competing ESG classification and reporting systems, global investment managers will be hard pressed to develop a one-size-fits-all approach to product marketing and investing that complies with all the various regulatory regimes, which may lead to a gravitation toward the SFDR as the lowest common denominator and most conservative ESG approach. To simplify matters given the long list of ESG factors that must now be considered, asset managers are likely to further focus their time and attention on climate change, which is the raison d'être of the SFDR and the European Green Deal it is designed to fund.

As they ratchet up over time, these new ESG mandates will have a distorting effect on the financial markets and create a perverse new reward system for investors. Despite the public reverse inquiry spin about protecting investors, ESG regulations are intended to control market prices through the technical factors of supply and demand while eliminating any fundamental or relative value considerations from the equation. As the regulators have noted, the best way to show sustainable investment impact is through changes in the cost of capital – lowering it for green energy and other ESG-favored industries and raising it for fossil fuels and similarly shunned sectors. Buying more of the former category and less of the latter group – regardless of price – will achieve this price control objective. Investing in expensive, overbought renewable power companies with utility-like returns while avoiding cheap, oversold oil and gas names with significant commodity price upside will be rationalized on a risk-adjusted basis and praised as an example of good ESG risk management.

The surest way for banks and asset managers to demonstrate ESG compliance and minimize the risk of regulatory action and activist lawsuits is by taking a definitive stand on climate change and pledging to decarbonize their loan and investment portfolios. More bans on fossil fuel lending and investing will likely be announced, along with the surgical removal of oil, gas, coal, and other industrial names from equity and debt benchmark indexes. Already, European financial institutions are getting the message, as evidenced by the recent announcements of oil and gas lending bans by France's BNP Paribas and Credit Agricole, Denmark's Danske Bank, and the UK's HSBC.[40]

To dispel any doubt about oil and gas divestment being the endgame of the current ESG regulatory onslaught, European bank regulators are now stepping in to make sure that the cost of doing banking business with fossil fuel companies becomes prohibitive, mainly through a combination of usurious risk-based capital charges and discriminatory industry-specific stress testing parameters. In its proposed amendments to the European banking system capital requirements due to take effect in 2025, the European Parliament has called for a sharply higher 150% risk weight for bank exposures to fossil fuel projects that received a final investment decision by end-2021, and an ultrahigh risk weight of 1,250% for any fossil-fuel-related exposures agreed to from January 2022 onward. Effectively, the latter ultrahigh capital charge would require all new bank exposures to fossil fuel activities to be funded 100% with their own equity. For perspective, under the current Basel III risk weighting for the global banking system, a 150% risk weight would only apply to highly speculative high-yield corporate credits rated B– or below, while the only lending category currently subject to a 1,250% risk weight would be crypto assets, which are the equivalent of ether in terms of collateral coverage.[41]

These new bank capital charges would apply to all hydrocarbon-related credits including coal, oil sands, crude oil, and natural gas and would encompass the full spectrum of energy activities from upstream production to midstream processing and transportation and downstream storage and distribution. In support of its aggressive amendments, the European Parliament has cited the IEA's view that fossil fuel exploration and expansion must cease immediately – by 2025 at the latest – for the world to achieve carbon neutrality by 2050. The European Parliament proposal was temporarily sidelined by a legislative committee in January 2023 despite enjoying cross-party support. If ultimately implemented, it could set the baseline for the OCC and other bank regulators around the world. Multilateral development banks such as the World Bank and its European regional counterparts, the European Investment Bank and the European Bank for Reconstruction and Development, along with European sovereign credit agencies such as Germany's KfW, have been phasing out concessional lending to fossil fuel projects since 2019, so it was only a matter of time before the same bans filtered down into the commercial banking arena.

In turn, a constricted bank lending market for the oil and gas industry will feed into the bond markets given its negative implications for the liquidity and overall credit profile of individual energy names. S&P

Global Ratings recently lowered many of its energy company ratings at the highest end of the spectrum due to climate considerations. Over the course of this decade, more downward ratings revisions are likely as the combination of increased regulatory risk and reduced bank availability more than offsets higher energy commodity prices – at least in the minds of the major credit rating agencies. Minimum ESG ratings or scores or green bond labels may also become a prerequisite for all debt issuances going forward, creating another gating mechanism to keep fossil fuel companies out of the market. Bondholders are already conditioned to look for credit ratings from the NRSROs for every new issue in the market. For all the ESG focus on shareholder resolutions and proxy voting, the credit markets were always going to be the kill switch for ESG activists, regulatory or otherwise. Debt is the cheapest source of capital, so forcing traditional energy companies to rely on equity financing – to the extent available – will challenge the economics and expected returns of new investment projects. While the details still need to be filled in, the lending and debt capital markets will become increasingly more hostile toward fossil fuels and traditional energy as well as other heavy industrial sectors between now and 2030, given the overriding focus of European and other financial regulators on climate change.

The current wave of Europe-led sustainable finance regulations now hitting the global markets will inaugurate the next, more rigid phase of the ESG movement. Ironically, the "sunshine" of sustainable disclosure will usher in a darker period for the capital markets. Since biblical times, increased disclosure and mandatory reporting have usually led to something bad happening – taxation, prohibition, expulsion, or worse – and it will be no different with sustainability. Sustainable disclosure reporting standards will be the first step toward screening out and excluding politically incorrect industries such as oil and gas from investment funds. Once carbon footprints must be calculated for bank loan portfolios and equity and bond funds based on the TCFD reporting framework, then those financial institutions aiding and abetting the energy sector and other emitting industries can be isolated and targeted. The tables will now be turned on banks and asset managers as the pressure tactics of ESG corporate engagement that they have been using on their portfolio companies the past few years will be used more aggressively on themselves – all backed by the explicit threat of legal action. In the new regulator-enforced sustainable financial system, ESG conformity will become the international norm, making the vision of the PRI a reality. Market participants, regardless of ideological view, will now be guided by the Japanese proverb "The nail that sticks out gets hammered down." Like foreign tourists visiting the Angkor Wat temple complex in Cambodia, Wall Street firms will stay on the beaten ESG path to avoid stepping on land mines.

We are now in the denouement of the ESG morality play. The financial regulators have entered stage left and are playing their all-important – and largely telegraphed – role of deus ex machina by imposing order on all the sustainability chaos in the financial markets. Absent a last-minute plot twist, an iron curtain will shortly be descending across Wall Street, from London to New York, as the final act of ESG draws to a close.

CHAPTER 12

A 2030 EXIT PLAN

I would prefer not to.
Herman Melville, "Bartleby, the Scrivener: A Story of Wall-Street"

If you are on the wrong road, progress means doing an about-turn and walking back to the right road; and in that case, the man who turns back soonest is the most progressive man.
C. S. Lewis

With the regulators now stepping in, the great Wall Street ESG capitulation trade will soon begin. Those firms that have tried to hold the line and quietly resist over the past few years in the hope that ESG would prove a passing Wall Street fad are now likely to throw in the towel given that the regulatory writing is on the wall. Those firms that have fully embraced ESG and publicly championed the sustainability cause will now have the political cover needed to take their internal investment policies to the next level and start discriminating more openly and aggressively with their capital without fear of being put at a competitive disadvantage. When ESG compliance is not optional, it really doesn't matter if a financial firm is a true ESG believer or a conscientious objector. Everyone on Wall Street is in the same boat.

Now that financial regulators are openly carrying the water of ESG activists by requiring more climate and other disclosure and mandating a sustainable approach to corporate policy and investment decision-making, how will things play out in the capital markets between now and 2030? For one, Wall Street will become much more bureaucratic. Every trading and investment decision will carry an extra layer of administrative complexity to make sure that all the sustainability boxes are being checked. More sustainability experts will be hired throughout Wall Street. Industry laypeople will be forced to take regular ESG training courses alongside the de rigueur diversity modules and annual anti–money laundering refreshers. Reporting and compliance costs will go up, as will the litigation risks associated with such regulatory compliance.

Since the ultimate sustainability goal is to impose capital controls on the financial markets, this will eventually deprive funding to politically incorrect companies – mainly in heavy industry, starting with oil and gas – which, in turn, will lead to a scarcity of industrial and agricultural goods, higher transportation costs, unreliable electricity grids, and increased prices for pretty much everything. The ripple effects on the broader economy of defunding fossil fuels and other industries, many of which are already starting to play out in Europe, will be profound. When civilization goes and social order breaks down, things tend to move quickly. As ESG spreads unchecked and infects the global financial system on the back of regulatory mandates, the timeline may be similarly accelerated. By 2030, Wall Street may be almost completely unrecognizable.

For those market players skeptical of such a dire financial industry outlook, pause a moment to look up from your Bloomberg screens and consider the current state of American society. Public schools are now willfully ignoring parental protests and openly teaching critical race theory and transgender ideology in the classroom. Colleges and universities are asking students to pick their personal pronouns and indoctrinating them with anticapitalist cant before sending them out to get a job in the business world. Churches drape themselves in the rainbow colors of the LGBTQ+ flag and host drag queen shows on consecrated ground, but when Roe v. Wade was finally overturned by the Supreme Court after nearly 50 years on the books and almost 60 million abortions in the US, the church bells all were broken. The traditional and social media have become the mouthpiece for government, much like *Pravda* during the glory days of the Soviet Union, championing every liberal policy initiative – including economic lockdowns, vaccine and mask mandates, unfettered illegal immigration, no-cash bail, legalized drugs, normalized homelessness, and uncontrolled welfare spending – no matter how bad the economic and social fallout. All of this would have been unthinkable just 10 years ago.

Now, as the last social institution to fall to the progressive agenda in the controlled demolition that began back in the 1980s, all the other pillars of society are set against and leaning on the financial industry. Climate change and sustainable development have been pushed on the public through schools, colleges, churches, and the media for the past two generations. Every year, another wave of liberal-minded college and business school graduates further weakens Wall Street from within, inexorably pushing the industry to an ideological and cultural inflection point. Given the current barbell between liberals at both the top and bottom echelons of most financial firms, this tipping point will come quickly.

The bill for the broad progressive agenda built around climate change is finally coming due in the form of ESG, with Wall Street expected to pick up the tab by funding the green transition and defunding the fossil fuels industry. Beyond climate change, everything else on the ESG wish list is largely superfluous, to be figured out down the road. The climate emergency is the immediate ESG issue to be addressed by the financial markets over the next six years and will set the precedent for implementing the rest of the liberal agenda of environmental and social causes. If things play out according to the ESG plan, Wall Street will become the dispenser of socially approved capital for companies and industries incubated in government-backed progressive circles and vetted by sustainability experts. Absent strong pushback by Wall Street at this point, it is only a matter of time before ESG holds "illimitable dominion over all" of the global financial markets, as Edgar Allan Poe wrote at the close of "The Masque of the Red Death."

To head off a complete reset and reengineering of the capital markets by 2030, what is required now, first and foremost, is greater situational awareness on the part of the financial industry. Like an epic work of Greek mythology, Wall Street is now *in medias res* with the sustainable investment scheme, with many still asleep and unaware about what is really going on. Admitting you have a problem is the first step in fixing the problem. ESG – or sustainable finance or responsible investing or whatever other euphemistic label you may choose – is clearly a problem for the financial markets since its intent is to change the purpose of a company and the meaning of investing. Acknowledging the scope of the problem is the second step. For those not keeping score, the ESG game clock for Wall Street is now ticking down and it is almost Hail Mary time.

The ESG movement, traced back to its climate change and sustainability beginnings, has more than a 30-year head start in terms of publicity, marketing, and organizational planning, and now enjoys explicit government backing through the financial regulators. Currently aligned against the financial industry is a global network of supranational agencies, international NGOs, environmental and social groups, academics, government officials, and regulatory agencies, all of which have significant political capital invested in the climate cum sustainability cum ESG movement.

Wall Street and the business sector are now living in the dystopian world described by Ayn Rand in *Atlas Shrugged.* Government looting of businesses and financial firms in the name of altruistic goals is ESG in a nutshell. Rand warned about the dangers of running businesses for the good of society – for "people and planet" in the current ESG parlance – calling it "the poison of death in the blood of Western civilization" that would reverse the "magnificent progress achieved by capitalism" since the Enlightenment. She also predicted how "unearned guilt" would be used to control companies, much as the current ESG system is built on virtue signaling and ethical peer pressure. While Rand intended her magnum opus as a prophetic warning for society of the downside of collectivism in the guise of stakeholder capitalism, that has not stopped liberals from using her epic novel as a kind of progressive playbook. Rand realized this unintended consequence early on. Shortly after its publication in 1957, she gave a speech in Boston titled "Is Atlas Shrugging?" wherein she discussed how her prophetic novel was rapidly becoming reality and turning into a work of history.[1] Fast-forward to the present, and even she would be appalled by the degree of her clairvoyance.

Most Wall Street analysts would kill for Rand's forecasting accuracy over the past 60 years about business, macroeconomics, and politics, particularly her prescient call around the energy sector. In Europe and certain regions of the US, failing electricity grids are now the norm, with periodic blackouts and forced demand reduction for industrial and retail customers alike – all due to a government-mandated overreliance on intermittent renewable power sources. One of the central themes of *Atlas Shrugged* is the importance of energy as a driver of industrial activity and economic growth. Over the course of the novel's nearly 1,200 pages, this truth is reinforced by the steady breakdown of modern society, with trains, factories, and airports all shutting down in serial fashion. While mainly intended as a metaphor for the creative power of the human mind and intellect, many progressives have interpreted it literally, with the main takeaway being that when you control energy, you control the motor of the economy. One of the most iconic scenes from *Atlas Shrugged* is when the oil tycoon Ellis Wyatt sets fire to his own oil wells, lighting up the Colorado sky with "a solid sheet of flame," before joining the shadowy John Galt on strike. Even though this scene of destruction was meant to shock, many progressives have taken it as an aspirational goal. Not since the "To Serve Man" episode of the *Twilight Zone* television series has a book been so completely misunderstood by its target audience.[2]

Through her popular works – misconstrued as they have been by many on the left – Rand was one of the staunchest defenders of capitalism during the 20th century, arguably a stronger advocate than most of the like-minded economists of the time, including Milton Friedman. Often described as intolerant and dogmatic, Rand was blunt-spoken and a woman of action. The characters that she uses in her novels to exemplify her economic philosophy are crude action figures – more immovable forces of nature – that put to shame every superhero currently residing in the Marvel Cinematic Universe. She believed that life requires a "constant process of self-sustaining action," and that the same holds true for the inherently moral system of capitalism. She loathed the passivity and indifference of libertarianism. A laissez-faire market approach only works if all sides agree to abide by the same rules; progressives have never observed the Marquess of Queensberry Rules when it comes to fighting. In her view, a hands-off libertarian market approach will only create a vacuum that progressivism, being a metastasizing ideological movement, will invariably move to fill. Rand realized that words must be muscled into deeds, and economic theories were nothing without dispositive force. Businesses and free markets must be perpetually defended from encroachment from the government, either directly or indirectly as in the case of ESG.

ESG will not go away of its own accord without a concerted, proactive effort on the part of all those opposed to the progressive takeover of Wall Street. Opponents should not waste time focusing on industry CEOs pandering to the sustainability mob with environmental sops, transgender product marketing, and ultra-inclusive advertising campaigns. No matter how many woke companies ultimately go broke, the other side is never going to give up the fight. Such C-suite culture war skirmishes are just a distraction from the real ESG battle now taking place in the financial markets. Given that pro-ESG government regulators have now started to take the field, a market-based solution to the ESG problem would not appear possible. Increased competition and simply offering a better nonsustainable mousetrap will do little to crack an entrenched ESG system built on moral duress and now cemented into place by regulation. ESG is not an example of market failure caused by a lack of competition.

While the backlash to ESG has been growing over the past two years, some in the anti-ESG crowd are losing sight of the bigger picture. Several state governments and pension plan administrators have tried to use their market power to reverse the ESG momentum on Wall Street, mainly by pulling their money from sustainability-focused investment managers such as BlackRock. Red-state governors and Republican attorneys general – many from oil and gas producing states – have attacked Larry Fink, the chairman and CEO of BlackRock, as the leading industry spokesperson for ESG. Using a shoot-the-messenger approach, 19 states have publicly called BlackRock on the carpet around ESG and started clawing back state business from the company. In 2022, nine different states – including Arizona, Florida, Louisiana, Missouri, Texas, and West Virginia – withdrew more than $4 billion in pension and state business from BlackRock due to its climate and other ESG policies.[3]

While sending a clear message, such a red-state divestment strategy is destined to fail based on demographics and fiscal reality. Definitionally, blue-state government pension plans – led by California, Illinois, and New York – are significantly larger than those for red states due to the combination of larger public sector workforces and more generous employee benefit packages in fiscally profligate Democrat-run states and municipalities. At year-end 2020, based on Federal Reserve statistics, total US state pension assets amounted to $5.2 trillion, of which blue states comprised $3.2 trillion or roughly 62% – nearly a two-to-one advantage.[4] The $4 billion of red-state business outflows suffered by BlackRock at year-end 2022 represented a drop in the bucket for the firm, being dwarfed by aggregate net capital inflows of $307 billion over the 12 months of that year.

The strategy of those opposed to ESG should not revolve around taking your marbles and giving them to an apolitical asset manager. The goal should not be to segregate out non-ESG funds from the rest of the market; rather, the objective should be to wall off funds with a sustainable mandate as separately managed and clearly delineated specialty accounts and shut down firm-wide ESG integration and corporate engagement to limit the contagion. Giving investors the choice of non-ESG funds on the margin will not address the core problem of ESG. Partial victory should not be the goal in the campaign against sustainability on Wall Street. Creating a safe space for ESG nonbelievers while ceding the public square of the global financial markets to sustainability zealots is not the answer. Moreover, the fight against ESG should not be viewed mainly as a market opportunity and something to profit from, since it was this kind of shortsighted, money-chasing response that suckered many Wall Street firms into initially supporting sustainability – a position from which they cannot now extricate themselves.

The battle to keep ESG in the specialized investment box where it belongs and limit its systemic spillover is larger than any one firm or individual. It is not a barroom brawl to be won by knocking out the biggest guy in the place. Picking a personal fight about woke politics with Larry Fink and BlackRock, as many have chosen to do, only serves to distract from the matter at hand. ESG is not a competition-driven market phenomenon. Wall Street firms are not following BlackRock's competitive lead because sustainable investing holds the key to improved financial returns. To the contrary, they are being pushed and coerced and pressured to comply by environmental and social activists and now financial regulators. Any permanent ESG solution must address these root causes and must cut through all the woke noise to focus on the immediate issue at hand: climate change.

The recent targeting of BlackRock by Republican politicians, mainly at the state level but also across the federal government, has led to the dismissal of any ESG criticism as politically motivated, echoing the same defensive strategy that has been used to shut down opposition to the climate change agenda for the last three decades. The partisan defense of the Democrat-leaning BlackRock's ESG policies is both instructive and constructive in that it gets the issue of politics out into the open. Why do liberal CEOs and politicians and US Democrats uniformly support ESG and stakeholder capitalism while most conservative politicians and US Republicans oppose it? Why do ESG activists discourage companies and financial institutions from making political contributions, and shame them with controversies if they do? To paraphrase Thomas Mann, everything about sustainability is progressive politics. Rather than shying away from the political fight, the anti-ESG movement should acknowledge and embrace it. Instead of shrinking when accused of being political, the opposition needs to resort to the same hardball tactics that have been used by progressives for years.

With regulators now picking sides, it will require significant government resources and selective state backing to mount a successful campaign to cast out ESG from the global financial system. With Europe now a lost cause, the US represents the last remaining hope for the markets. As the largest regional market in the world, if the US can become an ESG-free trading zone, it will blow a hole in the progressive ESG plot to take over Wall Street because ESG, like climate change and sustainable development, sets up as a prisoner's dilemma. Everyone must participate or the system doesn't work. If the US can remain an ESG holdout, it would effectively balkanize and cripple the global sustainable finance movement – much as the planned withdrawal of the US from the Paris Agreement during the Trump administration threatened to derail the entire global climate movement. Decoupling the US would allow the European economy and financial markets to follow their own chosen ESG path downward without pulling down the rest of the world with them.

Thus far, ESG has gained less traction in the US, giving the opposition a toehold from which to build. Despite outward appearances and all the press focus on BlackRock, there is still limited Wall Street consensus around sustainable investing – especially in the day-to-day trenches. Since the US has a federalist political system, with power distributed between the states and Washington, DC, this means that the political fight against ESG can be sustained regardless of which party controls the White House. While the ideological differences between Democrats and Republicans have blurred over the years – mainly because of a lack of principle and conviction on the part of the latter – there are still enough truly conversative Republicans around, many of whom are running economically and politically important states across the country, who are ready and willing to lead the fight against ESG. Some have already started.

Any successful strategy to counter sustainability must acknowledge the reality that ESG has now become a hostage situation for the financial markets. From an ESG perspective, Wall Street is occupied. Roughly a decade after street protestors camped out in Zuccotti Park in the Lower Manhattan financial district in 2011 raging against the wealthy 1% of society, their calls for the occupation of Wall Street have finally been answered, although not by brute mob force but through behind-the-scenes pressure from an international network of activist nonprofits and financial regulators. At present, nobody on Wall Street can speak out against ESG for fear of being personally attacked and likely fired or calling down the wrath of the ESG gods on their firm. The only ESG whistle-blowers who speak up are those who believe that financial firms should be doing more on the sustainability front, not less or nothing at all. You never hear any public ESG complaints going the other way, arguing that sustainability distracts from fiduciary duty and the business of making money for clients. Like France and the rest of continental Europe in the 1940s, Wall Street must now be liberated from ESG, mainly by rolling back recently enacted regulations and neutralizing the outside activist groups placing pressure on the entire financial industry.

The recent experience of Stuart Kirk, the former global head of responsible investing at the asset management division of HSBC, illustrates how no one on Wall Street is free to speak out against sustainability. In May 2022, Kirk gave an internally approved presentation at a conference hosted by the *Financial Times* wherein he opined that "investors need not worry about climate risk" because "unsubstantiated, shrill, partisan, self-serving, apocalyptic warnings are always wrong," adding that the "nut job" end-of-the-world claims of climate activists were no different than the Y2K market hysteria at the turn of the millennium. For speaking such truths out loud, he was roundly criticized by environmentalists and the sustainability community, immediately placed on suspension by HSBC management, and forced to resign his position shortly thereafter.[5] The Kirk incident shows the totalitarian, red-dot nature of the ESG movement and how it actively suppresses dissent. If a sustainability expert such as Kirk does not enjoy the right of free speech and the freedom to express his own personal and professional opinions about the field, then there is no hope for the rest of Wall Street. Even supportive CEOs must choose their words carefully for fear of offending someone's ESG sensitivities and triggering a board proxy fight and management coup.

Beating back ESG will require a direct – and long overdue – confrontation with the climate change movement and its legions of supporters. Most US business and political leaders – particularly Republicans – have not been willing to do this up until now, which is the main reason why the financial markets find themselves in their current ESG predicament. Climate change, with its decarbonization directive and its sanctified net-zero goal, is the one and only ESG factor that everyone can rally around. It provides structure, moral authority, and the oxygen needed to sustain the sustainability agenda. ESG activists readily agree about the need to defund fossil fuels and redirect capital toward clean energy and renewable power projects, but not much beyond that. Apart from climate change, ESG is just a ragtag collection of liberal policy wants. How many sustainable investors are championing strategies that exclusively target all-female firms or union-run manufacturers or industrial companies that carefully monitor their water and electricity usage or firms that pay their fair share of taxes?

Toppling the climate change bureaucracy, once and for all, would completely undercut the ESG movement. Those up for this climate challenge will need to educate themselves and screw up their courage for an ugly public fight. Questioning the climate orthodoxy at this late date – long after progressives told everyone to shut up and move on because the science had been settled – guarantees a knock-down, drag-out battle royal, although this was probably always going to be the case given how much the liberal left has riding on the issue.

All the information underlying the climate science is publicly available – with a little digging – on US government agency and UN body websites. Anyone with a logical mind and a basic understanding of science can see through the suspect data and flawed models being used to generate the dire climate forecasts that underlie all the extreme economic and regulatory measures now being proposed and implemented. For those requiring intellectual backup, there is no shortage of bona fide climate scientists – including physicists, astronomers, chemists, biologists, meteorologists, and oceanographers – who disagree with the so-called consensus. Many have spoken out in public and written extensively about their scientific views. The partial US list of dissenting scientists would include

Steven Koonin of NYU and Caltech, author of the 2021 book *Unsettled: What Climate Science Tells Us, What It Doesn't, and Why It Matters*; Judith Curry, former chair of the School of Earth and Atmospheric Sciences at Georgia Tech, president of the Climate Forecast Applications Network, and author of the 2023 book *Climate Uncertainty and Risk: Rethinking Our Response*; William Happer, Professor Emeritus of Physics at Princeton and cofounder of the CO_2 Coalition; Richard Lindzen, Professor Emeritus of Earth, Atmospheric, and Planetary Sciences at MIT; and Roy Spencer of the University of Alabama, a former NASA scientist and the author of several books on climate alarmism. For those needing additional moral support, a scientific declaration stating that there is no climate emergency has been making the global rounds in recent months. Specifically, the communiqué states that there are natural as well as anthropogenic factors contributing to global warming, which has been far slower than predicted by inadequate climate models and has not increased the frequency or severity of natural disasters. By October 2023, the declaration had garnered more than 1,800 scientist signatories from around the world.[6]

Doing the background reading on the climate science is meant more to steel the spines of the anti-ESG opposition and confirm the rationality of their position, rather than to serve as preparatory work for an argument with the other side. Progressives have avoided debating the merits of their climate, sustainability, and ESG policy prescriptions for years, dismissing critics as skeptics or deniers not worthy of being heard. Up until now, there has never been a public debate in the US about climate change, much less so for sustainability and ESG, despite the important implications for American commerce, the US economy, and the nation's financial markets. Likewise, there has never been a US election that has functioned as a national referendum on climate change. Most of the current body of rules and regulations has been implemented in backdoor fashion by executive agencies and the courts, rather than through the normal route of bipartisan legislation. Climate change and ESG have been the main handiwork of Democrats, although there has been nothing democratic about the process by which it has been foisted on the country.

There will be no Damascus moment for the liberal left when it comes to climate change, so now is not the time to start debating. As Jonathan Swift noted, "It is useless to attempt to reason a man out of a thing he was never reasoned into." Rather than getting distracted by a pointless discussion of what the climate *Futureworld* will look like decades down the road and bogged down in data minutiae, the ESG opposition should simply trust their minds, believe in the rightness of their cause, and be confident that their position will benefit the American people. Anti-ESG advocates should have the courage of their convictions by speaking out publicly against the climate hysteria at every turn. Most importantly, conservatives need to start using exact language – not the lexicon of the left – and refrain from making blithe, nonoffending statements whenever the topic of climate change comes up. Anodyne pronouncements like "I believe in climate change" fail to distinguish between natural and man-made factors. Saying that you "support clean air and water" is a non sequitur since carbon dioxide is not a particulate pollutant. And championing emissions reductions at every turn only concedes the central premise of climate change theory.

The anti-ESG movement should take an all-of-the-above political approach – which was the cynical phrase used during the Obama administration to mask its antienergy policies – to dismantle the climate change bureaucracy feeding the ESG machine. Rather than looking for a legislative solution and wasting valuable time on investigations and public hearings, the ESG resistance should adopt the same tactics that progressives have used for decades to achieve their environmental and social policy goals: exploiting the judicial system to leverage the regulatory state, only now in reverse. Successfully challenging federal climate regulations in court would result in them being kicked back to the legislature, which would effectively render them moot given the divided and dysfunctional nature of the US Congress. Anti-ESG plaintiffs should opportunistically venue shop the federal court system, taking full advantage of the 234 federal judges appointed by President Trump, including the three conservative associate justices who have now tipped the ideological balance of the Supreme Court.

The template for a successful ESG regulatory pushback strategy can be seen in the Supreme Court decision handed down in West Virginia v. Environmental Protection Agency in June 2022, wherein a 6–3 court majority found that the EPA did not have the authority to issue the 2015 Clean Power Plan (CPP) in the absence of clear congressional authority. The CPP was promulgated under President Obama and would have gone well beyond the site-specific regulatory oversight envisioned by the CAA by forcing a shift in US electricity generation from fossil-fuel-fired plants to renewable sources such as wind and solar over time. The Supreme Court held that such a sector-wide shift in generation mix was a major question of economic and political significance that was left to the Congress, not the EPA, to decide. As such, the EPA had exceeded its authority under the CAA when it issued the CPP, and the CPP was therefore unlawful. Notably, the Biden administration tried to withdraw the CPP at the last minute to avoid a legal precedent that potentially boxed it in regarding climate policy, which is exactly what happened. To their credit, West Virginia and its various state and corporate coplaintiffs persevered and, with their favorable ruling, have taken back important territory in the regulatory battle over climate change.

While the Supreme Court has stated its intention to reconsider its 1984 ruling in Chevron U.S.A., Inc. v. Natural Resources Defense Council – which laid down the doctrine of judicial deference to regulatory agency expertise, particularly regarding the environment – during its 2023–2024 term, Republicans should not wait for this potentially positive legal outcome since time is of the essence in the ESG fight. Building on the success of *West Virginia*, red-state plaintiffs should next focus on the EPA's 2009 Endangerment Finding, which labeled carbon dioxide as a pollutant and provided the legal justification for all the EPA's follow-on carbon regulations. Striking this politically driven agency ruling from the books would be a major setback for the climate cause. Despite protestations to the contrary about due process, there was a clear rush to judgment when this enabling ruling was rolled out by the Obama administration in its first year of office. Moreover, much of the scientific data upon which the agency's 2009 decision was predicated – chiefly, the AR4 of the IPCC released in 2007 – was already dated at the time of its publication and arguably not properly peer-reviewed as required by federal law. With the benefit of hindsight – including nearly two decades of actual-versus-modeled data – there would seem to be strong grounds to reargue the EPA's 2009 decision and reissue a new finding, particularly given the tenuous nature of the stated threat of carbon dioxide to the "public health and welfare of current and future generations."[7]

If President Biden should be reelected in 2024 or another Democratic candidate succeed him as the 47th president of the United States, then serious thought should be given to a potential state lawsuit to challenge the poorly reasoned 2007 Supreme Court decision that provided the underpinning for the EPA's 2009 Endangerment Finding. In Massachusetts v. Environmental Protection Agency, the court held that the EPA had the power to regulate carbon dioxide and other greenhouse gases under the CAA even though the US Congress amended the act twice over the 20 years after its passage into law in 1970 and both times declined to add carbon dioxide to the list of EPA-regulated air pollutants. Carbon dioxide, methane, and other greenhouse gases are not particulate pollutants but naturally occurring atmospheric gases. By the logic of the Supreme Court's 5–4 ruling in 2007, water vapor should also be regulated by the EPA given that it is the most abundant of Earth's greenhouse gases and is responsible for roughly one-half of planetary global warming.

Republican state governors should also revisit the renewable portfolio standards (RPS) passed by their respective public utility commissions, many of which have been dominated by liberal activists for years. By requiring that an ever-increasing percentage of electricity generation come from renewable sources such as wind and solar, these state RPS mandates have been an important driver of the power sector's shift away from coal and natural gas as a fuel source over the past two decades. In 2015, coal-producing West Virginia became the first US state to repeal its RPS, which was originally set in 2009 under Governor Joe Manchin and required the state's renewable generation share to rise from a target of 10% in 2015 to 25% by 2025. By the time it was repealed six years later, most of West Virginia's coal-mining production had already been bankrupted by the aggressive environmental policies of the Obama administration. Other red states have allowed their RPS mandates to lapse, but some governors are still asleep at the switch. Notably, Texas, which is not part of a regional transmission organization but operates its own statewide electricity grid called the Electric Reliability Council of Texas (ERCOT), has had an RPS in place since 1999. In 2023, roughly 40% of ERCOT's generation mix is slated to come from wind and solar power sources, even though such a heavy reliance on intermittent generation was one of the contributing causes to the ERCOT grid failure during the severe winter storm that hit Texas in February 2021, which killed 246 people across the Lone Star State.

The next time that a Republican takes up residence at 1600 Pennsylvania Avenue, the Paris Agreement should be formally submitted to the

US Senate for approval. Even though Senate approval is required of all binding international treaties negotiated by the executive branch – which clearly applies in the case of the Paris Agreement – this process was never observed for the climate accord. It was originally approved by executive order of President Obama rather than through the advice and consent of the Senate in 2016. It was then subsequently reversed by executive order of President Trump in June 2017, although given the withdrawal timeline stipulated in the deal, the US was not able to leave until November 4, 2020, notably the day after President Trump lost his reelection bid. On his first day in office in January 2021, President Biden issued his own executive order reinstating the agreement and calling for the US to rejoin the international climate body. While vividly highlighting the partisan politics of climate change and the extralegal tactics used by its proponents, this unconstitutional back-and-forth needs to be ended by the next Republican president. Since a treaty requires a two-thirds supermajority approval to pass the upper chamber, submitting the Paris Agreement to a Senate vote would effectively kill the agreement while setting a legal precedent that will be hard to reverse. Pulling the US out of the Paris Agreement would remove much of the justification for this country's climate policy push while seriously undermining international support for the deal. Given that the countdown clock to 2030 is now ticking, if the Democrats regain the White House in 2024, Republicans should give serious thought to legally challenging the constitutionality of the approval process used for the Paris Agreement up until now.[8]

The next step for Republican state attorneys general in the anti-ESG fight should be to challenge the SEC's climate-focused, TCFD-driven ESG disclosure rules once these are finalized in 2023. Red-state plaintiffs should make the argument that, as with the EPA's CPP rulemaking, the SEC's proposed ESG rules are not meant simply to improve disclosure and protect investors from fraud and deceptive practices but rather are designed to effect major economic and political change by shifting investment capital from fossil fuel producers to green energy companies. Moreover, the SEC requiring disclosures on nonmaterial, nonfinancial factors such as greenhouse gas emissions amounts to regulatory overreach exceeding its authority since, contrary to the view of ESG activists, most prudent investors do not consider climate risk to be an investment risk or a systemic financial threat. Also, the new SEC disclosure rules, by crossing over into the area of environmental regulation, are clearly beyond the SEC's financial market expertise and purview and, as such, are not authorized by the US Congress.

The last ESG-related regulation to be legally challenged would be the recent Biden DOL rule allowing ERISA trustees to consider climate and other ESG factors when looking at risk and return. The ruling, which took effect in January 2023, represents a game-changer since it creates a slippery slope by redefining fiduciary duty and normalizing ESG as part of the investment process – paving the way for all the follow-on ESG regulations noted above. Using risk and return to qualify the use of ESG factors will provide no protection for retirees and pension plan beneficiaries because ESG – as embodied in the 2030 Sustainable Development Goals of the UN – has also been sold as a risk management framework. Looking at returns on an ESG risk-adjusted basis will pretty much allow any environmental and social issue to be included when making asset allocation and security selection decisions. Particularly troubling is the new rule's call to action for ERISA fiduciaries around company engagement and the active management of proxy and other shareholder rights under the guise of asset stewardship. Since the Biden DOL rule codifies much of the ERISA guidance creep that has occurred under previous Democratic administrations and is clearly partisan in nature, the courts need to intervene to reestablish the primacy and exclusivity of pecuniary factors for ERISA plans by kicking the issue back to the US Congress. This process has already started with 26 Republican states suing the Biden administration in late January 2023 to block the rule's implementation. In September 2023, the case was surprisingly dismissed by US District Judge Matthew Kacsmaryk, a Trump appointee, who notably cited *Chevron* deference in his decision. The Kacsmaryk ruling has already been appealed to the US Circuit Court of Appeals and may ultimately need to go to the Supreme Court for a final decision.

Besides challenging the constitutionality of climate and ESG regulations promulgated by federal agencies, there should also be a parallel effort to leverage long-standing laws and regulations on the books to target the climate collusion at the core of the ESG movement. Once economic injury can be proved, state complainants should bring a cause of action under existing federal antitrust law against those companies, banks, and investment firms that are now working in concert with ESG activists and enablers to shut down the oil and gas industry through membership groups with stated net-zero emissions goals. As detailed in a 2021 report titled "Corporate Collusion: Liability Risks for the ESG Agenda" published by the Washington, DC, litigation firm Boyden Gray & Associates: "Federal law prohibits companies from colluding on group boycotts or conspiring to restrain trade, even to advance political and social goals." The report also found that federal antitrust law prohibits so-called "hub-and-spoke conspiracies" whereby "boycott agreements are instigated by a third party to coordinate firms that ordinarily compete against each other to unreasonably restrain market competition."[9] Such a description would apply to all the net-zero financial groups sponsored or supported by the PRI and other UN agencies. For example, the UN-convened NZAOA issued guidance in March 2023 that its members should immediately stop making new direct investments in oil and gas fields and greenfield energy infrastructure to "support a transition aligned with limiting the global temperature increase to 1.5°C."[10] Ironically, the best statute to use in suing these climate cartels would be the Sherman Antitrust Act of 1890, the same trust-busting law that was used more than a century ago to break up the Standard Oil Company and Trust because the Rockefeller-run energy conglomerate was restraining trade and commerce in the petroleum business. Now, in the ultimate payback, this progressive statute should be used to defend the petroleum business and all hydrocarbon-producing activities from a coordinated climate attack from without the industry.

Even ESG activists have acknowledged that companies working together to fight climate change through financial and business boycotts of entire industries presents a clear antitrust problem. Reed Hundt, the former chairman of the Federal Communications Commission under the Clinton administration and the current CEO of the Coalition for Green Capital, a green bank incubator platform, acknowledged as much in a September 2019 opinion piece in the *Washington Post*, writing that "major U.S. companies need protection from antitrust law so that they can feel free to work together in the fight against climate change, without fear of prosecution." To achieve this necessary protection, Hundt recommended that Fortune 500 companies "petition Congress to pass a law immunizing all joint action taken to adopt energy-reducing practices and curtail greenhouse gas emissions" from existing antitrust law.[11]

Absent such an unlikely legislative move, the only line of defense that participants in target-setting climate coalitions currently have is to argue that they maintain independent decision-making authority – even though every member invariably shoots at the same coordinated target and the group always flocks together, which is not a great fact pattern. Growing fears of collusion charges have started to spread across some of these net-zero groups. In January 2022, NZIA publicly backtracked from its previous commitment to stop insuring coal mines based on the legal advice that the group received regarding potential anticompetitive practices.[12] During the first half of 2023, several major European insurance companies including Allianz, AXA, Hanover Re, Lloyd's of London, Munich Re, Swiss Re, and Zurich Insurance opted to quietly leave the NZIA consortium.[13] Similarly, in December 2022, Vanguard, the world's second largest asset management firm, announced that it was withdrawing from NZAM,[14] which is a sector subset of GFANZ, to go it alone on climate policy, reportedly out of collusion concerns. Even though some of these climate cartels have started to go wobbly of late, an antitrust test case resulting in a final court ruling will still be necessary to shut down these net-zero groups once and for all.

Next, the anti-ESG movement should zero in on the banking sector since this source of corporate credit and liquidity is key to the fossil-fuel-defunding strategy of climate and ESG activists. Through collective action groups such as NZAB and company-targeted public confrontations staged by activist outfits such as Money Rebellion and Just Stop Oil, banks have been under pressure for years to stop lending to energy companies – starting with coal but then moving quickly up the hydrocarbon chain all the way to natural gas. Since the signing of the Paris Agreement in 2015, the amount of bank financing for the global energy industry has held fairly constant, averaging $781 billion per year as measured by the Rainforest Action Network.[15] Over 2016–2022, cumulative lending to the sector by the top 60 banks aggregated $5.5 trillion, which is money that ESG proponents believe would be better spent elsewhere. The IEA has decreed that there can be no new oil and gas investment from 2025 onward, and climate activists are now using this politicized energy policy statement to beat banks over the head. Financial regulations mandating a TCFD disclosure framework will only make matters worse. Many banks – mostly European – have already succumbed to this pressure by announcing a curtailment of energy-lending activity. Most have tried to finesse the issue by focusing their bans on new oil and gas development or specific geographic areas such as the Arctic region to hide the scope of the industry boycott. Based on data compiled by Energy Monitor, 48% of 101 major global banks had lending restrictions in place for unconventional energy projects as of October 2022.[16] The unconventional category includes all oil sands and shale extraction projects, the latter of which would encompass almost all onshore oil and gas development in the US.

To ensure a free flow of bank credit to fossil fuel companies, state plaintiffs should overlay any antitrust action against specific boycotting banks with an official request for the OCC, the national bank regulator, to bring an enforcement action against any banks announcing oil and gas lending bans. Based on long-standing OCC guidance, banks are required to conduct risk assessments of individual customers; they are not permitted to make broad-based decisions affecting whole categories or classes of customers when providing access to services, capital, and credit. Specifically, the OCC has instructed its regulated banks to "avoid termination of broad categories of customers without assessing individual customer risk." Even though the OCC has exhibited antienergy bias in the past – notably during the Obama administration, when the agency's deliberate inflexibility hamstrung senior bank lenders trying to work with their energy sector borrowing clients when crude oil prices dropped precipitously over 2014–2016 – and though the Biden administration paused the implementation of the Trump OCC's Fair Access Rule, which would have codified previous agency guidance against industry discrimination in bank lending, there is a sufficient body of supervisory guidance on the books to bring an enforcement action against banks discriminating against the energy sector.

Beyond the banks and other financial market players, the legal sights of the anti-ESG effort should be trained on the third-party actors behind all the net-zero affinity groups advocating for fossil fuel lending and investment boycotts. This would be the shadowy but well-funded and government-affiliated network of international NGOs and nonprofit organizations that has been applying the ESG pressure and pushing climate change and sustainability onto the financial markets for years now. Standing at the top of this list would be the PRI and all of its sister UN affiliates, along with the WEF. Throw in the various public protest groups such as Just Stop Oil, Extinction Rebellion, Money Rebellion, and Coal Action Network that target energy companies and their financing counterparties. For starters, these third-party groups should be charged with intentional tortuous interference with the conduct of business and contractual business relationships. Generally, such common law claims can be brought for conduct such as threats of physical violence, threatened litigation, or economic pressure. Actively promoting energy company bans through discriminatory decarbonization organizations and reinforcing this divestment message with incidents of corporate vandalism and property damage would seem to tick many of these boxes of unlawful activity. One need only gain log-in access to the PRI's Collaboration Platform to see the record of coordination, collective action, and regular corporate harassment of the energy industry. As the PRI openly admits on its website, the portal "allows investors to pool resources, share information and enhance their influence on ESG issues" by signing joint letters to companies, joining investor–company engagements, and coordinating responses on upcoming shareholder resolutions and proxy votes. Tellingly, the PRI includes disclaimer language reminding all 4,000+ users not to violate any antitrust statutes while using the collective hub.[17]

Republican lawmakers need to examine the role of the UN and the WEF in pushing climate change and ESG onto US corporations and financial firms. Since 2015, US companies have been voluntarily falling in line with the climate and sustainability goals of the UN and the WEF even though none of these policies is legally binding on this country or American businesses. Since 1945, the US has never submitted its military forces to UN command; yet somehow US companies feel obligated to make sure that their operations align with the Paris Agreement and their strategic business plans fit with the 17 Sustainable Development Goals of the UN.

Led by the PRI, it is a core group of UN affiliates that applies most of the climate and ESG pressure on Wall Street. It is quite amazing how much influence the PRI – with its more than 5,300 member signatories currently – exerts, both directly and indirectly, on the financial markets in terms of investment policy, capital allocation, financial reporting, and marketing disclosure despite it not being regulated by any government body or financial agency – particularly in the US and Europe, where most of its ESG business activities are focused. Like many of the most vocal advocates and policy drivers of climate change and sustainability, the PRI is also a nonprofit organization. Notwithstanding all the careful small-print disclaimers on the group's website and reams of publications stating that the group does not provide investment or legal advice, this is effectively what the PRI does through all its sustainability missives and ESG directives to its largely captive member audience. Moreover, by its own admission, the group actively coordinates with government officials worldwide over sustainable finance regulations.

The PRI hides behind platitudes about the Paris Agreement being adopted by 193 countries and the 2030 Agenda for Sustainable Development being the globally agreed sustainability plan, but neither of these multilateral compacts has any legal force. And yet, through the purpose-driven work of the PRI, both policy diktats are now being imposed on the global financial markets in full view of supposedly impartial financial regulators. How is it that the PRI, a nonprofit organization registered in England and Wales, is able to freely dispense ESG-related investment and legal advice in the US and regularly engage in national politics by lobbying US government officials over legislative and regulatory policy? This is something that US tax officials and the US Congress, which oversees the Internal Revenue Service, should take a closer look at, and not just for the PRI. There are many official-sounding nonprofit organizations formed by liberal billionaires – including Michael Bloomberg's SASB – that have been engaging in similar activities and behaving like unregistered lobbyists to influence ESG policy for years now, effectively setting economic and energy policy for the country. Also, many youth climate protest groups are funded by 501(c)(3) nonprofit organizations that are legally prohibited from financing criminal activities. Notably, Extinction Rebellion and Just Stop Oil have both received financial support from the Climate Emergency Fund, a 501(c)(3) formed – ironically enough – by Aileen Getty, the granddaughter of the oil tycoon J. Paul Getty.[18] Defacing priceless works of art in public museums and regularly disrupting traffic and commerce clearly qualify as criminal offenses. Defunding and defrocking these activist groups would do much to relieve the ESG pressure on Wall Street.

To up the ante, there is also a strong case to be made for bringing a racketeering charge against the network of environmental, climate, and

ESG activist groups that have been working in concert for so long to shut down the oil and gas industry. The Racketeer Influenced and Corrupt Organizations Act (RICO) was passed in 1970 to combat organized crime in the US but has been used against industry and Wall Street over the years and would be applicable to today's climate cartel. Under the law, members of a corrupt enterprise may be prosecuted and indicted en masse for a pattern of criminal activity affecting interstate or foreign commerce. Private plaintiffs need only point to the commission of two racketeering crimes over a 10-year period to demonstrate such a pattern. The list of 35 enumerated criminal racketeering activities includes mail fraud, wire fraud, financial institution fraud, economic espionage, interference with commerce, bribery, and extortion, all of which would seem to apply to the menu of tactics being used by climate groups to shut down the fossil fuels industry.[19] Given the stiff criminal and civil penalties involved, a guilty verdict at the federal level or under similar state RICO statutes would effectively shut down the activist climate groups now pressuring Wall Street and the financial markets. Even an ultimately unsuccessful RICO suit that went to trial would be helpful to the anti-ESG cause given all the intragroup coordination and communications that would doubtless come out in the legal discovery process, along with more transparency about the tactics and funding sources for these climate-driven NGOs. The sunshine of such disclosure would likely have a chilling effect on the influence of these activist organizations.

Energy Transfer, the midstream sponsor of the DAPL project, is currently showing the way on the RICO front. After the withering synchronized attack against its legally permitted, market-required oil pipeline – which continues until this day – the company brought a federal RICO lawsuit against Greenpeace, Earth First!, and various other environmental and Indigenous groups that opposed DAPL. While the federal lawsuit was dismissed before going to trial in 2019 by US District Judge Billy Roy Wilson, a Clinton appointee, Energy Transfer refiled the RICO case in North Dakota state court, with the litigation still ongoing. If successful, the treble damages of nearly $1 billion sought by the company would send a strong, stinging message to climate activists.

Lastly on the litigation front, it is axiomatic on Wall Street that any time anybody loses money, somebody is going to get sued. Whenever the financial markets experience a downturn or systemic shock, the number of private securities lawsuits invariably spikes. Over 1996–2022, investors filed a total of 6,314 federal securities class-action lawsuits that resulted in $109.3 billion of aggregate settlement payments, based on data compiled by Stanford Law School's Securities Class Action Clearinghouse and Cornerstone Research.[20] During this 27-year stretch, the peak year was 2001, when 498 lawsuits were filed after the dot-com bubble burst – an annual record that is almost certain to be beaten in the post-ESG financial markets. Once investors can prove actual injury from ESG policies – mostly likely through financial losses caused by climate-related strategic and investment decisions made by businesses and financial firms – then this will open the floodgates to class-action lawsuits by private parties. An oil and gas company that drives down its share price by diversifying into lower-return renewable power projects or sinking a significant amount of capital into unsuccessful decarbonizing technologies will likely face a lawsuit from shareholders. Investors in an open-end mutual fund that significantly underperformed versus its index benchmark and its peers because its investment managers deliberately screened out the energy sector due to its carbon emissions would have grounds to sue the fund adviser. Contrary to the party line of the PRI, litigation risk may become more of an issue for those companies and asset managers that adopt ESG policies rather than those that ignore sustainability altogether. Perhaps this is what it will take to stop the ESG madness on Wall Street once and for all: a massive class-action lawsuit resulting in an outsized financial payout to injured investors. Since sustainability activists love collective action, a debilitating class-action lawsuit would mark a fitting ironic end to the ESG movement.

Since the oil and gas industry is the main target for both the climate change and sustainability mobs, the energy sector should set the corporate example for ESG resistance by speaking out more vocally against climate change theory. The ESG response to date by the energy sector has been feckless, with many companies striving to conform rather than confronting the existential threat posed to fossil fuels by the combination of climate change theory and absolute government power, the latter of which is now being exerted on the financial markets. For the past two decades, the industry has allowed itself to be divided and conquered over time instead of using its technology edge and significant base of scientific knowledge to attack the suspect historical and computer-modeled data underlying climate science and redirect the public conversation.

When "dirty" coal was first being pushed out of the US generation mix by state and federal regulators, American energy producers played up the "clean" natural gas in their mix. During the 2000s, Aubrey McClendon, the cofounder of Chesapeake Energy Corporation, ran "Coal is Filthy" anticoal ads to showcase his upstream company's increasing leverage to natural gas. T. Boone Pickens, the founder of Mesa Inc. and another industry icon, pushed for using natural gas as a transportation fuel while proposing a "cash for clunkers" plan that would pay to shut down coal plants – a model later adopted by Michael Bloomberg. When oil sands were the next hydrocarbon to be targeted, most US companies sold off their Canadian assets and retreated back across the 49th parallel. Now, the protestors have already come for natural gas – with pipeline blockades, flaring restrictions, and fracking bans – and the industry response is to improve its emissions disclosure, talk up net-zero goals for the distant future, and waste precious capital on carbon capture, renewable natural gas, and green hydrogen science projects. Pushing back on climate change and questioning the global warming dogma is viewed, at this point, as déclassé in most corporate circles – including most management suites across the energy industry.

Oil and gas companies need to stop playing off their back foot and finally wake up to the fact that the endgame of the climate change and sustainable investment movements is fossil fuel cancellation. It is no longer just about squeezing more money out of energy companies to fund government spending and green initiatives. This financial bloodletting exercise will end in death for the industry. The only way for oil and gas producers to reduce their Scope 3 greenhouse gas emissions is by ceasing to operate. Tellingly, oil and gas producers are already referred to in the same breath as cluster munitions makers, predatory payday lenders, and manufacturers relying on child and slave labor. It is only a matter of time before the UN declares a global climate emergency – most likely by 2025, to sync up with the IEA's energy policy prescriptions – to justify a final assault on fossil fuels. For anyone who thinks that climate change is not a targeted vendetta against traditional energy, here is a thought exercise: If CCS technology, which is now all the theoretical rage but still just an economic fantasy, were to ultimately work at scale and remove all of the carbon dioxide emitted by the industry, both accumulated and going forward, would oil, gas, and coal companies be allowed to continue operating in such a new net-zero world? As Mattel's Magic 8 Ball would reply: "Don't count on it."

The current energy industry policy of collaboration needs to be replaced with confrontation and public arguments based on scientific data and economic analysis. Energy companies should be leading the energy policy discussion, not shrinking from it because they don't want to be perceived as self-serving or arguing in bad faith. While there has been more open criticism of the energy policies of the Biden administration by the US industry over the past three years, more needs to be done. In particular, the energy industry needs to give a more full-throated defense of the many positive contributions that fossil fuels make to society while calling out the impossibility of the current hurried, politically driven energy transition and the negative consequences that it will have for the US economy and American consumers.

In making the case for continued reliance on fossil fuels, the numbers do most of the talking. Based on the latest worldwide energy data compiled by BP and the Energy Institute, fossil fuels – including crude oil, natural gas, and coal – comprised 85% of global direct primary energy consumption in 2022, which is unchanged over the past 30 years from 85% in 1992.[21] After decades of government subsidies and other forms of support, renewable energy sources – excluding nuclear, hydropower, and biomass, the euphemism for wood burning – only accounted for 3%. Despite investing trillions of dollars to increase wind, solar, and biofuel production capacity, renewables still represent a rounding error for the global energy mix. All this sunk capital wasted on renewable power generation would have been better spent on fortifying power grids and expanding the reach of reliable electricity to more of the world's population. Based on IEA estimates, in 2022, the number of people globally living without access to reliable electricity rose for the first time in 20 years,[22] mainly because of the misplaced focus on intermittent renewable power generation capacity. And there needs to be more honesty about the true levelized cost of wind and solar electricity once you strip out government subsidies, adjust for much lower capacity factors, and layer on transmission system hookups. Lastly, aggressively electrifying the entire economy – including transportation, heating, and cooking activities – while at the same time dramatically shifting the generation mix toward intermittent wind and solar shows how far environmental activists and policymakers are willing to go in rolling the economic dice on climate change.

Before speaking up, though, the energy industry first needs to get its financial house in order to minimize its exposure to ESG defunding risk. US oil and gas companies should continue to focus on generating positive free cash flow as opposed to growing reserves or production, thereby reducing their external funding requirements and dependence on the financial markets. This should prove easier over the coming years as ratcheting climate policies perpetuate the current global energy crisis centered in Europe and keep energy commodity prices elevated. Going forward, the industry should run with higher balance sheet cash positions than in the past, as most US technology and European industrial companies currently do.

Rather than trying to appear woke and part of the sustainable in-crowd, energy companies need to start controlling the conversation when it comes to ESG. When dealing with investors, group ESG discussions should be avoided to prevent swarming. ESG-focused analysts should be frozen out of the conversation and put in the penalty box so that quarterly earnings calls are not hijacked. Every ESG engagement conversation with investors or activist groups should be recorded – much like the taped telephone lines used by Wall Street traders – and used as legal evidence to prove corporate harassment and collusion. Energy companies need to be more discriminating when it comes to their capital providers and realize that accounts who brag that they prefer to work with "dirty" or "brown" energy companies rather than divest are not quality investors.

No matter what it does, the energy industry will be criticized by the ESG activists for either not doing enough or talking their own book. Oil and gas companies need to finally accept this reality and go on a public relations offensive around climate change theory – even at this very late date. Instead of endlessly defending itself against frivolous climate cases filed by states, cities, children, and every environmental group under the sun, the energy sector needs to start filing its own lawsuits. If ExxonMobil can sue to block a windfall tax on oil companies in the EU, as it recently did in December 2022,[23] then the super major – along with its integrated peers – can start legally challenging US climate regulations at home. Turnabout is fair play. As the oil and gas industry stands the most to lose from climate change and ESG, this will help give a voice to the many others in the business world and across Wall Street that are currently afraid to speak up for fear of being canceled. It is only a matter of time before the decarbonization mob comes for the other heavy industries due to their large asset footprints and perceived environmental failings – ESG being, at its core, an anti-industrial movement targeted at developed countries and markets.

For those working on Wall Street opposed to the sustainability agenda, what is required now is across-the-board civil disobedience and resistance. It won't be easy. Everyone in the financial industry is under the gun to comply since sustainability policy is coming down from the CEO level. But even random acts of ESG defiance and insubordination would help to limit the spread of ESG across the US financial markets. Just focusing on making money, which is what Wall Street does best, would make an important contribution to the effort. The simple step of simply ignoring ESG considerations in every daily conversation about the financial markets, trade ideas, and investment recommendations would go a long way.

Senior business leaders – both on the sell side and the buy side – need to take the lead and set an example by subtly exposing the financial nonsense of nonfinancial ESG factors. In every internal meeting, sustainability experts should be challenged to explain the analysis and data behind their investment ideas and how their recommendations will necessarily lead to excess returns and market outperformance over a one-year investment horizon, which is still the most relevant time frame for Wall Street. Make them deal in specifics and back up their argument with market examples of past performance. Don't let them hide behind generalities and performance platitudes. Press them on why sustainability is the only investment strategy ever conceived that is impervious to both the economic and credit cycles and recommended in every market context for every asset class and every type of investor regardless of risk profile and return goals.

Sustainability colleagues should be treated like any other political rival by being boxed out and showed up at every turn. Otherwise, it is only a matter of time before such ESG specialists are running most trading and investment businesses on Wall Street, which is a dispiriting thought. Not crushing these political rivals now will mean reporting to them down the road. And if sustainability is allowed to take permanent hold, it is only a matter of time before industry compensation levels are reduced as a matter of equity and fairness and annual Wall Street bonuses are vested over the exceedingly long-term horizon of sustainability rather than the current three- to five-year industry standard.

The nonsustainable set on Wall Street needs to stop legitimizing ESG and giving lip service to the progressive reengineering of the financial markets because such silence does imply consent. More Ayn Rand–style blunt talk about ESG is in order, which shouldn't be a problem for Wall Street given that profanity is a dominant dialect on most trading floors. Rather than accepting every ESG assertion as gospel, start questioning the orthodoxy about sustainability. Don't be afraid to state obvious facts. Climate science, sustainable development, and ESG analysis are all contradictions in terms. The world cannot shut down and transition away from fossil fuels without crashing the global economy and, with it, the financial markets. None of the industry's financial VAR models worked in real time back in 2008, so why is Wall Street now placing any bets based on climate model projections for 2050 and beyond? Sustainable investing has not been shown to create long-term value or generate financial outperformance despite more than 30 years of trying. Stakeholder capitalism is not capitalism and the totalitarian system of ESG, with its pervasive investment integration and relentless corporate engagement, is incompatible with free markets. Two-sided financial markets cannot function when there is forced conformity of thought.

Wall Street's star producers, whether top-ranked sell-side analysts or top-decile buy-side portfolio managers, should not underestimate the power and the leverage that they have. Despite all the changes in Wall Street research departments over the past two decades, investment banks still covet the bragging rights associated with placing well in the *Institutional Investor* and other industry research polls for equity and fixed income. Sell-side research analysts – especially those with public personalities and investor followings – should avoid collaborating on joint research reports with their sustainability colleagues so as to not give credibility to the ESG argument and conflate the distinct concepts of fundamental analysis, relative value, and sustainability. To shut down all the ESG ratings and scoring noise in the market, sell-side analysts should simply default to the major credit rating agencies regarding any environmental, social, or governance issue that needs addressing. If an

ESG factor does not impact a company's long-term credit rating, then there is obviously no sustainability issue and no need to spend any time on it. Wherever possible, the subjective ESG belief system should be kept separate from the Wall Street business of picking stocks and bonds and making sector calls. ESG-labeled bonds should be regularly called out for their lack of relative value. Sell-side analysts need to learn how to deflect threats from their investing clients to "pull the wire" if they don't echo their views on sustainability.

Sell-side industry analysts can use their research platforms to expose the truth about ESG, both through their thematic pieces and their sector and company recommendations. For example, those analysts covering the oil and gas sector, either on the equity or debt side, should point out the obvious fact that forcing oil and gas companies to forgo their core business competencies will not make them better fundamental stories or more attractive investments. Moreover, energy analysts should not shy away from assigning an overweight to the sector or issuing buy recommendations on individual energy companies based on the current constructive commodity price outlook over the long term. Such a positive energy sector stance is, in and of itself, a refutation of the core climate argument and a tacit acknowledgment that the ESG system will not succeed. Regular research updates showing global oil and gas demand never peaking would also help to drive this message home.

Sell-side energy analysts also need to be more vocal about the inability of the global economy to transition away from fossil fuels based on current technologies without catastrophic results. Moreover, they should highlight how negative the green transition will be for the environment. For one, producing all the EVs and batteries that would be required to replace fossil fuels would be highly pollutive and environmentally devastating given the toxic minerals involved, with many questioning whether there is even enough resource base worldwide that can be mined and processed to meet the expected demand. Massive wind farms, both land-based and offshore, are killing thousands of birds – including eagles and other raptors – each year and disrupting underwater sea life, even though the environmentalists who regularly shout about climate-related biodiversity loss and mass extinction have chosen to look the other way.

Most importantly, Wall Street analysts should call out all the wasted economic motion associated with the green energy transition, including renewable power and EV businesses that can't stand on their own two economic feet without government subsidies, new technologies like CCS that will likely never work at commercial scale, and net-zero solutions such as carbon credits that add no economic value. With regard to the latter, paying third-world countries to abstain from cutting down forested land and then forcing carbon-emitting industries in the developed world to purchase such credits is a wealth transfer, no matter how many times you call it a trading system. Circular economies built on reusable products and raw materials and powered by an endless supply of renewable energy are a pipe dream because they would be closed economic loops marked by stagnant growth whose center would not hold in the face of creative destruction and innovation. Lastly, sell-side analysts should be honest in describing what a net-zero world would look like: less consumption and economic growth, limited mobility and human interaction, less-reliable supply chains and electricity grids, increased poverty and famine, and higher death rates. Decarbonization is synonymous with degrowth, deindustrialization, and depopulation. A world without fossil fuels would not be a better or more just place to live. To the contrary, it would resemble a Pieter Bruegel painting of hell.

In like manner, sell-side analysts covering the financial institutions sector can raise a red flag about ESG by highlighting the business and litigation risks posed to their coverage universe of companies. This is already starting to happen. In October 2022, an equity analyst at the Swiss bank UBS Group AG downgraded his rating on the stock of BlackRock to neutral and slashed his share price target for the company by 16% due to the growing backlash over the firm's ESG efforts.[24] In the sell-side analyst's view, BlackRock's sustainability push has increased political risk for the investment manager as well as the potential for lost fund mandates and heightened regulatory scrutiny. These same financial sector analysts should also remind their audiences that the chief responsibility for financing global sustainable development rests with the multilateral development banks and sovereign credit agencies, not the private sector.

Similarly, buy-side portfolio managers looking to resist should provide whatever minimal disclosure and reporting is required by regulators going forward but should exercise their discretion to opt out wherever possible when it comes to rebranding existing funds as sustainable, layering ESG integration and administrative costs onto actively managed assets after the fact, or submitting to European-style ESG regulation for simplicity's sake. Portfolio managers with strong performance track records have important leverage to influence the internal ESG discussion since investment advisers hate turnover that must be reported and explained to investors and consultants. Just maintaining the status quo by continuing to base every sector-weighting call and individual company pick on pecuniary factors will make a statement.

To take advantage of the current demand for sustainable investment products – some of which is organic in nature – every asset manager should probably have a box for sustainable or socially responsible or impact-oriented funds in their portfolio lineup. Raising new capital for separately managed ESG-targeted funds is how this demand should be met; this unique style of moral investing needs to be kept separate from economically driven strategies (both active and passive) and arguably should come with a black-box warning from fund managers about lost performance and forgone returns. Sustainable investing can and should be marginalized to minimize its negative externalities on the overall market. Under no circumstances should it be forced on financial firms or allowed to contaminate the rest of a firm's AUM or used as a cudgel against portfolio companies to get them to change their business strategy or financial policies. Company shares held by investment funds – particularly the passive kind – should, as a matter of policy, cede their voting proxy to company management and the board of directors when it comes to any shareholder resolution related to climate, sustainability, or ESG.

If investment managers and asset owners insist on dictating corporate and social policy to their portfolio companies, setting energy and broader economic policy for the country through the backdoor of capital controls, and replacing shareholder capitalism with stakeholder capitalism – all over an extremely rushed and completely arbitrary 2030 timeline set by the UN – then these firms should be designated as strategically important financial institutions or SIFIs under the Dodd–Frank Act, with all the heightened scrutiny and regulatory burden that such a label would entail. All the nonfinancial sustainable reporting and goal-setting being forced down the throats of corporations and banks by ESG investors is not a costless exercise. It seems only fair that those buy-side accounts pushing ESG onto the financial markets should also be subjected to the same type of costly business micromanagement at the hands of US regulators. Designating as SIFIs all the progressively minded investment firms now itching to show that they are saving the planet and society through ESG will provide a true test for their commitment to the sustainable finance agenda. It will also establish a clearing price for virtue signaling on Wall Street.[25]

While the ESG opposition has its work cut out for it, nothing about the sustainable investment movement is inevitable or irreversible, even with the formidable backing of government regulators worldwide. Market regulations have failed in the past – SEC Rule 144A, which was designed to inject liquidity into the US private placement market, being just one example. It is not a foregone conclusion that progressive activists will be able to complete their ESG takeover of Wall Street – even with government help – given the need to control asset prices, every pocket of available capital, and the animal spirits that animate the global markets to make the whole system work. If ESG regulatory relief never comes, then the market solution – and ultimate act of ESG resistance – would be for new market players to raise alternative pools of private capital to fill the funding gap for energy and other politically incorrect sectors as these companies are increasingly ostracized from the broader public markets. Such private investors, immune to ESG peer pressure and sustainability groupthink, are likely to make a killing. One of the major unintended market consequences of pushing ESG onto the global financial system may be a dramatic shift in capital from the public to the private markets, much as the 2008 global financial crisis resulted in a sharp swing of investment from active to passive funds.

And finally, Wall Street should resort to Alinsky's Rule #5 and use humor and ridicule as a "potent weapon" against ESG. Much like spritzing holy water on a vampire, mocking progressives tends to make them spitting mad, especially when they are trying to save the planet and the people of the world. It infuriates them because once you pierce their moral pretension, they are intellectually defenseless. Progressive liberals can't take a joke. This is why Jerry Seinfeld no longer does stand-up comedy routines on college campuses, why Chris Rock got slapped at the Academy Awards ceremony, why Dave Chappelle was assaulted on stage at the Hollywood Bowl, why the satirical newspaper *The Babylon Bee* was banned for two years by the previous management of Twitter, and why liberal media fact-checkers regularly pass judgment on the veracity of jokes, cartoons, and social media memes. Totalitarian regimes – like ESG, where every market participant must follow the same rules – also cannot tolerate humor since it represents a form of intellectual resistance and informal protest that undermines the legitimacy and authority of the overall system. The best example would be Communist China, where the authorities recently banned all *South Park* episodes and any public images of Winnie-the-Pooh, the latter due to the stuffed bear's uncanny resemblance to China's Supreme Leader Xi Jinping.

There is no shortage of comedic material when it comes to making fun of ESG. Starting with climate change, how about the decades-long mass hysteria about mass extinction and the end to life on Earth as we know it – even as people are living longer, and the human population continues to expand? How can anyone take the claims of the climate movement seriously at this point, especially after Al Gore's latest rant about "boiling oceans" and "one billion climate refugees" at the WEF's Davos meeting in January 2023? Why are we relying on ancient technologies such as windmills and sun mirrors to reconfigure the electricity grid of the 21st century, decades after the world mastered nuclear power and space travel? Why is every bad storm taken as a sign of the end of the world, which is clearly a medieval antiscience response more typical of a doomsday cult? And let's acknowledge the evidence of our eyes and ears, as George Orwell would say. Septuagenarians like the UN's António Guterres propping up and hiding behind teenagers and young children to sell climate change to the public is more than a little creepy. Klaus Schwab of the WEF does look and sound like a megalomaniacal James Bond villain – or perhaps the caricature of one, like Doctor Evil in the *Austin Powers* movies. And there really is something sinister about all the WEF's unsolicited recommendations for improving society by turning technology on mankind along the lines of Skynet in the *Terminator* movies.

The idea of hijacking Wall Street to provide a permanent funding source for progressive environmental and social causes is audaciously comical, almost slapstick with equal parts Karl Marx and Marx Brothers. Sustainability experts with little to no experience in finance and investing are telling Wall Street traders and portfolio managers that nonfinancial ESG factors will create financial value over the long term – a gigantic "Trust me" trade where ESG activists, like Wimpy in the Popeye comic strip, promise that you will be paid sometime in the future. Wall Street analysts and strategists are being told to plug climate models into their financial projections and market predictions which, like the latest ACME device mail-ordered by the hapless Wile E. Coyote in the Road Runner cartoons, are likely to blow up in their faces. Broad ESG integration means that every company equity or debt discussion now kicks off like the setup for a Johnny Carson punch line: How sustainable is she? In the Abbott and Costello world of ESG, everyone knows that climate change is what's on first. With regular ESG engagement, every company meeting offers a chance to dress down management and hurl insults like Don Rickles in his "Hello Dummy!" routine. Like the classic chocolate factory episode of *I Love Lucy*, financial professionals are being forced to look at hundreds of ESG factors and metrics for each company, with activists now telling them to speed it up because 2030 is fast approaching. For anyone cutting corners on sustainability, the financial regulators are now swooping in like the Keystone Kops to slap the cuffs on those breaking the ESG law and not doing enough to save the planet. That ESG is such a serious threat to the global financial system does not mean it offers nothing to laugh at. God knows, some old-school boomer humor would help give some much-needed perspective to many of the uptight and overly serious millennials now working on Wall Street.

A humorous countermovement is what is now needed on Wall Street to laugh ESG out of town. Here the financial industry should take a page out of the protest playbook of the 1960s. In 1967, Arlo Guthrie, the son of folk-singing legend Woody Guthrie, released "Alice's Restaurant Massacree," a satirical talking song to protest the US draft for the Vietnam War. In the more-than-18-minute-long song, which became the younger Guthrie's signature piece, he recounted the largely true story of how his arrest and conviction for dumping trash illegally in Stockbridge, Massachusetts, one Thanksgiving weekend had endangered his suitability for the military draft because, as Guthrie noted, he wasn't "moral enough to join the army, burn women, kids, houses and villages after being a litterbug." Outraged by the "damn gall" of the army for questioning his ethical character, Guthrie called for an antidraft movement driven by song and symbolized by the singing of "a bar of Alice's Restaurant" whenever and wherever possible, in groups of one or more. The song became a hit because of its preposterous premise, its lighthearted treatment of a serious subject, and its comic deconstruction of a pointless, bloody war waged by a Democratic administration. In many ways, Guthrie's protest song should serve as a template for dealing with ESG, which is no less ridiculous in terms of core argument and policy implementation, and which will also require a loud voice to shout down. That said, singing "with four-part harmony and feeling," as Guthrie recommended, would probably not be viewed kindly on most Wall Street trading and investment banking floors.[26]

The American psychologist and philosopher William James, brother of Henry, once observed: "Common sense and a sense of humor are the same thing, moving at different speeds. A sense of humor is just common sense, dancing." Both senses are now required in earnest on Wall Street to combat the spread of the intertwined ideologies of sustainable finance and stakeholder capitalism based on the preposterous notion that the financial markets need reimagining and redemption, which is the most laughable part of ESG. No apologies are necessary for Wall Street or the corporations that it funds. The worlds of business and finance are already moral universes. Neither needs to earn progressive merit badges to achieve a higher ethical state. Until and unless the many good people working on Wall Street rediscover and embrace some of the core tenets of Ayn Rand's philosophy – including her view that capitalism is based on a ruling principle of justice and "holds integrity and trustworthiness as cardinal virtues," and her belief that "a free mind and a free market are corollaries" – then they are asking for the industry's destruction, and the ESG joke will be on them.

ACKNOWLEDGMENTS

There are many people to thank on the long and winding journey to writing this book – otherwise known as my life.

First and foremost, I am grateful for my wife, Pat, the love of my life and my best friend since we were teenagers, and our two sons, Matt and Andrew. The three of them are my rock. They have supported me throughout my professional life – even though growing up my sons weren't quite sure what I did for a living – and always given me the very best of reasons to get in early, work more efficiently, and get home at a reasonable time. Now, after years of working long hours on Wall Street with way too much travel and lost weekends, they have indulged me one more time so that I can cross off "Write a book" from my bucket list. I thank them for their tolerance of my wandering mind and my endless note-scribbling these past few months, as well as for all their helpful suggestions and ideas to improve this book and make it a better read.

I would like to thank my parents, Marion and David Tice, for providing me with every opportunity to succeed in life. My mother taught kindergarten and music classes in the New York City public school system; my father was a cardiovascular surgeon and professor of surgery at NYU School of Medicine. Both were great teachers, each in their own way, as well as choir directors and church organists in their spare time. While the Fates did not allow either to be part of my adult life, their lessons about the value of an education, the joy of music, the importance of family and heritage (Norwegian, *uff da*), and the need for faith have stayed with me until the present day. I could not have asked for a better environment to grow up in than the Brooklyn of the 1960s and 1970s.

My lifelong interest in writing was sparked at an early age, and much of the credit goes to my high school English teacher, Michael D'Ambrosia. Every student should have at least one teacher like "Mr. D" who lights a similar spark for them. My love of writing has stayed with me since Fort Hamilton High School, through college, and into my working life, where I was very lucky to have found a job on Wall Street where I could write for a living.

I must also thank Glenn Reynolds, the best fixed income analyst on Wall Street since the Carter administration, for taking a chance and hiring an English major from Columbia into the research group at Shearson Lehman Hutton back in 1989. That risky, ill-considered managerial move – along with the subsequent years of his mentoring and friendship – forever changed the arc of my Wall Street career, for which I am forever grateful.

One of the main reasons why I felt compelled to write this book was to give voice to the many people in business and finance who are not currently able to speak up about ESG for fear of retribution – something that I have experienced firsthand in recent years. Over the course of my career, I have been blessed and honored to work with many fine people in both the energy industry (the real world) and on Wall Street (the surreal world), making many good friends along the way. My simple goal with this book, much like Ellis Wyatt in *Atlas Shrugged*, is to leave both the energy patch and Wall Street the same way that I found each of them. Hopefully, this book will also have an incendiary impact.

Lastly, I would like to thank Roger Kimball, Sam Schneider, Malcolm Salovaara, Elizabeth Bachmann, Lauren Miklos, and the rest of the team at Encounter Books for agreeing to publish this book and for all their hard work getting it across the finish line, sanding down the rough edges, and polishing up the final product. A special shoutout to freelancers David Hornik, Robert Erickson, and Steve Cooley, the former two for their meticulous work editing and proofing the manuscript and imposing order on all the style chaos and the latter for designing the perfect racy cover to go with the title of the book. All the opinions and all the Brooklyn attitude contained herein are mine and mine alone.

ABOUT THE AUTHOR

Paul H. Tice spent 40 years working on Wall Street in a variety of roles at some of the industry's most recognizable firms, including JPMorgan Chase, Lehman Brothers, Deutsche Bank/Bankers Trust, and BlackRock. A long-time veteran of the fixed income and credit markets, he specialized in the global energy sector for most of his career, both as a top-ranked Wall Street research analyst and a buy-side investment manager.

He spent 17 years in sell-side credit research, both as an analyst and producing manager, and was the #1-ranked analyst on *Institutional Investor*'s All-America Fixed Income Research Team for Investment Grade Energy in 1998 and 2006. During his 16 years on the buy side, he was mainly a public and private energy investor while holding a series of senior positions – including senior investment analyst, portfolio manager, board director, partner, chief operating officer, and co–chief investment officer – at various hedge fund, private equity, and asset management firms.

His work with the oil and gas industry since the mid-1990s has made him an expert in climate policy and environmental regulation and its financial offshoot, the ESG and sustainable investment movement. In recent years, he has taught about the energy, infrastructure, and project finance markets as an adjunct professor of finance at NYU Stern School of Business, where he has also authored several academic case studies and a joint faculty research white paper on infrastructure finance. His opinion pieces on energy, climate change, infrastructure policy, higher education, ESG, and the financial markets have appeared in the *Wall Street Journal*, the *Washington Examiner*, the *New York Post*, the *Epoch Times*, and *The Hill*. He is also regularly quoted by news outlets in their reporting on the energy and infrastructure markets.

He graduated magna cum laude with a BA in English from Columbia University and is a member of Phi Beta Kappa. He also holds an MBA in finance from NYU Stern. Born and raised in Bay Ridge, Brooklyn, he now lives with his family in suburban New Jersey.

ENDNOTES

Chapter 1: Sustainability: A Theory about Everything

1 Paul Johnson, *Modern Times* (HarperCollins, 1983), 49.
2 David Satter, "100 Years of Communism—and 100 Million Dead," *Wall Street Journal*, November 6, 2017, https://www.wsj.com/articles/100-years-of-communismand-100-million-dead-1510011810.
3 United Nations General Assembly, "Report of the World Commission on Environment and Development: Our Common Future," A/42/427 (August 4, 1987), 14, https://documents-dds-ny.un.org/doc/UNDOC/GEN/N87/184/67/img/N8718467.pdf?OpenElement.
4 A/42/427, 13.
5 A/42/427, 14.
6 A/42/427, 52, 62.
7 A/42/427, 24.
8 A/42/427, 13–14.
9 A/42/427, 51.
10 Johnson, *Modern Times*, 493–94.
11 A/42/427, 176.
12 A/42/427, 31, 72, 56.
13 A/42/427, 16, 222.
14 A/42/427, 31.
15 Milton Friedman, "A Friedman Doctrine—The Social Responsibility of Business Is to Increase Its Profits," *New York Times*, September 13, 1970, https://www.nytimes.com/1970/09/13/archives/a-friedman-doctrine-the-social-responsibility-of-business-is-to.html.
16 Friedman, "A Friedman Doctrine."
17 Adam Smith, *An Inquiry into the Nature and Causes of the Wealth of Nations*, ed. S. M. Soares (MetaLibri Digital Library, 2007), 349.
18 David Hume, *Essays, Moral, Political, and Literary*, ed. Eugene F. Miller (Liberty Fund, 1987), 271.
19 John Locke, *Second Treatise of Government* (Project Gutenberg, 2003), chap. 5.
20 F. A. Hayek, *The Road to Serfdom*, ed. Bruce Caldwell (University of Chicago Press, 2007), 86, 172.
21 Ayn Rand, "America's Persecuted Minority: Big Business," in *Capitalism: The Unknown Ideal* (Penguin Books, 1967), 45.

22 Ayn Rand, *Atlas Shrugged* (Penguin Books, 1957), 412.
23 Klaus Schwab and Hein Kroos, *Modern Company Management in Mechanical Engineering* (VDMA, 1971), 21.
24 WEF, "The Davos Agenda 2021: What is stakeholder capitalism?" (January 22, 2021), accessed February 1, 2023, https://www.weforum.org/agenda/2021/01/klaus-schwab-on-what-is-stakeholder-capitalism-history-relevance.
25 WEF, "The World Economic Forum: A Partner in Shaping History, 1971–2020," 26, https://www.weforum.org/about/history.
26 William Conrad Kessler, "The German Corporation Law of 1937," *American Economic Review* 28, no. 4 (1938): 653–62.
27 Klaus Schwab has publicly acknowledged that his father was Eugen Schwab, most recently in the dedication for his 2021 book on stakeholder capitalism. A fact-checking report by Deutsche Presse-Agentur has confirmed that Eugen Schwab moved his family from Switzerland to Germany during the 1930s so that he could manage the Ravensburg factory of Escher Wyss, which was recognized as a National Socialist Model Company by the Nazi regime. The Ravensburg factory's use of forced labor during World War II was confirmed in an August 24, 2000, statement by the National Swiss Press Agency, which was produced as part of the Holocaust Victim Assets Litigation brought against Swiss banks in 1996 in the US District Court for the Eastern District of New York. The postwar German denazification process was mainly accomplished through hearings and questionnaires (*Fragebögen*).
28 Randall K. Morck and Bernard Yeung, "Corporatism and the Ghost of the Third Way," *Capitalism and Society* 5, no. 3 (2010): 16–25.
29 Klaus Schwab and Peter Vanham, *Stakeholder Capitalism: A Global Economy that Works for Progress, People and Planet* (John Wiley & Sons, 2021), 176–79.
30 A/42/427, 16.
31 United Nations Department of Economic and Social Affairs, "The 17 Goals," accessed January 26, 2023, https://sdgs.un.org/goals.
32 United Nations Department of Economic and Social Affairs, "Transforming our world: the 2030 Agenda for Sustainable Development," accessed July 25, 2023, https://sdgs.un.org/2030agenda.
33 United Nations Department of Economic and Social Affairs, "Harnessing Climate and SDGs Synergies," accessed July 25, 2023, https://sdgs.un.org/climate-sdgs-synergies.
34 Klaus Schwab, *The Fourth Industrial Revolution* (Penguin Random House, 2016).
35 WEF, "Now Is the Time for a Great Reset," accessed January 27, 2023, https://www.weforum.org/agenda/2020/06/now-is-the-time-for-a-great-reset.
36 *Back to the Future Part II*, directed by Robert Zemeckis, Amblin Entertainment, Universal Pictures, 1989.

37 "The Pitch," *Seinfeld*, season 4, episode 3, written by Larry David, directed by Tom Cherones, aired September 16, 1992.
38 Friedman, "A Friedman Doctrine."
39 United Nations Sustainable Development Group, "Decade of Action," accessed January 27, 2023, https://unsdg.un.org/16019-decade-action.

Chapter 2: It's All about Climate Change

1 EPA, "Our Nation's Air: Trends through 2021," accessed January 27, 2023, https://gispub.epa.gov/air/trendsreport/2022/#home.
2 David A. Keiser and Joseph S. Shapiro, "Consequences of the Clean Water Act and the Demand for Water Quality," *Quarterly Journal of Economics* 134, no. 1 (February 2019): 373, doi:10.1093/qje/qjy019.
3 White House Report of the Environmental Pollution Panel, President's Science Advisory Committee, "Restoring the Quality of Our Environment" (November 1965), 111–33, https://www.climatefiles.com/climate-change-evidence/presidents-report-atmospher-carbon-dioxide.
4 The Nobel Prize, "The Nobel Peace Prize 2007," accessed July 26, 2023, https://www.nobelprize.org/prizes/peace/2007/summary.
5 NOAA Global Monitoring Laboratory, "Atmospheric CO_2 at Mauna Loa Observatory," accessed January 27, 2023, https://gml.noaa.gov/ccgg/trends/data.html.
6 NOAA National Centers for Environmental Information, "Climate Change: Atmospheric Carbon Dioxide," accessed January 27, 2023, https://www.climate.gov/news-features/understanding-climate/climate-change-atmospheric-carbon-dioxide.
7 Andrew Moseman, "How much carbon dioxide does the Earth naturally absorb?," Ask MIT Climate, January 4, 2022, https://climate.mit.edu/ask-mit/how-much-carbon-dioxide-does-earth-naturally-absorb.
8 NOAA National Centers for Environmental Information, "International Surface Temperature Initiative (ISTI) Global Land Surface Temperature Databank," accessed October 27, 2023, https://www.ncei.noaa.gov/access/metadata/landing-page/bin/iso?id=gov.noaa.ncdc:C00849.
9 Anthony Watts, "Corrupted Climate Stations: The Official U.S. Temperature Record Remains Fatally Flawed," Heartland Institute (2022), 3, https://heartland.org/wp-content/uploads/documents/2022_Surface_Station_Report.pdf.
10 Daniel T. C. Cox, Ilya M. D. Maclean, Alexandra S. Gardner, and Kevin J. Gaston, "Global variation in diurnal asymmetry in temperature, cloud cover, specific humidity and precipitation and its association with leaf area index,"

Global Change Biology (2020): 7099–7111, https://onlinelibrary.wiley.com/doi/epdf/10.1111/gcb.15336.

11 NOAA National Centers for Environmental Information, "Climate Change in the Context of Paleoclimate," accessed January 27, 2023, https://www.ncei.noaa.gov/news/climate-change-context-paleoclimate.

12 NOAA National Centers for Environmental Information, "Assessing the Global Climate in 2022," accessed January 27, 2023, https://www.ncei.noaa.gov/news/global-climate-202212.

13 NASA Goddard Institute for Space Studies, "The Elusive Absolute Surface Air Temperature," accessed January 27, 2023, https://data.giss.nasa.gov/gistemp/faq/abs_temp.html.

14 NOAA, "Layers of the Ocean," accessed July 25, 2023, https://www.noaa.gov/jetstream/ocean/layers-of-ocean.

15 NOAA Global Ocean Monitoring & Observing, "The Argo Program," accessed July 25, 2023, https://globalocean.noaa.gov/research/argo-program.

16 NOAA Climate.gov, "Climate Change: Ocean Heat Content," accessed January 28, 2023, https://www.climate.gov/news-features/understanding-climate/climate-change-ocean-heat-content.

17 NASA Global Climate Change, "Vital Signs: Ocean Warming," accessed August 3, 2023, https://climate.nasa.gov/vital-signs/ocean-warming.

18 EPA, "Climate Change Indicators: Snow and Ice," accessed January 28, 2023, https://www.epa.gov/climate-indicators/snow-ice.

19 Julia R. Andreasen, Anna E. Hogg, and Heather L. Selley, "Change in Antarctic ice shelf area from 2009 to 2019," *The Cryosphere* 17 (May 16, 2023): 2059–72, https://doi.org/10.5194/tc-17-2059-2023.

20 NOAA Climate.gov, "Climate Change: Global Sea Level," accessed January 28, 2023, https://www.climate.gov/news-features/understanding-climate/climate-change-global-sea-level.

21 UNEP Intergovernmental Science-Policy Platform on Biodiversity and Ecosystem Services, "IPBES Global Assessment Report on Biodiversity and Ecosystem Services" (May 4, 2019), https://zenodo.org/record/6417333.

22 WWF, "Fossil fuel addiction driving polar bears to extinction says WWF-Canada" (May 4, 2006), https://www.wwf.mg/en/?67880/Fossil-fuel-addiction-driving-polar-bears-to-extinction-says-WWF-Canada.

23 IUCN Polar Bear Specialist Group, "Status Report on the World's Polar Bear Subpopulations, July 2021," accessed January 29, 2023, https://www.iucn-pbsg.org/wp-content/uploads/2021/11/July-2021-Status-Report-Web.pdf.

24 AIMS, "Annual Summary Report of Coral Reef Condition 2021/2022," accessed January 29, 2023, https://www.aims.gov.au/sites/default/files/2022-08/AIMS_LTMP_Report_on%20GBR_coral_status_2021_2022_040822F3.pdf.

25 NOAA National Centers for Environmental Information, "Climate Moni-

toring Products by Category," accessed January 29, 2023, https://www.ncei.noaa.gov/access/monitoring/products.

26 Hannah Ritchie, Pablo Rosado, and Max Roser, "Natural Disasters," Our World in Data, 2022, accessed January 29, 2023, https://ourworldindata.org/natural-disasters.

27 Kenneth Skrable, George Chabot, and Clayton French, "World Atmospheric CO_2, Its 14C Specific Activity, Non-fossil Component, Anthropogenic Fossil Component, and Emissions (1750–2018)," *Health Physics* 122, no. 2 (February 2022): 291–305, https://journals.lww.com/health-physics/Abstract/2022/02000/World_Atmospheric_CO2,_Its_14C_Specific_Activity,.2.aspx.

28 Hannah Ritchie and Max Roser, "Forests and Deforestation," Our World in Data, 2021, accessed January 29, 2023, https://ourworldindata.org/forests-and-deforestation.

29 Sean Twomey, "Cloud Physics Considerations in Global Climate Change Studies," DOE Office of Energy Research, 1995, https://www.osti.gov/servlets/purl/232602.

30 Gregory Duveiller, Federico Filipponi, Andrej Ceglar, Jedrez Bojanowski, Ramdane Alkama, and Alessandro Cescatti, "Revealing the widespread potential of forests to increase low level cloud cover," *Nature Communications* 12 (2021): 4337, https://doi.org/10.1038/s41467-021-24551-5.

31 Zeke Hausfather, "How well have climate models projected global warming?," Carbon Brief, 2017, accessed January 29, 2023, https://www.carbonbrief.org/analysis-how-well-have-climate-models-projected-global-warming.

32 IPCC, "Sixth Assessment Report, Working Group I: The Physical Science Basis" (2021), accessed January 29, 2023, https://www.ipcc.ch/report/ar6/wg1/chapter/summary-for-policymakers.

33 Global Carbon Project, "Global Carbon Budget 2022," accessed January 29, 2023, https://essd.copernicus.org/articles/14/4811/2022.

34 United Nations, "Secretary-General's statement on the IPCC Working Group 1 Report on the Physical Science Basis of the Sixth Assessment" (August 9, 2021), https://www.un.org/sg/en/content/secretary-generals-statement-the-ipcc-working-group-1-report-the-physical-science-basis-of-the-sixth-assessment.

35 Frank Jordans and Seth Borenstein, "UN warns Earth 'firmly on track toward an unlivable world,'" Associated Press, April 4, 2022, https://apnews.com/article/climate-united-nations-paris-europe-berlin-802ae4475c9047fb6d82ac88b37a690e.

36 United Nations, "Secretary-General's remarks to High-Level opening of COP27" (November 7, 2022), https://www.un.org/sg/en/content/sg/speeches/2022-11-07/secretary-generals-remarks-high-level-opening-of-cop27.

37 Peter James Spielmann, "U.N. Predicts Disaster if Global Warming Not

Checked," Associated Press, June 29, 1989, https://apnews.com/article/bd45c372caf118ec99964ea547880cd0.

38 John Cook, Dana Nuccitelli, Sarah A. Green, Mark Richardson, Bärbel Winkler, Rob Painting, Robert Way, Peter Jacobs, and Andrew Skuce, "Quantifying the consensus on anthropogenic global warming in the scientific literature," *Environmental Research Letters* 8 (2013), https://doi.org/10.1088/1748-9326/8/2/024024.

39 Mark Lynas, Benjamin Z. Houlton, and Simon Perry, "Greater than 99% consensus on human caused climate change in the peer-reviewed scientific literature," *Environmental Research Letters* 16 (2021), https://doi.org/10.1088/1748-9326/ac2966.

40 Vatican, "Encyclical Letter *Laudato Si* of the Holy Father Francis on Care for our Common Home" (May 24, 2015), 3, 18, https://www.vatican.va/content/dam/francesco/pdf/encyclicals/documents/papa-francesco_20150524_enciclica-laudato-si_en.pdf.

41 IPCC, "Sixth Assessment Report, Working Group III: Climate Change 2022, Mitigation of Climate Change" (2022), accessed July 28, 2023, https://www.ipcc.ch/report/ar6/wg3.

Chapter 3: The UN Wants to Be Your Investment Adviser

1 Paraphrased in speech given by UN Secretary-General Dag Hammarskjöld on May 13, 1954, but widely attributed to Henry Cabot Lodge Jr.

2 A/42/427, 12.

3 Paul Johnson, "In Praise of Richard Nixon," *Commentary*, October 1988, https://www.commentary.org/articles/paul-johnson-3/in-praise-of-richard-nixon.

4 American Committee on Africa, "Divestment Action on South Africa by US and Canadian Colleges and Universities" (August 1988), https://kora.matrix.msu.edu/files/50/304/32-130-E6E-84-AL.SFF.DOCUMENT.acoa000194.pdf.

5 UNEP FI, "About Us," accessed August 4, 2023, https://www.unepfi.org/about.

6 UNGC, "See who's involved," accessed August 4, 2023, https://unglobalcompact.org/what-is-gc/participants.

7 PRI, "What is the PRI's mission?," accessed January 29, 2023, https://www.unpri.org/about-us/about-the-pri.

8 PRI, "Quarterly signatory update," accessed August 4, 2023, https://www.unpri.org/signatories/signatory-resources/quarterly-signatory-update.

9 PRI, "PRI brochure 2021," accessed January 29, 2023, https://www.unpri.org/download?ac=10948.

10 UNCTAD, "World Investment Report 2014," 11, https://unctad.org/system/files/official-document/wir2014_en.pdf.
11 S&P Dow Jones Indices, "S&P 500 Bond Index Factsheet, April 28, 2023," accessed May 18, 2023, https://www.spglobal.com/spdji/en/indices/fixed-income/sp-500-bond-index/#overview.
12 PRI, "The SDG Investment Case" (2017), 16, https://www.unpri.org/download?ac=5909.
13 PRI, "The SDG Investment Case," 24.
14 PRI, "Climate risk: An investor resource guide" (January 21, 2022), accessed January 29, 2023, https://www.unpri.org/climate-change/climate-risk-an-investor-resource-guide/9329.article.
15 PRI, "A Blueprint for Responsible Investment" (2017), https://www.unpri.org/download?ac=5330.
16 World Bank, "Global GDP (current US$), 1960–2021," accessed January 30, 2023, https://data.worldbank.org/indicator/NY.GDP.MKTP.CD.
17 SIFMA, "2022 Capital Markets Fact Book" (July 12, 2022), 10, https://www.sifma.org/wp-content/uploads/2022/07/CM-Fact-Book-2022-SIFMA.pdf.

Chapter 4: Wall Street: In the Shadow of the Mushroom Cloud

1 Ken Auletta, "The Fall of Lehman Brothers: The Men, The Money, The Merger," *New York Times*, February 24, 1985, https://www.nytimes.com/1985/02/24/magazine/the-fall-of-lehman-brothers-the-men-the-money-the-merger.html.
2 CNBC, "JPMorgan Froze Lehman Assets Ahead of Bankruptcy," October 6, 2008, https://www.cnbc.com/2008/10/06/jpmorgan-froze-lehman-assets-ahead-of-bankruptcy.html.
3 Lehman Brothers, "Minutes of the Board of Directors, September 14, 2008," https://ypfs.som.yale.edu/library/minutes-lehman-brothers-board-directors.
4 Laurence Ball, "The Fed and Lehman Brothers: Introduction and Summary," National Bureau of Economic Research Working Paper 22410 (July 2016), http://www.nber.org/papers/w22410.
5 Thaya Brook Knight, "Court Finds Government Actions in AIG Bailout Were Illegal," Cato Institute, June 15, 2015, https://www.cato.org/blog/court-finds-government-actions-aig-bailout-were-illegal.
6 Christina Rexrode and Emily Glazer, "Big Banks Paid $110 Billion in Mortgage-Related Fines. Where Did the Money Go?," *Wall Street Journal*, March 9, 2016, https://www.wsj.com/articles/big-banks-paid-110-billionin-mortgage-related-fines-where-did-the-money-go-1457557442.
7 Sam Batkins and Dan Goldbeck, "Six Years After Dodd-Frank: Higher Costs, Uncertain Benefits," American Action Forum, July 20, 2016, https://www.

americanactionforum.org/insight/six-years-dodd-frank-higher-costs-uncertain-benefits.

8 US Department of the Treasury, "About FSOC," accessed January 30, 2023, https://home.treasury.gov/policy-issues/financial-markets-financial-institutions-and-fiscal-service/fsoc/about-fsoc.

9 Yahoo Finance, "Price Chart for S&P 500 Index, 12/31/08 to 12/30/16," accessed January 30, 2023, https://finance.yahoo.com/quote/%5EGSPC/history?period1=1230681600&period2=1483142400&interval=1d&filter=history&frequency=1d&includeAdjustedClose=true.

10 S&P Dow Jones Indices, "Price Graph for S&P 500 Index, 9/28/18 to 12/31/18," accessed January 30, 2023, https://www.spglobal.com/spdji/en/indices/equity/sp-500/#overview.

11 Federal Reserve Bank of St. Louis Economic Research, "Federal Debt: Total Public Debt," accessed July 28, 2023, https://fred.stlouisfed.org/series/GFDEBTN#0.

12 Antoine Gara, James Fontanella-Khan, Eric Platt, and Brooke Masters, "Private equity titans dance until the music stops under the California sun," *Financial Times*, May 6, 2022, https://www.ft.com/content/ebefa5d6-c0a3-4589-8e7a-389d24eed4fe.

13 BLS, "Data Retrieval: Employment, Hours, and Earnings (CES)," accessed February 3, 2023, https://www.bls.gov/webapps/legacy/cesbtab1.htm.

14 FINRA, "2022 FINRA Industry Snapshot" (2022), 7, 26, https://www.finra.org/sites/default/files/2022-03/2022-industry-snapshot.pdf.

15 SIFMA, "U.S. Securities Industry Employment Report, First Quarter 2013" (2013), https://www.sifma.org/wp-content/uploads/2017/05/us-securities-industry-employment-2013-q1.pdf.

16 Office of the New York State Comptroller, "The Securities Industry in New York City" (October 2022), 6, https://www.osc.state.ny.us/files/reports/osdc/pdf/report-11-2023.pdf.

17 SIFMA, "Guiding Principles to Promote the Integrity of Fixed Income Research" (May 19, 2004), https://www.sifma.org/wp-content/uploads/2017/08/Cross-Product_Guiding-Principles-to-Promote-Integrity-of-Fixed-Income-Research.pdf.

18 Greenlight Capital, "Third Quarter 2008 Letter to Investors" (October 1, 2008), https://celestri.files.wordpress.com/2008/10/greenlight-capital-letter-1-oct-081.pdf.

19 Nicole Jao, "Passive US funds poised to overtake active, ISS says," *Financial Times*, January 25, 2023, https://www.ft.com/content/bac54be7-55af-4a61-bbe6-5171d29fcb42.

20 Adam Sabban, CFA, and Ryan Jackson, "US Fund Flows: Investors Bail in 2022," Morningstar, January 17, 2023, https://www.morningstar.com/articles/1129741/us-fund-flows-investors-bail-in-2022.

21 "Imaginationland Episode 1," *South Park*, season 11, episode 10, written and directed by Trey Parker, aired October 17, 2007.
22 Ian Hall, "'Time of Troubles': Arnold J. Toynbee's twentieth century," *International Affairs* 90, no. 1 (January 2014): 23–36, https://www.jstor.org/stable/24538250.
23 Yahoo Finance, "Price Chart for S&P 500 Index, 3/9/09 to 12/31/21," accessed January 30, 2023, https://finance.yahoo.com/quote/%5EGSPC/history?period1=1236556800&period2=1640908800&interval=1d&filter=history&frequency=1d&includeAdjustedClose=true.
24 NYS Comptroller, "Wall Street's 2021 Bonuses Set a New Record" (March 23, 2022), https://www.osc.state.ny.us/files/press/pdf/2021-wall-street-bonus-pool.pdf.
25 Bloomberg, "Bloomberg Billionaires Index," accessed January 30, 2023, https://www.bloomberg.com/billionaires.
26 Hannah Arendt, *Crises of the Republic: Thoughts on Politics and Revolution* (Harcourt Brace, 1972), 206.

Chapter 5: ESG: The Social Control Network

1 Friedman, "A Friedman Doctrine."
2 Schwab, *Stakeholder Capitalism*, 176.
3 John Butters, "Do S&P 500 Companies That Discuss 'ESG' on Earnings Calls Have Higher 'ESG' Ratings?," FactSet, April 18, 2022, https://insight.factset.com/do-sp-500-companies-that-discuss-esg-on-earnings-calls-have-higher-esg-ratings.
4 Business Roundtable, "Business Roundtable Redefines the Purpose of a Corporation to Promote 'An Economy That Serves All Americans'" (August 19, 2019), https://www.businessroundtable.org/business-roundtable-redefines-the-purpose-of-a-corporation-to-promote-an-economy-that-serves-all-americans.
5 Insightia, "Shareholder Activism in 2022," https://www.insightia.com/press/reports.
6 Governance & Accountability Institute, "Examining 2020 sustainability reporting trends of the largest publicly-traded companies in the U.S." (2021), 2, https://www.ga-institute.com/fileadmin/ga_institute/images/FlashReports/2021/Russell-1000/G&A-Russell-Report-2021-Final.pdf?vgo_ee=umptzb7JXEdM1kJT1y5IzqRTDKblZmj7B7iJo6gYJ%2Bs%3D.
7 Corporate Register, "Welcome to Corporate Register," accessed August 5, 2023, https://www.corporateregister.com.

8 UNFCCC, "Race To Zero Campaign," accessed August 4, 2023, https://unfccc.int/climate-action/race-to-zero-campaign.

9 SBTi, "Companies Taking Action," accessed August 4, 2023, https://sciencebasedtargets.org/companies-taking-action.

10 The Climate Pledge, "About The Climate Pledge," accessed August 4, 2023, https://www.theclimatepledge.com/us/en/the-pledge/About.

11 PRI, "Active Ownership 2.0: The Evolution Stewardship Urgently Needs" (2019), https://www.unpri.org/download?ac=9721#:~:text=Active%20Ownership%202.0%20is%20a,and%20effort%20over%20narrow%20interests.

12 As You Sow, Sustainable Investments Institute, and Proxy Impact, "Proxy Preview 2023" (March 22, 2023), https://www.proxypreview.org/press-release.

13 Merel Spierings, "Linking Executive Compensation to ESG Performance," ESG Center, The Conference Board, October 28, 2022, https://www.conference-board.org/pdfdownload.cfm?masterProductID=41301.

14 Exxon Valdez Oil Spill Trustee Council, "NOAA Timeline of Recovery from the Exxon Valdez Oil Spill," 2014, https://evostc.state.ak.us/media/4451/exxon-valdez-timeline-of-recovery-5jun14_noaa.png.

15 Adam Vaughan, "BP's Deepwater Horizon bill tops $65bn," *The Guardian*, January 16, 2018, https://www.theguardian.com/business/2018/jan/16/bps-deepwater-horizon-bill-tops-65bn.

16 Jennifer Larino, "Gulf Coast beaches, marshes show 'substantial recovery' after 2010 oil spill, BP witness testifies," nola.com, January 28, 2015, https://www.nola.com/news/business/gulf-coast-beaches-marshes-show-substantial-recovery-after-2010-oil-spill-bp-witness-testifies/article_2ad25277-c7c8-59a8-a965-0711d0dd3486.html.

17 NYU Stern Spring Symposium 2018, "The Infrastructure and Real Estate Nexus: Three Case Studies" (April 25, 2018), https://www.stern.nyu.edu/sites/default/files/assets/documents/Conference%20Write-Up%20-%20Spring%20Symposium%202018.pdf.

18 The $16 million request made by the SRS in return for supporting DAPL was confirmed to this author by Energy Transfer's then-CFO and current co-CEO, Tom Long, at a company analyst meeting hosted by Barclays Capital as part of its "Investment Grade Energy & Pipeline Corporate Days" conference in New York, February 28–March 1, 2018.

19 Paul Tice, "The ESG attack on energy becomes personal," *Washington Examiner*, March 4, 2023, https://www.washingtonexaminer.com/restoring-america/faith-freedom-self-reliance/the-esg-attack-on-energy-becomes-personal.

20 Paul Tice, "Theatrical corporate-climate protesters deserve Tony Awards of their own," *New York Post*, June 9, 2022, https://nypost.com/2022/06/09/theatrical-corporate-climate-protesters-deserve-tony-awards.

21 Paul Tice, "Theatrical corporate-climate protesters," *New York Post*, June 9, 2022.
22 RepRisk, "Spotting greenwashing with ESG data" (July 2022), accessed January 30, 2023, https://www.reprisk.com/news-research/reports/spotting-greenwashing-with-esg-data.
23 Hannah Miao, "Hundreds of corporations, business leaders, celebs sign statement against voting restrictions," CNBC, April 14, 2021, https://www.cnbc.com/2021/04/14/corporations-business-leaders-celebrities-sign-statement-against-voting-restrictions.html.
24 Human Rights Campaign Foundation, "Corporate Equality Index 2022," accessed August 5, 2023, https://www.hrc.org/resources/corporate-equality-index.

Chapter 6: It Takes a Village of ESG Enablers

1 MSCI, "ESG Investing," accessed July 29, 2023, https://www.msci.com/our-solutions/esg-investing.
2 MSCI, "ESG Ratings & Climate Search Tool," accessed July 29, 2023, https://www.msci.com/our-solutions/esg-investing/esg-ratings-climate-search-tool/issuer. All MSCI ESG ratings and scores cited are valid as of July 29, 2023.
3 Sustainalytics, "ESG Risk Ratings," accessed July 29, 2023, https://www.sustainalytics.com/esg-data.
4 Sustainalytics, "Company ESG Risk Ratings," accessed July 29, 2023, https://www.sustainalytics.com/esg-ratings. All Sustainalytics ESG ratings and scores cited are valid as of July 29, 2023.
5 MSCI, "Implied Temperature Rise," accessed July 29, 2023, https://www.msci.com/our-solutions/climate-investing/implied-temperature-rise.
6 The Impact Investor, "9 Best ESG Rating Agencies—Who Gets to Grade?" (June 9, 2023), https://theimpactinvestor.com/esg-rating-agencies.
7 Refinitiv, "Refinitiv ESG company scores," accessed July 29, 2023, https://www.refinitiv.com/en/sustainable-finance/esg-scores.
8 FTSE Russell, "ESG Scores," accessed July 29, 2023, https://www.ftserussell.com/data/sustainability-and-esg-data/esg-ratings.
9 Leslie Norton, "Complaints About ESG Ratings Reflect 'Maturing, Robust' Industry, Morningstar's Jantzi Says," Morningstar, September 23, 2021, https://www.morningstar.com/articles/1059115/complaints-about-esg-ratings-reflect-maturing-robust-industry-morningstars-jantzi-says.
10 Emile Hallez, "ESG downgrades show complicated nature of sustainability ratings," *InvestmentNews*, April 6, 2023, https://www.investmentnews.com/esg-downgrades-show-complicated-nature-of-sustainability-ratings-236117.

11 Moody's, "ESG Credit and Sustainable Finance," accessed July 29, 2023, https://www.moodys.com/newsandevents/topics/ESG-Credit-00702C.
12 S&P Global, "ESG Scores," accessed July 29, 2023, https://www.spglobal.com/esg/solutions/data-intelligence-esg-scores.
13 Fitch, "ESG Products," accessed July 29, 2023, https://www.fitchratings.com/topics/esg/products.
14 RepRisk, "RepRisk methodology overview," accessed July 29, 2023, https://www.reprisk.com/news-research/resources/methodology.
15 ESG Book, "Making ESG data accessible, comparable and transparent," accessed July 29, 2023, https://www.esgbook.com/the-platform.
16 Nasdaq, "Nasdaq Launches ESG Data Hub" (June 29, 2021), https://www.nasdaq.com/articles/nasdaq-launches-esg-data-hub-2021-06-29.
17 FactSet, "ESG Investing Solutions," accessed July 29, 2023, https://www.factset.com/solutions/esg-investing.
18 Bloomberg, "ESG Data," accessed July 29, 2023, https://www.bloomberg.com/professional/product/esg-data.
19 CDP, "CDP Media Factsheet" (March 2023), https://cdn.cdp.net/cdp-production/comfy/cms/files/files/000/007/666/original/CDP_Media_Factsheet__March_2023.pdf.
20 GRI, "About GRI," accessed July 29, 2023, https://www.globalreporting.org/about-gri.
21 IFRS, "ISSB issues inaugural global sustainability disclosure standards" (June 26, 2023), https://www.ifrs.org/news-and-events/news/2023/06/issb-issues-ifrs-s1-ifrs-s2.
22 TCFD, "About," accessed July 30, 2023, https://www.fsb-tcfd.org/about.
23 TCFD, "Recommendations of the Task Force on Climate-related Financial Disclosures" (June 2017), https://assets.bbhub.io/company/sites/60/2021/10/FINAL-2017-TCFD-Report.pdf.
24 ISS, "ISS ESG," accessed July 30, 2023, https://www.issgovernance.com/esg.
25 ISS, "United States Sustainable Proxy Voting Guidelines: 2023 Policy Recommendations" (January 17, 2023), https://www.issgovernance.com/file/policy/active/specialty/Sustainability-US-Voting-Guidelines.pdf?v=1.
26 Glass Lewis, "ESG Profile," accessed July 30, 2023, https://www.glasslewis.com/esg-profile.
27 McKinsey & Company, "The net-zero transition: What it would cost, what it could bring" (January 2022), 2, https://www.mckinsey.com/~/media/mckinsey/business%20functions/sustainability/our%20insights/the%20net%20zero%20transition%20what%20it%20would%20cost%20what%20it%20could%20bring/the-net-zero-transition-what-it-would-cost-and-what-it-could-bring-final.pdf.
28 Network for Business Sustainability, "For Sustainability Centre Leaders," accessed July 30, 2023, https://nbs.net/for-sustainability-centres.
29 Tensie Whelan, Jamie Friedland, and Ellen Knuti, "U.S. Corporate Boards

Suffer From Inadequate Expertise in Financially Material ESG Matters," NYU Stern Center for Sustainable Business, January 2021, https://www.stern.nyu.edu/sites/default/files/assets/documents/U.S.%20Corporate%20Boards%20Suffer%20From%20Inadequate%20%20Expertise%20in%20Financially%20Material%20ESG%20Matters.docx%20%282.13.21%29.pdf.

30 Kevin Eckerle, Brian Tomlinson, and Tensie Whelan, "ESG and the Earnings Call: Communicating Sustainable Value Creation Quarter by Quarter," NYU Stern Center for Sustainable Business, May 27, 2020, https://ssrn.com/abstract=3607921.

31 Chet Van Wert, "Case Study: The Campaign to Reenergize ExxonMobil," NYU Stern Center for Sustainable Business, November 2021, https://www.stern.nyu.edu/sites/default/files/assets/documents/Case%20Study%20-%20The%20Campaign%20to%20Reenergize%20ExxonMobil%20-%2011-11-2021.pdf.

32 Ulrich Atz, Tracy Van Holt, Elyse Douglas, and Tensie Whelan, "The Return on Sustainability Investment (ROSI): Monetizing Financial Benefits of Sustainability Actions in Companies," *St. John's University Review of Business* 39, no. 2 (June 2019): 1–31, https://www.stjohns.edu/sites/default/files/uploads/Review-of-Business-June-2019.pdf.

33 Randi Kronthal-Sacco and Tensie Whelan, "Sustainable Market Share Index™, 2021 Report," NYU Stern Center for Sustainable Business, April 2022, https://www.stern.nyu.edu/sites/default/files/assets/documents/FINAL%202021%20CSB%20Practice%20Forum%20website_0.pdf.

34 Allie Griffin, "NYU Professor Maitland Jones Jr. fired for being too hard says colleges 'coddle students'," *New York Post*, October 20, 2022, https://nypost.com/2022/10/20/nyu-professor-fired-for-being-too-hard-said-colleges-coddle-students-for-tuition-money.

35 NYU Stern, "Full-time MBA Tuition & Cost of Attendance," accessed July 30, 2023, https://www.stern.nyu.edu/programs-admissions/full-time-mba/financial-aid/tuition-cost-attendance.

36 PRI, "PRI Academy," accessed July 30, 2023, https://priacademy.org.

37 CFA Institute, "Future of Sustainability in Investment Management: From Ideas to Reality" (2020), 3, https://www.cfainstitute.org/-/media/documents/survey/future-of-sustainability.pdf.

38 Ford Foundation, "Ford Foundation commits $1 billion from endowment to mission-related investments" (April 5, 2017), https://www.fordfoundation.org/news-and-stories/news-and-press/news/ford-foundation-commits-1-billion-from-endowment-to-mission-related-investments.

39 TCFD, "Task Force member—Chairman: Michael Bloomberg," accessed January 31, 2023, https://www.fsb-tcfd.org/members/michael-r-bloomberg.

40 PRI, "Fiduciary duty in the 21st century final report," accessed July 30, 2023, https://www.unpri.org/fiduciary-duty/fiduciary-duty-in-the-21st-century-final-report/4998.article.

Chapter 7: A Paralysis of Analysis

1 Alex Gray, "Around 90% of all river-borne plastic that ends up in the ocean comes from just 10 rivers," WEF, June 8, 2018, https://www.weforum.org/agenda/2018/06/90-of-plastic-polluting-our-oceans-comes-from-just-10-rivers.
2 Hess ESG scores and ratings from MSCI and Sustainalytics are valid as of July 30, 2023.
3 Chevron and ExxonMobil ESG scores and ratings from MSCI and Sustainalytics and credit ratings from Moody's and S&P Global Ratings are valid as of July 30, 2023.
4 S&P Global Ratings, "2021 Annual Global Corporate Default and Rating Transition Study" (April 13, 2022).
5 Veronika Henze, "Carbon Offset Prices Could Increase Fifty-Fold by 2050," BloombergNEF, January 10, 2022, https://about.bnef.com/blog/carbon-offset-prices-could-increase-fifty-fold-by-2050.
6 Toby Lockwood, "The Kemper County CCS project—what went wrong and what next?," Only Natural Energy, November 13, 2017, https://www.onlynaturalenergy.com/the-kemper-county-ccs-project-what-went-wrong-and-what-next.
7 S&P Dow Jones Indices, "Price Graph for S&P 500 Index, 12/31/21 to 12/30/22," accessed January 31, 2023, https://www.spglobal.com/spdji/en/indices/equity/sp-500/#overview.
8 S&P Dow Jones Indices, "Price Graph for S&P 500 Energy Index, 12/31/21 to 12/30/22," accessed January 31, 2023, https://www.spglobal.com/spdji/en/indices/equity/sp-500-energy-sector/#overview.
9 Alyssa Stankiewicz, "U.S. Sustainable Funds Suffer a Worse Quarter Than Conventional Peers," Morningstar, January 25, 2023, https://www.morningstar.com/sustainable-investing/us-sustainable-funds-suffer-worse-quarter-than-conventional-peers.

Chapter 8: Sustainable Returns and ESG Performance Art

1 PRI, "PRI brochure 2021," accessed July 31, 2023, https://www.unpri.org/download?ac=10948.
2 PwC, "Asset and wealth management revolution: The power to shape the future" (2020), https://www.pwc.com/gx/en/industries/financial-services/assets/wealth-management-2-0-data-tool/pwc_awm_revolution_2020.pdf.
3 S&P Dow Jones Indices, "Price Graph for S&P 500 Index, 12/31/20 to 12/31/21," accessed January 31, 2023, https://www.spglobal.com/spdji/en/indices/equity/sp-500/#overview.

4 S&P Dow Jones Indices, "Price Graph for S&P 500 Energy Index, 12/31/20 to 12/31/21," accessed January 31, 2023, https://www.spglobal.com/spdji/en/indices/equity/sp-500-energy-sector/#overview.
5 Yahoo Finance, "Price Chart for Devon Energy Corporation Common Stock, 12/31/20 to 12/31/21," accessed January 31, 2023, https://finance.yahoo.com/quote/DVN/history?period1=1609372800&period2=1640908800&interval=1d&filter=history&frequency=1d&includeAdjustedClose=true.
6 S&P Dow Jones Indices, "Price Graph for S&P 500 Energy Index, 12/31/21 to 12/30/22," accessed January 31, 2023, https://www.spglobal.com/spdji/en/indices/equity/sp-500-energy-sector/#overview.
7 BlackRock, "Sustainable investing: Resilience amid uncertainty," accessed January 31, 2023, https://www.blackrock.com/uk/about-us/sustainability-resilience-research.
8 Gunnar Friede, Timo Busch, and Alexander Bassen, "ESG and Financial Performance: Aggregated Evidence from More than 2000 Empirical Studies," *Journal of Sustainable Finance & Investment* 5, no. 4 (October 22, 2015): 210–33, https://ssrn.com/abstract=2699610.
9 Ulrich Atz, Tracy Van Holt, Zongyuan Zoe Liu, and Christopher Bruno, "Does Sustainability Generate Better Financial Performance? Review, Meta-analysis, and Propositions," *Journal of Sustainable Finance and Investment* 13, no. 1 (July 22, 2022), https://ssrn.com/abstract=3708495.
10 George Serafeim, "Investors as Stewards of the Commons?" *Journal of Applied Corporate Finance* 30, no. 2 (August 7, 2017), https://ssrn.com/abstract=3014952.
11 Mozaffar Khan, George Serafeim, and Aaron Yoon, "Corporate Sustainability: First Evidence on Materiality," *Accounting Review* 91, no. 6 (November 9, 2016), 1697–1724, https://ssrn.com/abstract=2575912.
12 George Serafeim, "Public Sentiment and the Price of Corporate Sustainability," *Financial Analysts Journal* 76, no. 2 (October 12, 2018): 26–46, https://ssrn.com/abstract=3265502.
13 Cam Simpson, Akshat Rathi, and Saijel Kishan, "The ESG Mirage," *Bloomberg Businessweek*, December 10, 2021, https://www.bloomberg.com/graphics/2021-what-is-esg-investing-msci-ratings-focus-on-corporate-bottom-line.
14 Morgan Stanley Institute for Sustainable Investing, "Sustainable Reality: Analyzing Risk and Returns of Sustainable Funds" (2019), https://www.morganstanley.com/content/dam/msdotcom/ideas/sustainable-investing-offers-financial-performance-lowered-risk/Sustainable_Reality_Analyzing_Risk_and_Returns_of_Sustainable_Funds.pdf.
15 Barclays Capital, "The Case for Sustainable Bond Investing Strengthens" (2018), https://www.cib.barclays/content/dam/barclaysmicrosites/ibpublic/documents/our-insights/ESG2/BarclaysIB-ImpactSeries4-ESG-in-credit-5MB.pdf.

16 Soohun Kim and Aaron Yoon, "Analyzing Active Fund Managers' Commitment to ESG: Evidence from the United Nations Principles for Responsible Investment," *Management Science* (March 17, 2020), https://ssrn.com/abstract=3555984.

17 Giovanni Bruno, Mikheil Esakia, and Felix Goltz, "'Honey, I Shrunk the ESG Alpha': Risk-Adjusting ESG Portfolio Returns," Scientific Beta, April 2021, https://cdn.ihsmarkit.com/www/pdf/0521/Honey-I-Shrunk-the-ESG-Alpha.pdf.

18 Ingo Walter, "Sense and Nonsense in ESG Ratings," *Journal of Law, Finance and Accounting* (July 23, 2020), https://ssrn.com/abstract=3568104.

19 David F. Larcker, Lukasz Pomorski, Brian Tayan, and Edward Watts, "ESG Ratings: A Compass without Direction," Rock Center for Corporate Governance at Stanford University Working Paper (August 2, 2022), https://ssrn.com/abstract=4179647.

20 George Serafeim, "ESG: Hyperboles and Reality," Harvard Business School Research Paper Series Working Paper 22-031 (November 8, 2021), https://ssrn.com/abstract=3966695.

21 Natalie Kenway, "Global sustainable flows bounce back in Q4," ESG Clarity, January 26, 2023, https://esgclarity.com/global-sustainable-flows-bounce-back-in-q4.

22 All Vanguard index pricing as of July 31, 2023.

23 S&P Dow Jones Indices, "Price Graph for S&P 500 ESG Index, 12/31/20 to 12/30/22," accessed July 31, 2023, https://www.spglobal.com/spdji/en/indices/esg/sp-500-esg-index/#overview.

24 Isla Binnie, "Green bonds are set to drive corporate ESG debt out of slump in 2023—Barclays," Reuters, January 5, 2023, https://www.reuters.com/business/sustainable-business/green-bonds-are-set-drive-corporate-esg-debt-out-slump-2023-barclays-2023-01-04.

25 IEA, "World Energy Investment 2023" (May 2023), https://iea.blob.core.windows.net/assets/54a781e5-05ab-4d43-bb7f-752c27495680/WorldEnergyInvestment2023.pdf.

26 IEA, "Net Zero by 2050: A Roadmap for the Global Energy Sector" (May 2021), https://iea.blob.core.windows.net/assets/7ebafc81-74ed-412b-9c60-5cc32c8396e4/NetZeroby2050-ARoadmapfortheGlobalEnergySector-SummaryforPolicyMakers_CORR.pdf.

27 BloombergNEF, "Global Low-Carbon Energy Technology Investment Surges Past $1 Trillion for the First Time" (January 26, 2023), https://about.bnef.com/blog/global-low-carbon-energy-technology-investment-surges-past-1-trillion-for-the-first-time.

28 All BlackRock fund return data sourced from BlackRock public website as of July 31, 2023.

29 Data used to calculate price return from 12/29/17 to 12/31/22 for all individual

company stocks noted sourced from Yahoo Finance as of January 31, 2023.

30 S&P Dow Jones Indices, "Price Graph for S&P 500 ESG Index, 12/29/17 to 12/31/22," accessed January 31, 2023, https://www.spglobal.com/spdji/en/indices/equity/sp-500/#overview.

Chapter 9: The Children's Hour

1 PRI, "A blueprint for responsible investment," accessed January 31, 2023, https://www.unpri.org/about-us/a-blueprint-for-responsible-investment.

2 Paul H. Tice, "On Climate, the Kids Are All Wrong," *Wall Street Journal*, March 12, 2019, https://www.wsj.com/articles/on-climate-the-kids-are-all-wrong-11552430379.

3 United Nations, "Secretary-General's Remarks at 2019 Climate Action Summit" (September 23, 2019), https://www.un.org/sg/en/content/sg/speeches/2019-09-23/remarks-2019-climate-action-summit.

4 António Guterres (@antonioguterres), "My message to the youth of today: Do not take up careers with the climate wreckers. I urge you to be the generation that succeeds in addressing the planetary emergency of climate change," Twitter, October 29, 2022, 1:00 p.m., https://twitter.com/antonioguterres/status/1586402493315121154.

5 Our Children's Trust, "Legal Actions," accessed October 31, 2023, https://www.ourchildrenstrust.org/juliana-v-us.

6 Douglas Holtz-Eakin, Dan Bosch, Ben Gitis, Dan Goldbeck, and Philip Rossetti, "The Green New Deal: Scope, Scale, and Implications," American Action Forum, February 25, 2019, https://www.americanactionforum.org/research/the-green-new-deal-scope-scale-and-implications.

7 United Nations, "Climate Action: Youth in Action," accessed January 31, 2023, https://www.un.org/en/climatechange/youth-in-action#:~:text=The%20world%20is%20home%20to,generation%20of%20youth%20in%20history.

8 Caroline Hickman, Elizabeth Marks, Panu Pihkala, Susan Clayton, R. Eric Lewandowski, Elouise E. Mayall, Britt Wray, Catriona Mellor, and Lise van Susteren, "Climate anxiety in children and young people and their beliefs about government responses to climate change: a global survey," *The Lancet* 5 (December 2021): 863–73, https://www.thelancet.com/action/showPdf?pii=S2542-5196%2821%2900278-3.

9 United Nations, "Climate Action: Education is key to addressing climate change," accessed January 31, 2023, https://www.un.org/en/climatechange/climate-solutions/education-key-addressing-climate-change.

10 UNESCO, "Climate change education," accessed August 1, 2023, https://www.unesco.org/en/climate-change/education.

11 Paul H. Tice, "Schoolroom Climate Change Indoctrination," *Wall Street*

Journal, May 27, 2015, https://www.wsj.com/articles/schoolroom-climate-change-indoctrination-1432767611.

12 BLS, "Labor Force Statistics from the Current Population Survey," accessed January 30, 2023, https://www.bls.gov/cps/cpsaat11b.pdf.

13 Morgan Stanley Institute for Sustainable Investing, "Sustainable Signals: New Data from the Individual Investor" (2017), https://www.morganstanley.com/pub/content/dam/msdotcom/ideas/sustainable-signals/pdf/Sustainable_Signals_Whitepaper.pdf.

14 Stephen Haber, John D. Kepler, David F. Larcker, Amit Seru, and Brian Tayan, "2022 Survey of Investors, Retirement Savings, and ESG," Rock Center for Corporate Governance at Stanford University Working Paper (November 2, 2022), https://www.hoover.org/sites/default/files/research/docs/2022_Survey_Of_Investors_Retirement_Savings_And_ESG.pdf.

15 Federal Reserve, "Distributional Financial Accounts," accessed May 24, 2023, https://www.federalreserve.gov/releases/z1/dataviz/dfa/distribute/table/#quarter:119;series:Net%20worth;demographic:generation;population:all;units:shares.

16 Arwa Mahdawi, "'Blah, blah, blah': Greta Thunberg lambasts leaders over climate crisis," *The Guardian*, September 28, 2021, https://www.theguardian.com/environment/2021/sep/28/blah-greta-thunberg-leaders-climate-crisis-co2-emissions.

17 Tyler Durden, "Greta Thunberg Calls For 'Overthrow of Whole Capitalist System,'" ZeroHedge, November 1, 2022, https://www.zerohedge.com/geopolitical/greta-thunberg-calls-overthrow-whole-capitalist-system.

18 Stuart Basden, "Extinction Rebellion isn't about the Climate," Medium, January 10, 2019, https://medium.com/extinction-rebellion/extinction-rebellion-isnt-about-the-climate-42a0a73d9d49.

19 Jack Crowe, "AOC's Chief of Staff Admits the Green New Deal Is Not about Climate Change," Yahoo, July 12, 2019, https://www.yahoo.com/video/aoc-chief-staff-admits-green-124408358.html.

Chapter 10: The Fiduciary Rule: Broken, Not Bent

1 BLS, "Industries at a Glance: NAICS 523," accessed February 1, 2023, https://www.bls.gov/iag/tgs/iag523.htm.

2 SIFMA, "2022 Capital Markets Fact Book" (July 12, 2022), 56, 60, https://www.sifma.org/wp-content/uploads/2022/07/CM-Fact-Book-2022-SIFMA.pdf.

3 SEC, "SEC Announces Enforcement Results for FY 2021" (November 18, 2021), https://www.sec.gov/news/press-release/2021-238.

4 Michael V. Seitzinger, "Federal Securities Law: Insider Trading," Congres-

sional Research Service, March 1, 2016, https://sgp.fas.org/crs/misc/RS21127.pdf.

5 Patrick Purcell and Jennifer Staman, "Summary of the Employee Retirement Income Security Act (ERISA)," Congressional Research Service, May 19, 2009, https://crsreports.congress.gov/product/pdf/RL/RL34443/6.

6 Freshfields Bruckhaus Deringer, "A legal framework for the integration of environmental, social and governance issues into institutional investment" (October 2005), https://www.unepfi.org/fileadmin/documents/freshfields_legal_resp_20051123.pdf.

7 UNEP FI, "Fiduciary responsibility: Legal and practical aspects of integrating environmental, social and governance issues into institutional investment" (July 2009), https://www.unepfi.org/fileadmin/documents/fiduciaryII.pdf.

8 PRI, UNEP FI, and UNGC, "Fiduciary Duty in the 21st Century" (September 2015), https://www.unepfi.org/fileadmin/documents/fiduciary_duty_21st_century.pdf.

9 Freshfields Bruckhaus Deringer, "A Legal Framework for Impact: Sustainability impact in investor decision-making" (October 2021), https://www.unpri.org/download?ac=13902.

10 FRC, "The UK Stewardship Code, 2020" (2020), https://www.frc.org.uk/getattachment/5aae591d-d9d3-4cf4-814a-d14e156a1d87/Stewardship-Code_Dec-19-Final-Corrected.pdf.

11 FRC, "FRC lists successful signatories to UK Stewardship Code" (February 15, 2023), https://www.frc.org.uk/news/february-2023/frc-lists-successful-signatories-to-uk-stewardship#:~:text=The%20list%20now%20includes%20successful,235%20in%20September%20last%20year.

12 EU, "Commission Delegated Regulation (EU) 2021/1253" (April 21, 2021), https://eur-lex.europa.eu/legal-content/EN/TXT/PDF/?uri=CELEX:32021R1253.

13 OECD, "Pension Markets in Focus, Preliminary 2022 Data" (June 26, 2023), 2, https://www.oecd.org/daf/fin/private-pensions/PMF-2023-Preliminary-2022-Data.pdf.

14 DOL, "Prudence and Loyalty in Selecting Plan Investments and Exercising Shareholder Rights" (December 1, 2022), https://www.govinfo.gov/content/pkg/FR-2022-12-01/pdf/2022-25783.pdf.

15 PRI, "Fiduciary duty in the 21st century—from a legal case to regulatory clarification around ESG" (November 25, 2019), https://www.unpri.org/fiduciary-duty/fiduciary-duty-in-the-21st-century-from-a-legal-case-to-regulatory-clarification-around-esg/5137.article.

16 PRI, "The modern interpretation of fiduciary duty" (November 6, 2020), https://www.unpri.org/fiduciary-duty/the-modern-interpretation-of-fiduciary-duty/6538.article.

Chapter 11: Europe Attacks!

1 Russell Investments, "2020 Annual ESG Manager Survey: Turning up the volume" (2020), https://russellinvestments.com/-/media/files/kr/insights/annual-esg-manager-survey-2020-results-kor-eng.pdf.
2 Thomas Shingler and Hannah Vieira, "Callan Survey Sees First Decline in ESG Incorporation Since 2019," Callan Institute, November 28, 2022, https://www.callan.com/blog-archive/2022-esg-survey.
3 PRI, "Policy Frameworks for Long-Term Responsible Investment: The Case for Investor Engagement in Public Policy" (2014), https://www.unpri.org/download?ac=1420.
4 PRI, "Regulation database," accessed February 1, 2023, https://www.unpri.org/policy/regulation-database.
5 Eurostat, "Greenhouse gas emission statistics—emission inventories" (June 2022), https://ec.europa.eu/eurostat/statistics-explained/index.php?title=Greenhouse_gas_emission_statistics_-_emission_inventories.
6 European Commission, "A European Green Deal: Striving to be the first climate-neutral continent," accessed February 1, 2023, https://commission.europa.eu/strategy-and-policy/priorities-2019-2024/european-green-deal_en.
7 Jefferson Airplane, "White Rabbit," written by Grace Slick, produced by Rick Jarrard, RCA, track 5, side 2 on *Surrealistic Pillow*, 1967.
8 Norwegian Petroleum, "The Petroleum Tax System," accessed August 2, 2023, https://www.norskpetroleum.no/en/economy/petroleum-tax.
9 Trine Jonassen, "The Green Shift: Norwegian Climate Minister: The Foundation for Norwegian High North Policy is Radically Changed," *High North News*, May 20, 2022, https://www.highnorthnews.com/en/norwegian-climate-minister-foundation-norwegian-high-north-policy-radically-changed.
10 European Commission, "State aid: Commission approves €1.47 billion Dutch schemes to reduce nitrogen deposition on nature conservation areas" (May 2, 2023), https://ec.europa.eu/commission/presscorner/detail/en/IP_23_2507.
11 World Bank, "Nitrous oxide emissions (thousand metric tons of CO_2 equivalent)—Netherlands, 1990–2020," accessed August 2, 2023, https://data.worldbank.org/indicator/EN.ATM.NOXE.KT.CE?locations=NL.
12 Amrou Awaysheh and Christine J. Picard, "5 reasons why eating insects could reduce climate change," WEF, February 9, 2022, https://www.weforum.org/agenda/2022/02/how-insects-positively-impact-climate-change.
13 Kate Whiting, "How soon will we be eating lab-grown meat?," WEF, October 16, 2020, https://www.weforum.org/agenda/2020/10/will-we-eat-lab-grown-meat-world-food-day.

14 Thomas Birr and Carsten Stocker, "Goodbye car ownership, hello clear air: welcome to the future of transport," WEF, December 16, 2016, https://www.weforum.org/agenda/2016/12/goodbye-car-ownership-hello-clean-air-this-is-the-future-of-transport.

15 Kunal Kumar and Mridul Kaushik, "'My Carbon': An approach for inclusive and sustainable cities," WEF, September 14, 2022, https://www.weforum.org/agenda/2022/09/my-carbon-an-approach-for-inclusive-and-sustainable-cities.

16 Arthur Wyns, "How our responses to climate change and the coronavirus are linked," WEF, April 2, 2020, https://www.weforum.org/agenda/2020/04/climate-change-coronavirus-linked.

17 Carlton Reid, "France's Plan To Ban Short-Haul Domestic Flights Wins Approval From European Commission," *Forbes*, December 3, 2022, https://www.forbes.com/sites/carltonreid/2022/12/03/frances-plan-to-ban-short-haul-domestic-flights-wins-approval-from-european-commission/?sh=29c9619e2385.

18 UK Local Government Association, "Delivering local net zero: How councils could go further and faster," accessed February 1, 2023, https://www.local.gov.uk/delivering-local-net-zero.

19 Oxfordshire County Council, "About the Central Oxfordshire Travel Plan (COTP)," accessed February 1, 2023, https://www.oxfordshire.gov.uk/residents/roads-and-transport/connecting-oxfordshire/central-oxon-travel-plan.

20 Kelly Henaughen, "City of Edinburgh Council changes its policy for meat on menus," *The Scottish Farmer*, January 26, 2023, https://www.thescottishfarmer.co.uk/news/23276791.city-edinburgh-council-changes-policy-meat-menus.

21 Gregory Claeys and Simone Tagliapietra, "A trillion reasons to scrutinize the Green Deal Investment Plan," Bruegel, January 15, 2020, https://www.bruegel.org/blog-post/trillion-reasons-scrutinise-green-deal-investment-plan.

22 European Commission, "EU taxonomy for sustainable activities," accessed August 2, 2023, https://finance.ec.europa.eu/sustainable-finance/tools-and-standards/eu-taxonomy-sustainable-activities_en.

23 European Commission, "Corporate sustainability reporting," accessed August 2, 2023, https://finance.ec.europa.eu/capital-markets-union-and-financial-markets/company-reporting-and-auditing/company-reporting/corporate-sustainability-reporting_en.

24 European Commission, "Sustainability-related disclosure in the financial services sector," accessed August 2, 2023, https://finance.ec.europa.eu/sustainable-finance/disclosures/sustainability-related-disclosure-financial-services-sector_en.

25 Lydia Linna, "Morningstar: €175bn of article 9 funds downgraded in Q4

2022," Delano, February 2, 2023, https://delano.lu/article/morningstar-175bn-of-article-9.

26 PwC, "Asset and wealth management revolution" (2020).

27 FCA, "Sustainability Disclosure Requirements (SDR) and investment labels" (October 2022), https://www.fca.org.uk/publication/consultation/cp22-20.pdf.

28 SEC, "Fact Sheet: Enhancement and Standardization of Climate-Related Disclosures" (March 2022), https://www.sec.gov/files/33-11042-fact-sheet.pdf.

29 SEC, "Fact Sheet: ESG Disclosures for Investment Advisers and Investment Companies" (May 2022), https://www.sec.gov/files/ia-6034-fact-sheet.pdf.

30 Moody's, "FED Proposes Principles for Climate Risk Management at Large Banks" (December 8, 2022), https://www.moodysanalytics.com/regulatory-news/dec-08-22-fed-proposes-principles-for-climate-risk-management-at-large-banks.

31 CFA Institute, "The Evolving Future of Fiduciary Duty in an ESG World: A Survey of CFA Institute EU-Based Members" (2018), https://www.cfainstitute.org/-/media/documents/survey/esg-survey-2018.pdf.

32 PRI, "Climate risk: An investor resource guide," accessed August 2, 2023, https://www.unpri.org/climate-change/climate-risk-an-investor-resource-guide/9329.article.

33 BlackRock, "Larry Fink's 2020 Letter to CEOs: A Fundamental Reshaping of Finance" (January 14, 2020), https://www.blackrock.com/us/individual/larry-fink-ceo-letter.

34 Catherine Clifford, "BlackRock and Mike Bloomberg agree that measuring climate risk and investing in clean energy is smart capitalism," CNBC, September 9, 2022, https://www.cnbc.com/2022/09/09/blackrock-bloomberg-measuring-climate-investment-risk-is-capitalism.html.

35 CDP, "Are Companies Developing Credible Climate Transition Plans?" (February 2023), https://www.cdp.net/en/articles/climate/new-cdp-data-shows-companies-are-recognizing-the-need-for-climate-transition-plans-but-are-not-moving-fast-enough-amidst-incoming-mandatory-disclosure.

36 SEC, "Enforcement Task Force Focused on Climate and ESG Issues," accessed August 2, 2023, https://www.sec.gov/securities-topics/enforcement-task-force-focused-climate-esg-issues.

37 Ewan Palmer, "Deutsche Bank HQ Raided by Police in DWS Greenwashing Probe," *Newsweek*, May 31, 2022, https://www.newsweek.com/deutsche-bank-hq-police-raid-germnay-greenwashing-1711596.

38 SEC, "SEC Charges BNY Mellon Investment Adviser for Misstatements and Omissions Concerning ESG Considerations" (May 23, 2022), https://www.sec.gov/news/press-release/2022-86.

39 SEC, "SEC Charges Goldman Sachs Asset Management for Failing to Follow its Policies and Procedures Involving ESG Investments" (November 22, 2022), https://www.sec.gov/news/press-release/2022-209.

40 Philippe Roos, "European Banks Get Tougher on Oil, Gas," Energy Intelligence, February 8, 2023, https://www.energyintel.com/00000186-2894-d0a2-a3e7-3ef485c40000.
41 Fitch Ratings, "Proposed Fossil Fuel Penalties for EU Banks Likely to Be Challenged" (September 21, 2022), https://www.fitchratings.com/research/banks/proposed-fossil-fuel-penalties-for-eu-banks-likely-to-be-challenged-21-09-2022.

Chapter 12: A 2030 Exit Plan

1 Ayn Rand, *Capitalism: The Unknown Ideal* (Penguin Books, 1967), 164–83.
2 "To Serve Man," *The Twilight Zone*, season 3, episode 24, directed by Richard L. Bare, aired March 2, 1962.
3 Lananh Nguyen and Simon Jessop, "Davos 2023: BlackRock U.S. lost $4 billion in ESG backlash, CEO says," Yahoo, January 17, 2023, https://www.yahoo.com/now/davos-2023-blackrock-u-inflows-125746960.html.
4 Federal Reserve, "Enhanced Financial Accounts: State Pensions," accessed February 2, 2023, https://www.federalreserve.gov/releases/z1/dataviz/pension/comparative_view/bar_chart.
5 Julie Steinberg and Ben Dummett, "HSBC Suspends Executive for Climate Comments," *Wall Street Journal*, May 23, 2022, https://www.wsj.com/articles/hsbc-suspends-executive-for-climate-comments-11653313199?mod=article_inline.
6 Climate Intelligence, "World Climate Declaration: There is no climate emergency," accessed November 2, 2023, https://clintel.org/world-climate-declaration.
7 Paul H. Tice, "Trump's Next Step on Climate Change," *Wall Street Journal*, March 28, 2017, https://www.wsj.com/articles/trumps-next-step-on-climate-change-1490740870.
8 Steve Milloy, "How to Stop the Paris Climate Accord," *Wall Street Journal*, November 29, 2020, https://www.wsj.com/articles/how-to-stop-the-paris-climate-accord-11606684590.
9 C. Boyden Gray, "Corporate Collusion: Liability Risks for the ESG Agenda to Charge Higher Fees and Rig the Market," Texas Public Policy Foundation, June 2021, https://thecannononline.com/wp-content/uploads/2021/06/2021-06-RR-Gray-LP-Corporate-Collusion.pdf.
10 UNEP FI, "UN-convened Net-Zero Asset Owner Alliance: Position on the Oil and Gas Sector" (March 2023), https://www.unepfi.org/wordpress/wp-content/uploads/2023/03/NZAOA-Position-on-the-Oil-and-Gas-Sector.pdf.
11 Reed Hundt, "Companies colluding to fight climate change don't need to

worry about antitrust laws," *Washington Post*, September 11, 2019, https://www.washingtonpost.com/opinions/2019/09/11/companies-colluding-fight-climate-change-dont-need-worry-about-antitrust-laws.

12 Alastair Marsh, "Net-Zero Insurers' Climate-Friendly Plans to Exit Coal Impeded by Antitrust Laws," *Insurance Journal*, January 19, 2022, https://www.insurancejournal.com/news/international/2022/01/19/649921.htm.

13 Jon McGowan, "Insurers Leave U.N. Climate Alliance Over ESG Pushback And Antitrust Claims," *Forbes*, May 26, 2023, https://www.forbes.com/sites/jonmcgowan/2023/05/26/insurers-leave-un-climate-alliance-over-esg-pushback-and-anti-trust-claims/?sh=478006946e13.

14 Kristen McGachey, "Vanguard exit from $66tn net-zero coalition could trigger 'domino effect,' ESG expert warns," *Financial News*, December 8, 2022, https://www.fnlondon.com/articles/vanguard-exit-from-66tn-net-zero-coalition-could-trigger-domino-effect-esg-expert-warns-20221208.

15 Rainforest Action Network, "Banking on Climate Chaos: Fossil Fuel Finance Report 2023" (April 2023), https://www.bankingonclimatechaos.org.

16 Nick Ferris, "Why banks are key to turning the tide on oil and gas," Energy Monitor, December 2, 2022, https://www.energymonitor.ai/finance/banking/why-banks-are-key-to-turning-the-tide-on-oil-and-gas.

17 PRI, "Terms of Use—PRI Collaboration Platform" (December 3, 2020), 7, https://www.unpri.org/download?ac=6970.

18 Damien Gayle, "Just Stop Oil's 'spring uprising' protests funded by US philanthropists," *The Guardian*, April 29, 2022, https://www.theguardian.com/environment/2022/apr/29/just-stop-oils-protests-funded-by-us-philanthropists.

19 Charles Doyle, "RICO: A Brief Sketch," Congressional Research Service, August 3, 2021, https://crsreports.congress.gov/product/pdf/RL/96-950/12.

20 Stanford Law School, "Securities Class Action Clearinghouse," accessed February 2, 2023, https://securities.stanford.edu/list-mode.html.

21 Our World in Data, "Global direct primary energy consumption," accessed July 20, 2023, https://ourworldindata.org/grapher/global-primary-energy.

22 Laura Cozzi, Daniel Wetzel, Gianluca Tonolo, and Jacob Hyppolite II, "For the first time in decades, the number of people without access to electricity is set to increase in 2022," IEA, November 3, 2022, https://www.iea.org/commentaries/for-the-first-time-in-decades-the-number-of-people-without-access-to-electricity-is-set-to-increase-in-2022.

23 Melissa Eddy, "Exxon Mobil sues to try to block a European windfall tax," *New York Times*, December 28, 2022, https://www.nytimes.com/2022/12/28/world/europe/exxon-mobil-european-union-windfall-tax.html#:~:text=European%20subsidiaries%20of%20the%20American,cost%20it%20billions%20of%20dollars.

24 Andrew Moran, "BlackRock Downgraded by UBS Over Growing ESG Investing Risks," *Epoch Times*, October 14, 2022, https://www.theepochtimes.

com/blackrock-downgraded-by-ubs-over-growing-esg-investing-risks_4796030.html.

25 Paul H. Tice, "A Regulatory Solution to the ESG Problem on Wall Street," *Epoch Times*, July 11, 2023, https://www.theepochtimes.com/a-regulatory-solution-to-the-esg-problem-on-wall-street_5385046.html.

26 Arlo Guthrie, "Alice's Restaurant Massacree," written by Arlo Guthrie, produced by Fred Hellerman, Warner Brothers, track 1, side 1 on *Alice's Restaurant*, 1967.

INDEX

A Note on the Type

The Race to Zero has been set in Kingfisher, a family of types designed by Jeremy Tankard. Frustrated by the paucity of truly well-drawn fonts for book work, Tankard set out to create a series of types that would be suitable for a wide range of text settings. Informed by a number of elegant historical precedents – the highly regarded Doves type, and Monotype's Barbou and Ehrhardt among them – yet beholden to no one type in particular, Kingfisher attains a balance of formality, detail, and color that is sometimes lacking in types derived or hybridized from historical forms. The italic, designed intentionally as a complement to the roman, has much in common with earlier explorations in sloped romans like the Perpetua and Joanna italics, yet moderates the awkward elements that mar types like Van Krimpen's Romulus italic. The resulting types, modern, crisp, and handsome, are ideal for the composition of text matter at a variety of sizes, and comfortable for extended reading.

DESIGN & COMPOSITION BY CARL W. SCARBROUGH